DRIVES AND REINFORCEMENTS: BEHAVIORAL STUDIES OF HYPOTHALAMIC FUNCTIONS

Drives and Reinforcements:

Behavioral Studies of Hypothalamic Functions

James Olds, Ph.D.
Division of Biology
California Institute of Technology
Pasadena, California

Raven Press ■ New York

Raven Press, 1140 Avenue of the Americas, New York, New York 10036

Made in the United States of America

Library of Congress Cataloging in Publication Data

Olds, James.
Drives and reinforcements.

Bibliography: p. 115
Includes index.
1. Reinforcement (Psychology) 2. Hypothalamus.
3. Brain stimulation. 4. Brain—Localization of functions. I. Title. [DNLM: 1. Drive. 2. Electric stimulation. 3. Hypothalamus—Physiology.
4. Neurohumors. 5. Reinforcement (Psychology)
WL312 044d]
QP383.7.056 152.5 75-31480
ISBN 0-89004-087-7

Foreword

The neural basis of drives and reinforcements, the topic to which Jim Olds devoted the major portion of his professional life, is a central problem of great significance to neuroscience. Random variations in the genetic code have been selected by their survival value over hundreds of millions of years to produce animals with complex repertoires of innate adaptive behavior. A fundamental step in the line of evolution leading to human behavior was the development of learning, a new process of adaptation that could occur far more rapidly within the lifetime of the individual instead of slowly during the evolution of the species. In determining which particular response will be performed and learned, the selective factor is reinforcement which, in turn, is closely related to the drives that are active at a given time.

The capacity for learning appears to be dependent on the nervous system; the reliance of different species on it is roughly correlated with the ratio of brain weight to body weight, which is relatively high in mammals and, among mammals, increases steeply from monkeys to apes to man.

Until about 20 years ago, the goal of determining the neural basis for reinforcement seemed remote indeed. The primary method available was the creation of lesions in certain areas of the brain and the observation of the defects that were produced. The major conclusion was that greater volumes of destruction produced greater deficits in learning.

Jim Olds played a key role in the events that led to an almost explosive development of interdisciplinary work that produced new information about the role of the brain in the reinforcement of learned behavior. He was among those who pioneered in combining a variety of powerful new neurophysiological and pharmacological techniques with a variety of behavioral techniques to discover new relationships between the brain and behavior.

His initial and greatest discovery resulted from his having the wit to notice and exploit a totally unexpected outcome—an important aspect of science inadequately understood by the general public or by those legislators who believe that it is efficient to concentrate most research funds on specific planned programs to attack targeted practical problems, such as a cure for cancer. Olds was using a technique new to psychologists, the use of a chronically implanted electrode to stimulate a specific point in the brain of an unanesthetized, freely moving animal. He was learning this technique from Peter Milner in Hebb's laboratory at McGill University. He had aimed his

[1]Olds, J. (1973): Commentary on Olds and Millner's "Positive reinforcement produced by electrical stimulation of septal area and other regions of rat brain." In *Brain Stimulation and Motivation: Research and Commentary* (E. S. Valenstein, editor). Glenview, Ill., Scott, Foresman & Co., pp. 81–99.

electrode at the reticular formation in order to study the recently discovered arousing effects of stimulating that structure. But the difficulties of implanting such an electrode on the thin skull of a rat in those early days were so great that his probe missed its target by approximately four millimeters, which is roughly equivalent to the whole longitudinal dimension of the rat's diencephalon. When stimulating this rat with a weak electrical current as it wandered throughout a large table-top enclosure, he noticed that it tended to return to the place where it had been stimulated. Seizing on this chance observation, he systematically stimulated the rat for approaching other points randomly chosen by an independent observer, and demonstrated that it would learn to approach any distinctive place where the brain stimulation was regularly delivered. In short, the stimulation had the properties of a reinforcement or, in other words, a reward.

Because of difficulties in finding another rat showing similar behavior, Olds developed a small Skinner box with a large lever as a simple screening device and embarked on a systematic mapping procedure. After he learned where to aim the electrodes, he showed that the stimulation did have all the functional properties of a reinforcement; it could be used not only to cause rats to learn to approach a place and to press a lever, but also to cause them to learn to run progressively more rapidly down a straight alley, and to eliminate errors in a maze. Rats would even cross a grid that delivered foot shocks in order to reach the place where they received the electrical stimulation in the brain. Instructive details of this early history have been described elsewhere (Olds, 1973).

From this early work, he proceeded to further studies, systematically mapping rewarding, aversive, and drive-inducing areas of the rat brain, studying the effects of lesions and of drugs administered both systemically and via chronic cannulas into a specific area of the brain, and devising ingenious ways of training the rat to stand still so that single cells could be recorded. His wife, Marianne Olds, became a valuable collaborator. He trained students, generously sharing with them his bountiful fountain of original ideas. He helped to inspire much work in other laboratories.

In this book he presented his most recent and comprehensive summary of his own work on brain mechanisms of drives and reinforcements. He also brought together relevant work from many other laboratories and with other origins. In this book the pattern of a fascinating puzzle emerges, many parts of which seem to fit beautifully together, but in other cases there are obvious misfits that provide tantalizing contradictions to the main pattern. The reader is left with the challenge of finding the missing pieces and/or reorganizing the existing ones to achieve a better fit. With his boundless energy and warm, vital enthusiasm, Jim Olds would have loved to continue to work on the completion of this task. His sudden recent death is a tragic loss to us all.

Neal E. Miller
The Rockefeller University
New York, New York

Contents

Introduction

The rewarding effects of electric stimulation applied in some parts of the brain are well known. The electric shocks are pursued as if they were the positive goals of active drives, or as if they were of such a hedonically appetizing character that no drive was needed to provoke pursuit behavior. The brain centers involved are to a large degree the same as those shown by other stimulation and lesion experiments to be involved in the control of drive behaviors. They are also the same as or heavily interdigitated with the main hormone control centers of the brain. Pharmacological experiments show that reward, drive, and hormone systems are controlled by drugs that appear to have their main influence on a special neurochemical messenger system, the catecholamine system. The catecholamines involved are two specialized "transmitters"—norepinephrine and dopamine—which convey neuronal messages to smooth muscles, glands, and other neurons.

Neuroanatomical evidence shows that fibers containing catecholamines pervade the critical brain areas and course through them to targets in many other parts of the brain. Because the catecholamine systems pervade the hormone systems in the same areas where reward systems pervade drive systems, it is tempting to suppose the pair of chemical messengers underlies the pair of behavior processes. Because the catecholamine transmitters are slower than other well-known transmitters, and hormones are slower still, it is possible to imagine a chain from fast neuronal processes, through slower catecholamine events, to still slower neurohormonal states which would then possibly exert an influence back on the fast processes. If this were a reward-drive cycle, it would be involved in determining priorities and stabilizing behavioral directions. Studies of the brain reward systems, related drive systems, catecholamine fibers that pervade them, coresident hormone systems, and large neurons that make up the main dramatis personae in the critical brain centers are brought together here with a view to moving toward a clarification of some of the mechanisms.

Electric Stimulation

A. Reward

Psychologists have long identified "positive reinforcements" (i.e., rewards) by their effects on behavior. The behavior involved is easy to describe: The rewarding stimulus causes the animal to come back for more. It is more difficult to formulate a definition that is scientifically precise. Usually rewards used in animal experiments cause repetition of behaviors which immediately precede them. However, it is possible to conceive a reward which, being sought only once a day, would not have any important effect on the frequency of a normal antecedent behavior. In such a case the reward is often defined in terms of some obstruction the animal crosses or some other "cost" the animal "pays" to get it. In the end, obstruction-crossing, and cost-paying are behaviors chosen for their prior infrequency. Their frequency therefore *is* increased by infrequently sought rewards. Thus we are back again to defining reward in terms of changed frequencies or repetition rates of normal behaviors or of originally infrequent behaviors. Following Skinner's (1938) terminology, behaviors that can be controlled in this way are called operant behaviors; they are distinguished from reflex behaviors, whose incidence cannot be modified by manipulation of consequences. Operant behaviors, because they can be modified by manipulation of outcomes or effects, are said to obey the "law of effect."

"Negative reinforcements" (i.e., punishments) are similarly identified by their effects on behavior. On the operant side there is (1) failure to repeat punished responses, and (2) repetition of responses which terminate the punishment. On the reflex side there is (3) general activation of the animal during application of the punishing stimulus, and (4) some set of aversive or withdrawal reflexes.

Thus in relation to operant behavior, the application of a rewarding stimulus and the termination of a punishing one have similar effects; both cause repetition of the preceding operant responses. This similarity has led many psychologists to postulate a single hypothetical mechanism for appetitive and aversive behaviors (Miller, 1957).

In experiments used to demonstrate positive reinforcement, the animal, usually deprived of food, water, or sexual stimulation, is placed in a situation where a certain response previously decided on by the experimenter leads to the stimulus that has been withheld. The response initially exists in the animal's repertory, but it occurs rarely. The experiment is begun by placing the animal in the apparatus and waiting until the response occurs at first by "accident." Immediately thereafter the previously withheld stimulus is presented either mechanically or by the experimenter. As a consequence of this correlation between response and stimulus, either at once or after several repetitions, the response becomes more frequent.

In experiments used to demonstrate the effects of negative reinforcement, the animal is not deprived; instead, a noxious stimulus is presented repeatedly or in a steady train. As in the positive reinforcement experiment, a response rare at the outset is selected by the experimenter as the response whose frequency is to be augmented. When the response occurs, the experimenter or the apparatus terminates the train of noxious stimulation for some period of time. After one or several repetitions of this correlation between response and cessation of noxious stimulation, an obvious change in response frequency occurs, the response becoming more frequent while the animal is subjected to the noxious stimulation.

B. Rewarding Stimulation of the Brain

A new window on the brain was opened in 1953 when a rat fortuitously evidenced a neural rewarding effect by returning to the place in an open field where it had been when an electric stimulus was applied to the brain via chronically implanted electrodes (Olds, 1955). The ensuing studies provided not only a neural substrate as a focal point for further study of a key psychological concept (i.e., the "law of effect") but also a stable preparation, and thereby a method of studying many brain-behavior relationships. On the basis of accomplishments to date, the method bodes well in its own way to prove as fruitful as other well-known landmarks in the behavioral sciences, e.g., Skinner's method for studying operant behavior or Lashley's method for studying discrimination and choice on a jumping stand.

The initial observation led to studies which showed that electrical excitation in a restricted region of the central nervous system caused rats to work steadily at arbitrarily assigned tasks (Fig. 1) in order to obtain the electric stimulus (Olds and Milner, 1954). The behavior was called "self-stimulation" by Brady (1960), and this designation is widely used. The behavior was easily reproducible from animal to animal; it was sustained during extended periods of testing; and it was not accompanied by any other obvious pathological signs. It seemed possible, therefore, to view this self-stimulation behavior in terms of an artificial activation of the brain's normal positive reinforcement mechanism.

Since that time similar effects have been obtained in many vertebrates from fish to primates (Olds, 1962). There is evidence from therapeutic procedures that human brains do not differ from those of other vertebrates in this regard (Bishop, Elder, and Heath, 1963). Most of the experiments on brain reward behavior, however, were carried out on rats. The goal of the experiments was to determine what parts of the brain were involved, if the rewarding effects were valid and general rather than being limited to irrele-

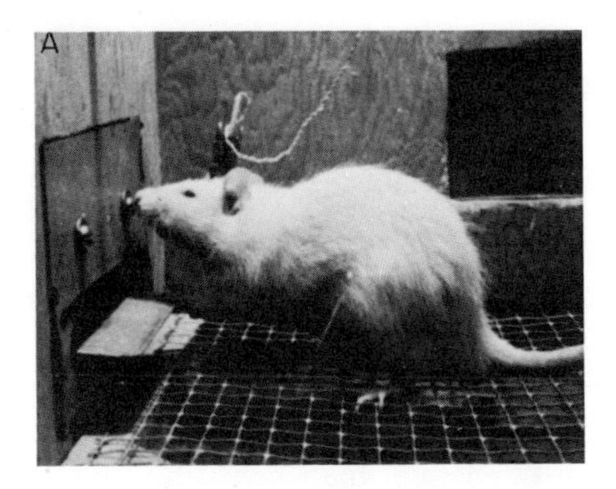

FIG. 1. A and B: Rat pedal-pressing to stimulate itself in the lateral hypothalamus. C: X-ray film showing wires penetrating the brain and screws holding plaque to the skull.

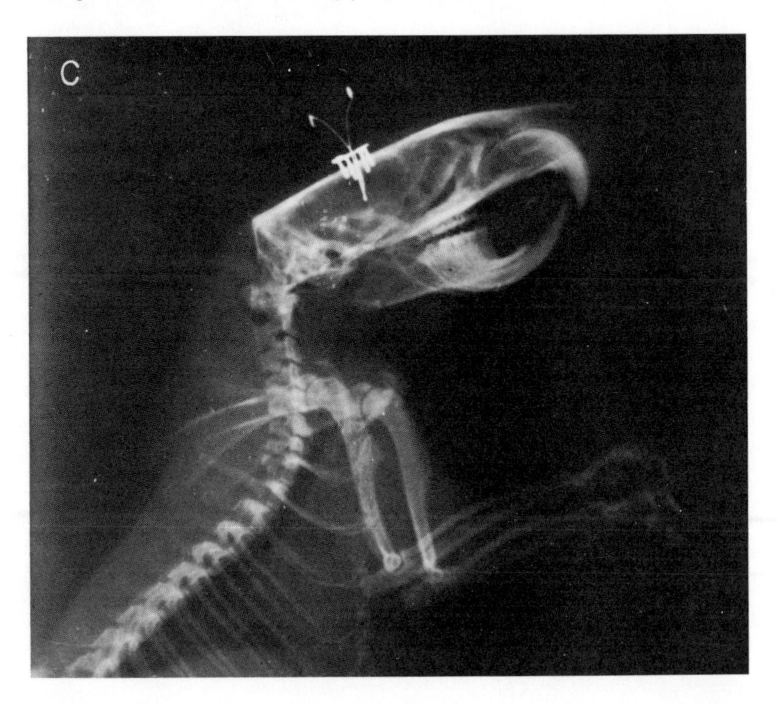

vant features of the testing situation, and how these "brain rewards" matched ordinary ones (and which kinds of ordinary ones they might match). The overriding goal, of course, was to look at brain function in the hope that these experiments would clarify the brain mechanisms of reward.

My strategy in the next subsection is to answer a set of questions that are regularly asked about the brain areas and the behaviors involved. I believe that this direct question and answer format is the clearest way to present this part of the material.

C. Reward and Drive Behaviors Caused by Electric Stimulation of the Brain

1. *What parts of the brain were involved?* The answer in the form of a list starting from the front includes: (1) olfactory bulbs; (2) primary olfactory centers such as the prepyriform cortex; (3) secondary olfactory centers (septal area, amygdala, and pyriform cortex); (4) tertiary olfactory centers (e.g., cingulate cortex and hippocampus); (5) *main subcortical area related to this olfactory system, i.e., hypothalamus;* (6) a part of the thalamus which is also tied into the olfactory system, i.e., the anterior thalamus; (7) certain parts of the midbrain which have strong fiber connections with the hypothalamus and with olfactory systems of the telencephalon; (8) a set of fibers (possibly dopamine secretors) connecting two main subcortex motor centers; and (9) a set of fibers (possibly norepinephrine secretors) originating near the gustatory centers of the medulla and projecting to near the hypothalamus and elsewhere (Olds, 1956*a;* Olds and Peretz, 1960; Olds, Travis, and Schwing, 1960; Olds and Olds, 1963; Wurtz and Olds, 1963; Valenstein and Campbell, 1966; Wetzel, 1968; Routtenberg and Malsbury, 1969; Phillips and Mogenson, 1969; Routtenberg, 1971; Crow, 1971, 1972*b;* Crow, Spear, and Arbuthnott, 1972; Ritter and Stein, 1973; Routtenberg and Sloan, 1974; German and Bowden, 1974).

The neuroanatomical systems seemed to form a single topographical continuum. The system originating in the medulla, the one originating in the extrapyramidal motor system, and the one related to the olfactory bulb could nevertheless be quite different; and other grounds suggested that even more different systems might be involved. It was not clear, therefore, whether there were several systems or one. Planting a probe in a given area did not give assurance that the effect of stimulation would be rewarding. There were different probabilities for different locations ranging from near certainty for some specifiable locations in or near the hypothalamus (Olds and Olds, 1963) to near 20% or 30% for the cingulate cortex and the hippocampus (Olds, 1956*a;* Ursin, Ursin, and Olds, 1966). In the last two areas it was even suspected that the stimulation was not actually rewarding but that some special artifact gave the appearance but not the substance of reward (e.g., hippocampal seizures might cause repetitive behavior giving the illusion of reward behavior). However, I believe this suspicion to be false.

There were also reports of self-stimulation from points that appeared originally to be totally outside the system. These were questioned at first but are now treated as valid. The brain areas involved included the neocortex (Routtenberg and Sloan, 1974; G. Ball, *private communication*), the cerebellum (J. Lilly, *private communication*), and the midline system of the thalamus (Cooper and Taylor, 1967). In the neocortex the best results were achieved with probes in those parts that were on the boundaries of the pyriform, cingulate, and hippocampal regions (Routtenberg and Sloan, 1974).

When probes were planted in the midline thalamus, reports of negative, positive, and no reinforcement were sufficiently stable in different experiments to suggest that slight differences in method or location would move marginal areas into or out of the set of "brain reward areas." The probe size, stimulating parameters, or behavior used for testing could make large differences. One possibility I entertain seriously is that there may be no areas of the brain where the reward effect is completely absent. Nevertheless, there were clear differences in the brain. In some central locations the phenomenon was stable and strong through any modification of methods. At the other extreme there were areas where most methods failed to demonstrate any sign of reward, and those that succeeded showed an extremely weak effect. The lateral hypothalamus was at the center of the class where the effect was stable and strong (Olds and Olds, 1963). Most parts of the neocortex lay at the other extreme (Olds, 1956*a*).

2. *Were there any fiber systems that pervaded all the reward areas and thus might be candidates for "reward neurons?"* The descending fibers from the olfactory bulb and olfactory centers in and near the cortex, the ascending amine fiber systems from medulla, midbrain, and hypothalamus, and the large path neurons of the medial forebrain bundle were alternate candidates for the "reward neuron" status. The lower fifth of the brain hangs together (see Fig. 2). Its parts are interconnected by large numbers of fibers. Its connections to the rest of the brain are by comparison sparse, although by no means absent (Crosby, Humphrey, and Lauer, 1962). It is made up of the lower part of the neocortex and all parts of the paleocortex (including central parts that surround the ventricles). In the system also are the olfactory bulbs. All parts are tied bidirectionally to the hypothalamus which lies at the center and coordinates the actions of the diverse structures (Haymaker, Anderson, and Nauta, 1969). The hypothalamus is a subcortical collection of cell groups which works in consort with two other similar sets, two outposts of the hypothalamus. These are the septal area up front and the amygdala at the sides. The system is like a wheel—the cortex and paleocortex comprising the tire, and the hypothalamus with its outposts the hub and spokes. Just as the hypothalamus lies at the central base of the paleocortical system, the pituitary lies at the central base of the hypothalamus.

Anatomists divide the hypothalamus into 12 to 20 parts, but this number may be reduced for convenience. This is partly because the behavioral studies

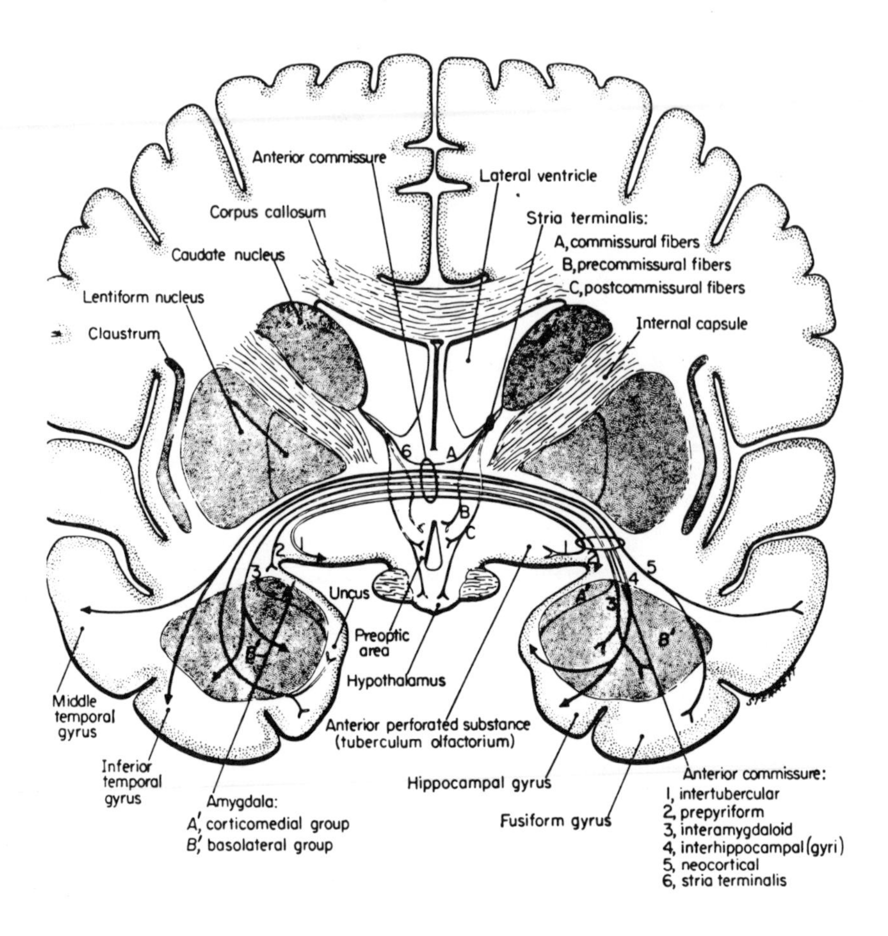

FIG. 2. The lower fifth of the brain hangs together. This is well shown on this section from the human brain (Crosby et al., 1962). At bottom center is the hypothalamus. Above that, in ascending order are: (1) between the lateral ventricles, the preoptic area; (2) the anterior commissure, which connects the basal cortical and paleocortical systems of the two sides; (3) the septum pellucidum (in rats this area contains the septal nuclei; in humans those nuclei are just in front of the septum pellucidum); (4) the corpus callosum, which is not part of the "lower fifth," but just above that is the "cingulate gyrus" (central cortex, which is closely connected to the septal nuclei and to the other systems of the lower fifth). On the sides, the middle temporal gyrus, inferior temporal gyrus, and fusiform gyrus are the parts of the neocortex closely tied into this motivational system; the hippocampal gyrus begins the olfactory or paleocortex (closely tied to the cingulate cortex on top). Following the line of the hippocampal gyrus we come to the uncus and the olfactory tubercle, and this brings us back to the hypothalamus. The gray areas marked A′ and B′ are the two main parts of the amygdala; the lentiform and caudate nuclei are two parts of the extrapyramidal system (these are sometimes called the striatum). Sometimes the amygdala and the striatum are grouped together and called the basal ganglia (often the thalamus, which does not appear here, is also included in the term "basal ganglia"). The stria terminalis is a strange, looping pathway from the amygdala to the preoptic area and hypothalamus; it is shown coming through the septal region, but its origin in amygdala is not shown.

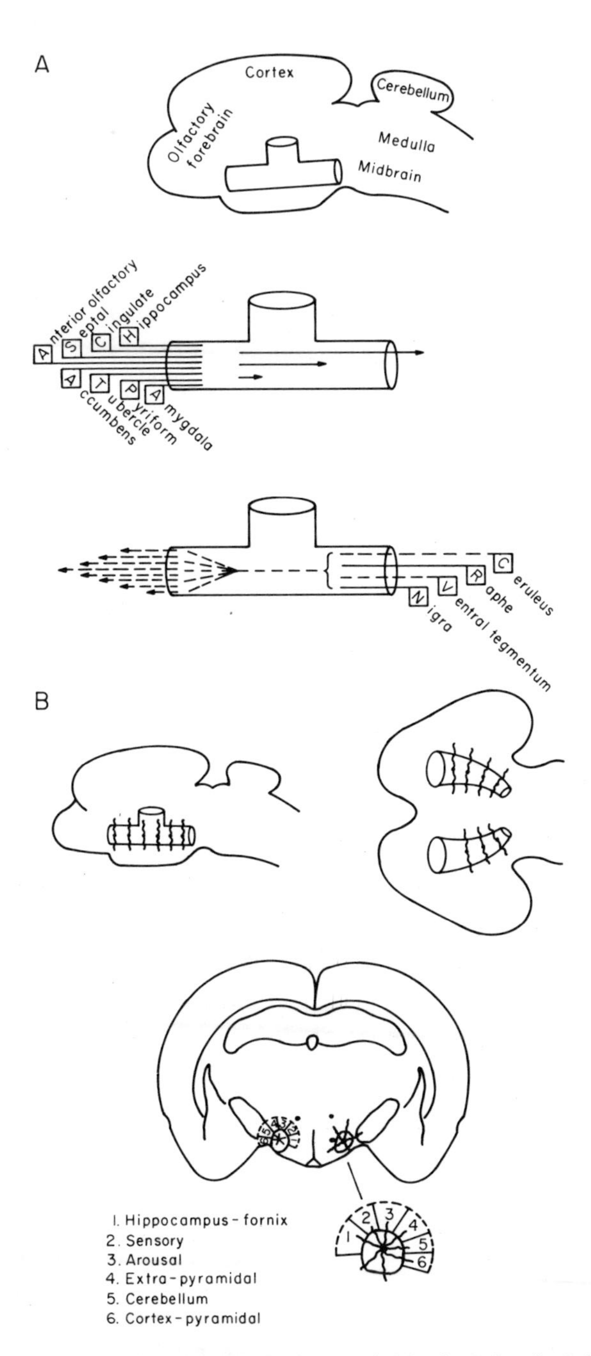

FIG. 3. A: Descending and ascending components of the medial forebrain bundle. B: Wheel-like neurons (i.e., the path neurons) spread to monitor the medial forebrain bundle and the shell of ascending and descending pathways that surrounds it. In the shell the fiber systems are identified by the functional systems which they are related to.

have been relatively gross and partly because the maps of behavioral functions have not followed either the fine or the coarse divisions drawn by the anatomists.

The following subdivisions of hypothalamus are appropriate to begin with. First there are medial and lateral sectors. The lateral sector is a tube that runs the full length. A fiber pathway, the medial forebrain bundle (Fig. 3A), runs through the tube occupying 30% to 50% of its cross section. Eight or 10 different olfactory forebrain structures project bundles downward into this pathway. Several different areas in the midbrain, pons, and medulla project bundles upward into it. Many of these ascending fibers carry one of the three monoamine neurotransmitters: norepinephrine, dopamine, or serotonin. These are specialized chemicals which form a bridge and a compromise between neuronal and endocrine functions. Beside and between the fiber pathways, the tube is populated by cell bodies (Fig. 3B). The most prominent family of cell bodies has dendrites, like the spokes of a wheel, spread as if to monitor all the bundles in the tube, plus another set of bundles which forms a partial shell around it (Millhouse, 1969). In the surrounding shell there is a great concourse of sensory and motor systems: (1) the three main motor pathways (from cortex, extrapyramidal motor systems, and cerebellum); (2) special sensory fibers from olfactory and gustatory receptors (Scott and Pfaffman, 1967; Norgren and Leonard, 1973); (3) side paths from the other sensory systems (Findlay, 1972); (4) a bundle of fibers from the "arousal" system; and (4) a special bundle from the computer-like hippocampus of the paleocortex. The spokes of the wheel-like neurons penetrate into these and must therefore receive afferents from many if not all.

The medial sector of the hypothalamus has three main subsets: anterior, middle, and posterior. These subsets are even more heavily populated with cells than their lateral neighbor. They also contain a system of "tubules," (Bleier, 1972) from the blood and possibly also from the cerebrospinal fluid. These may carry hormones from the body and possibly from the hypothalamus itself or other parts of the brain (Knigge, Scott, and Weindl, 1972). The medial sector contains some cells very like the wheel-like neurons of the lateral sector. The medial and lateral families of large neurons interdigitate their dendrites in a border region along the medial edge of the medial forebrain bundle, and they project to one another (Millhouse, 1969) (Fig. 4A). Neuronal input-output systems for both the medial and lateral sectors run (1) through the medial forebrain bundle to the olfactory forebrain structures and to the several midbrain and lower structures; (2) across the medial forebrain bundle toward the amygdala and the extrapyramidal motor system; (3) up toward the thalamus; and (4) toward the "central gray" (Fig. 4B). From both of the last two, the messages are relayed through "nonspecific" pathways to cortex and probably also to outgoing motor centers.

Many bidirectional pathways appear to be common between medial and lateral sectors. The main differences seem to be the hormonal message sys-

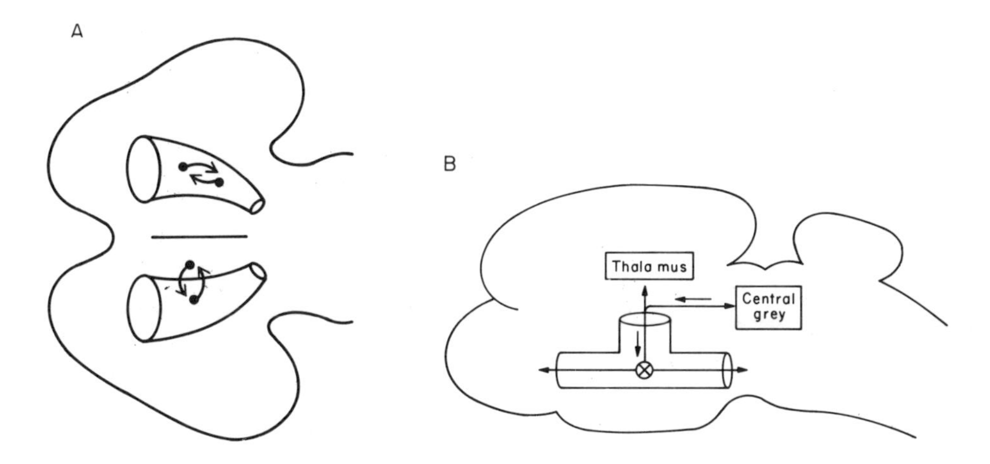

FIG. 4. A: Communication of path neurons with one another and with their medial neighbors. B: Outputs from medial and lateral hypothalamic neurons. Wheel-like neurons project four ways.

tems (which have more access to the medial sector) and the shell of fiber systems (which appear to have more effect on the dendrites of the lateral wheel-like neurons). This puts the medial set in a position to monitor the hormonal actions and the lateral set to monitor the activities of the brain.

3. *Were all the "reward areas" similar in respect to brain reward behavior?* By no means. For many of the questions that follow there were different answers for different areas.

4. *Were seizures associated with brain rewards?* When probes were planted in the anterior thalamus, the septal area, the anterior hypothalamus, and in telencephalic locations, seizures were often produced by stimulations near the reward thresholds (Porter, Conrad, and Brady, 1959). Stimulations in hippocampus seemed to be rewarding only so long as they induced periodic seizures. Stimulations in the amygdala appeared quite the opposite; as soon as the stimulus caused a seizure it ceased to be rewarding for a period of 24 hr or so. With probes in the ventral tegmental area (just in back of the hypothalamus), however, there were no seizures associated with brain reward behavior. Very high self-stimulation rates were achieved with very low currents, and even very high currents gave no recordable seizure activity (Bogacz, St. Laurent, and Olds, 1965). I conclude that seizures, insofar as they match or add to the effect of brain rewards, may be rewarding; but seizures are not necessary to produce the phenomenon (unless it be argued that the momentary and local effect of the brain stimulus is itself a seizure).

5. *Did animals press pedals at different rates to stimulate different parts of the brain?* Yes. There appeared to be a continuum spreading from central areas in lateral posterior hypothalamus and ventral tegmentum where rates

were high. In a second tier, including parts of anterior hypothalamus and parts of pons and medulla, rates were somewhat lower although still quite high. When probes were planted in the medial hypothalamus, the rates were often lower; although stable high rates occurred in the case of some medial probes. When probes were placed in cingulate cortex or hippocampus, rates were very low (but still far above chance levels). The septal area, amygdala, and pyriform cortex fell between anterior hypothalamus and cingulate cortex, both anatomically and in self-stimulation rates (Olds, 1956*a;* Olds et al., 1960; Olds and Olds, 1963; Wurtz and Olds, 1963; Routtenberg and Malsbury, 1969; Routtenberg, 1971; Atrens and von Vietinghoff-Riesch, 1972).

6. *Did animals run mazes as well as press pedals?* With probes in some places they did not run mazes at all or did so very poorly. When probes were placed elsewhere, however, they learned mazes with ease (Fig. 5). The best locations for maze behavior did not correlate perfectly with the best locations for high pedal rates. Animals with septal area probes had low rates and poor maze performance (so this correlation was good). Those with medial hypothalamus probes had lower rates than if probes were in the lateral hypothalamus; but medial stimulation supported equal maze or runway behavior (Olds, 1956*b;* Newman, 1961; Spear, 1962; Wetzel, 1963; Scott, 1967).

7. *Did the brain reward impart its rewarding properties to objects with which it was associated?* To some degree associating a signal with a brain reward caused it to become rewarding; but learned reward experiments of this kind did not work as readily with brain rewards as with ordinary rewards. In one experiment rats were presented with two pedals. One activated a brief tone signal; the other did not. At the outset animals pressed the two pedals about equally but showed a slight preference for the one that did not cause a tone. The tone was then paired with a brain reward (with no pedals available). When retested with pedals after this "training," the rats pressed the tone pedal more frequently than the other (Stein, 1958). This showed that the tone had acquired some of the rewarding property. In a second try this experiment did not work (Mogensen, 1965), but in a third case the experiment was repeated successfully (Knott and Clayton, 1966). Other experiments of different detail have also been successful in showng that signals associated with brain rewards became rewarding (Trowill and Hynek, 1970; Wald and Trowill, *in press*).

8. *How much work would animals do for brain rewards?* In "ratio" experiments, tests were made for the number of pedal responses a rat would make for just one brain reward. The number was smaller than would have been guessed from the very rapid pedal rates that occurred if each pedal response was rewarded (Sidman, Brady, Boren, Conrad, and Schulman, 1955; Brady, 1960; Brodie, Moreno, Malis, and Boren, 1960; Keesey and Goldstein, 1968). Rats working for food would pedal 50 to 100 times for a single reward. Rats working for brain reward were usually stopped if the

ratio was raised to 20:1 or 30:1. There were individual differences, some animals doing much more work for a brain stimulus than others. The difference was thought to be due mainly to probe locations, but no anatomical mapping differentiated those sites which sustained high ratios from those that did not. Certain methods could be used to increase the ratios. The first

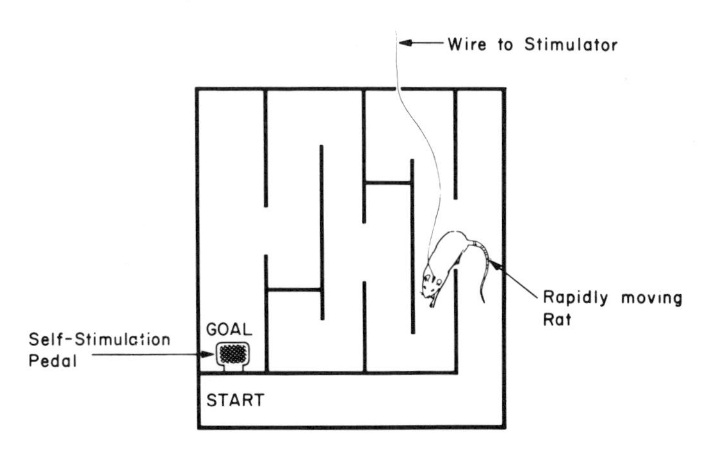

FIG. 5. Rats with probes positioned near the preoptic area sector of the medial forebrain bundle ran this maze well, eliminating errors from trial to trial and from day to day. On the first runs of the third and fourth days (each being 23 hr after the last previous stimulation), behavior was rapid and nearly errorless, indicating that it did not require immediate prior stimulation to sustain it.

was to make each "reward" a multiple one. For example, a repeated train of stimulations was applied as the brain reward (Brown and Trowill, 1970), or the animal could be rewarded by presenting it with a second pedal (automatically introduced into the cage after a ratio of responses on the first pedal) with which it could stimulate its brain several times (Pliskoff, Wright, and Hawkins, 1965). In a different kind of experiment with a puzzling outcome a signal coming just before the brain reward greatly augmented the number of pedal responses the animal would make for a single reward, up to ratios of 200:1 in one instance (Cantor, 1971). The animal thus gave many responses for one brain reward as long as there was some way to anticipate its exact time of application (as if the rat needed to prepare for it).

Several arguments have been made to explain the discrepancy between the very high rates on one for one pedal schedules and the poor behavior on some schedules that required several responses for one reward. One explanation was that the multiple reinforcement of a 100% schedule might contain a reinforcement that was more than the sum of the individual trains. In other words, 10 reinforcements in rapid succession would be reinforcing even though each one alone would not be positive at all. This would match the observation that hungry or thirsty animals often refuse to work for very small amounts of food or water. A second argument was that the brain stimulus triggered both a reward and a "drive," and the drive provoked by the first stimulus in a set was required to make the next one be pursued. Both of these arguments are probably true for some cases, especially the first one. They clearly did not account for all cases, as when a single reinforcement preceded by a signal was rewarding, but without the signal it was not. There were other puzzling cases of a similar nature. In some experiments animals avoided the same temporal pattern of stimulation as they self-administered (Steiner, Beer, and Shaffer, 1969). Animals were first allowed to pedal-press for brain reward. The sequence of self-administration was recorded and an exactly similar sequence applied later by a programming device. Animals were then permitted to escape from this by performing an operant response. This they did at a rate which was substantially above the chance level. The predictability of the stimulus when self-administered apparently made it rewarding; its unpredictability during program administration apparently made it aversive.

9. *How long would the animal keep working after the brain reward was stopped?* Brain-rewarded behavior usually subsided rapidly when the brain stimulus was withdrawn. Hungry animals working for food kept trying longer, but the brain-rewarded behavior matched that of rats motivated by the incentive of highly appetizing foods rather than by deprivation (Gibson, Reid, Sakai, and Porter, 1965). In these cases, when the reward was withdrawn, the animal turned readily to other pursuits. The rapid subsidence of brain reward behavior has been used as an argument for the view that the animal needs a drive caused by one brain stimulus to sustain the motivation for a second one (Deutsch and Howarth, 1963). Extinction was said to occur rapidly because this drive component dropped rapidly after stimulation. One main truth in this formulation is that all behavior which depends heavily on incentive and very little on drive loses motivation rapidly when the incentive is withdrawn. If the concept of drive is expanded to lump together the drive caused by deprivation and that caused by signaling or titillating with an appetizing incentive, the "drive decay" view becomes true (by definition). However, brain reward behavior did not require some electrical activation of an artificial deprivation state to start it. This was shown by the fact that the extinguished behavior could be started by a signal which promised brain reward just as well as by a brain reward stimulus itself. Moreover, extinction could be prolonged by a variety of procedures. One was to arrange the training so the animal became used to periodic withdrawal and return of rewards (Herberg, 1963*b*).

Clarifying this problem further, subsidence of the behavior in "extinction" experiments was shown to depend on inhibition emanating from the higher brain centers rather than on a subsidence of stimulated drive emanating from lower centers (Huston and Borbely, 1974); this was demonstrated by destroying the higher centers. Almost all of the "higher centers," including cortex, hippocampus, striatum, amygdala, and septum, were removed bilaterally. The lesioned animals then learned to perform gross behaviors such as sitting, climbing, or moving the tail in return for stimulation in the lateral hypothalamus. In the cases where the response was discrete and clearly observable, it did not appear to subside at all after withdrawal of the brain stimulus. This remarkable absence of extinction was observed as long as 2 weeks after training. The paradox of rapid subsidence of behavior in normal animals and long-lasting behavior after lesions is best interpreted in terms of a special inhibition emanating from the higher centers. A mechanism for conservation of effort might bring behaviors to a halt by some inhibitory process when drive or incentive was withdrawn.

10. *Did animals accept pain in order to get brain rewards?* This depended on where the brain probes were placed and on the amount of electric current used. With probes in some hypothalamic locations animals crossed an electrified grid (Fig. 6), which gave 0.5-mA shocks to the feet, to get to a pedal where currents approximately half that large were delivered to the brain (Olds and Sinclair, 1957; Olds, 1958*c*). The 0.5-mA shocks to the feet were more than five times as large as shocks which stopped hungry animals (deprived for 24 hr) on the path to food. Making a similar point was the fact that these animals with rewarding lateral hypothalamus probes and high currents were also quite undistractable and looked compulsive in their brain-rewarded behaviors. With smaller "reward" currents or other probe locations, however, it was quite easy to stop animals by imposing a foot shock on the path to brain reward. Such animals were easy to disturb and would self-stimulate only when distracting events were absent from the environment.

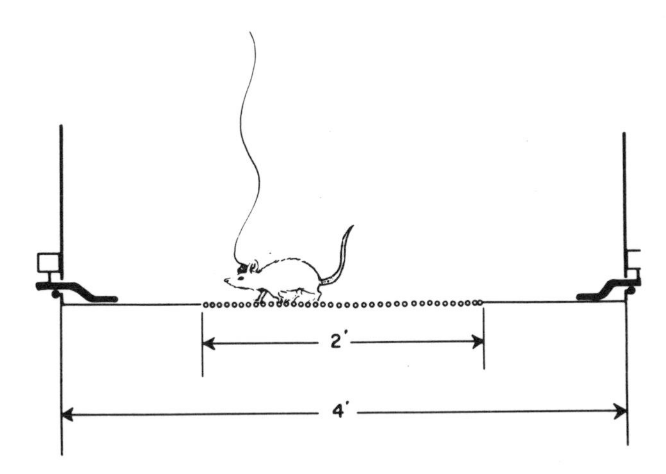

FIG. 6. Obstruction box. Pedal responses were rewarded with brain shocks. After every three of these the rat was required to cross a foot-shock grid to get more.

11. *Would animals give up food and starve to get rewarding brain stimulations?* This did happen with some probes and some stimulation levels, but it was quite unusual (Routtenberg and Lindy, 1965; Spies, 1965; Miliaressis and Cardo, 1973). When probes were planted in some parts of the hypothalamus and in some parts of the ventral tegmental area, with the currents set at several times threshold, animals gave up eating to devote themselves to brain reward behavior. In one experiment the animals were first trained to get food by pedal-pressing in a Skinner box (one 45-mg pellet for each pedal response). The Skinner box feeding time was limited to about 45 min/day. (Actually the amount of time was determined to be that required to maintain body weight at a steady level; the animals did not gain weight.) Then a second pedal whose depression yielded a rewarding brain shock was introduced. For some animals this was fatal or nearly so. They split their time between brain reward and food on the first 2 or 3 days, thus losing weight. After this they gave up food altogether and died if they were not rescued by termination of the experiment. In a different experiment, deprived rats consistently chose the arm of a T-maze equipped for self-stimulation in preference to the one with a feeding mechanism.

12. *How was the rewarding brain stimulation related to aversive factors?* In most areas where brain rewarding effects could be obtained, the same electric stimulation was shown to have aversive effects as well (Fig. 7) in experiments where the animal could reduce or interrupt an ongoing brain

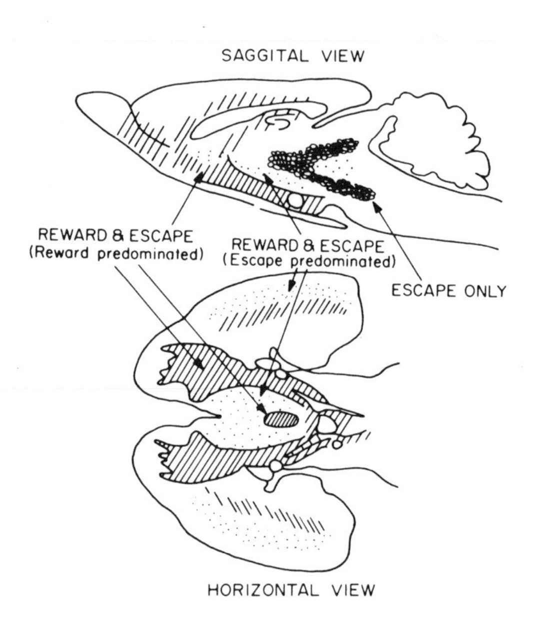

FIG. 7. Reward-escape overlaps. Stimulation in single-hatched areas was mainly rewarding. In stippled areas it was mainly aversive. In both it was mixed. In scrambled areas there was escape only.

stimulus series by some measurable behavior (Bower and Miller, 1958; Roberts, 1958; Kent and Grossman, 1969; Steiner et al., 1969; Steiner, Bodnar, Ackerman, and Ellman, 1973). Either longer trains had aversive effects, or the selfsame train appeared to be positive when the animal was allowed to generate a series of trains by its own behavior, and negative when it later responded to reduce or interrupt a "replay" of that same series of trains programmed now from a tape recorder (Steiner et al., 1969). With probes in the lateral hypothalamus when animals were given free control over stimulus duration, they did not turn the stimulus on and leave it on. Instead, they stopped the stimulus after brief trains (often approximately 0.5 sec). If probes were planted in parts of the medial hypothalamus animals would sometimes take much longer trains (Atrens and von Vietinghoff-Riesch, 1972). If probes were planted in some parts of the cingulate cortex, longer trains were also taken (*unpublished observations*). With probes in some places (e.g., on the boundaries between the tectum and the tegmental reticular formation) electric stimulation of the brain was mainly aversive (Delgado, Roberts, and Miller, 1954; Olds and Olds, 1963), and there was no appreciable tendency for animals to turn the stimulus on at all.

A surprising finding about most of the areas where both positive and negative effects could be demonstrated was that the self-selected train duration was not usually optimal in other tests. Animals self-selected short trains if allowed to control the duration by pressing a pedal to start and releasing it to stop. However, if they were forced to do much work for a single train, trains longer than the self-selected ones turned out to be optimal (Keesey, 1964; Hodos, 1965).

Between brain rewards and aversive stimulations, there were different interactions. Some rewarding brain stimulation counteracted aversive stimulation so that if a negative stimulus was applied within the 0.25-sec period just after the brain stimulus it had no influence at all (Cox and Valenstein, 1965; Valenstein, 1965). In quite different tests some reinforcing brain stimulation (in hypothalamus) augmented aversive behavior (Olds and Olds, 1963), whereas other rewarding brain stimulation (in septal area) suppressed the same escape behavior (Routtenberg and Olds, 1963).

13. *Was rewarding brain stimulation arousing or quieting?* The answer depends on the probe location. When stimulation was applied near the septal area it arrested overt behavior (Olds, 1956*b*). In these cases it also had parasympathetic effects, lowering the heart rate, blood pressure, and respiratory rate (Malmo, 1961). It slowed or halted escape behavior (Routtenberg and Olds, 1963). It sometimes even slowed the avid brain reward behavior that could be simultaneously provoked by stimulating a hypothalamus electrode (Keesey and Powley, 1968). When stimulation was applied in lateral hypothalamus it had quite the opposite effect (Perez-Cruet, Black, and Brady, 1963; Perez-Cruet, McIntire, and Pliskoff, 1965). It excited the animal and caused much overt locomotor activity and sympathetic peripheral

effects, raising respiratory rate and blood pressure. In this case it also increased aversive behavior (Olds and Olds, 1962; Stein, 1965).

14. *When stimulated in brain reward centers, what did humans feel?* If it was in the telencephalic centers, there were some reports of great reduction of pain or even hedonic experiences that seemed to be related to basic drives such as sex. If it was in hypothalamus there were no clear reports of positive affect in spite of behavioral signs of reward (patients manipulated switches to stimulate probes that were most likely in the hypothalamus). The actual location of probes in human studies was poorly determined (Fig. 8). These tests were carried out during therapeutic procedures or during medical researches aimed at developing therapeutic procedures; the patients were ill with major diseases, and all other therapeutic efforts had failed (Heath, 1954, 1964; Bishop, Elder, and Heath, 1964; Sem-Jacobsen, 1968; Delgado, 1969; Mark and Ervin, 1970).

15. *What was the relation, if any, to drug addiction?* Some addictive drugs (e.g., cocaine, amphetamine, and apomorphine) appeared to have strong relations to the brain reward behavior itself and to the neurochemical systems thought to underlie it (Stein, 1964*a,b,* 1966; Crow, 1970; Broekkamp and van Rossum, 1974). These drugs promoted the brain reward behaviors and most likely activated some of the same synaptic mechanisms as the brain reward stimulations. Other addictive drugs (e.g., morphine) did not have known relations to the underlying neurochemical systems and did not promote the behavior. There were signs, however, that morphine might affect

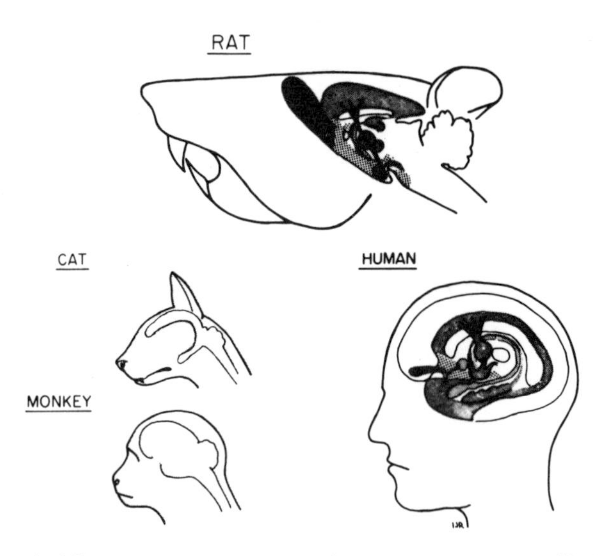

FIG. 8. Reward maps in different animals. The most detailed map is the one for rats (Olds and Olds, 1963). The ones for cats (Wilkenson and Peele, 1963) and monkeys (Bursten and Delgado, 1958) are in less detail, and the pictures presented here involve some speculative additions based on analogies. The human map (Bishop et al., 1963) is based on even less data and more speculation.

the same neurons as the rewarding brain stimulus (Kerr, Triplett, and Beeler, 1974). Animals "addicted" to morphine had neurons "turned on" during the active high drive condition evidenced by withdrawal symptoms; these neurons were turned off by morphine administration. In other experiments neurons recorded from the same areas fired actively during periods intervening between self-administered brain shocks but were turned off by the brain shocks themselves. A similarity of function between brain reward and morphine was shown by experiments in which the rewarding brain stimulation exhibited pain-reducing properties (Rose, 1974). Quite different studies showed a regional distribution of an "opiate receptor" in the brain that seemed to parallel the reward map to some degree (Kuhar, Pert, and Snyder, 1973). Therefore although the evidence is fragmentary, it is fair to suppose that a strong connection may be established between self-stimulation and drug-induced behaviors.

16. *Was there a period of addiction or incubation involved in brain reward behaviors?* The answer is yes and no (but mainly no). Brain stimulation often appeared to be rewarding when first applied. I have observed several times in my own laboratory, however, that there was an improvement in brain reward behavior that accumulated for 2 or 3 weeks. It first suggested a growing addiction, but this interpretation was wrong. This was shown by the fact that the improvement occurred regardless of whether the animals were stimulated (*unpublished observations*). In other words, if the first stimulations were delayed for several weeks, the improvement had already occurred by that time. The animals performed better than controls that had received implants more recently. Furthermore, when tests were started this late there was no further improvement. Thus the improvement occurred even without practice and without stimulation. It appeared at first as if it depended entirely on recovery from the effects of surgery. It now appears equally likely that it depends on some proliferation of nerve fibers which is surprisingly triggered by surgery; this proliferation required a period of growth to develop fully (Pickel, Segal, and Bloom, 1974*b*). Thus although there was a period of improvement in the brain-rewarding effects after probes were planted, there did not appear to be any addiction to the brain stimulation necessary to make it rewarding. Anecdotal observations from almost all "brain reward laboratories" tell of some animals pressing the pedal avidly within a minute or two of their first experience.

17. *Was there satiation of brain reward behavior?* The behavior often continued at high rates for substanial periods. If animals were permitted continuous access for hours or days, however, there were usually long pauses while eating, drinking, and sleeping occurred (Olds, 1958*b;* Valenstein and Beer, 1964). With probes in some locations the animals pedal-pressed at a slow but very steady pace when permitted only an hour of this behavior daily. When there was a shift to "continuous access," however, behavior gradually dropped to a new and much lower level. After this there were periodic rises

and falls. In most cases of slow or moderate self-stimulation rates, diurnal rhythms (sometimes mixed with faster rhythms) could be detected (Terman and Terman, 1970). When the behavior rates were maintained at higher levels by higher stimulating currents or by probes in locations yielding higher rates, the diurnal rhythms were not clear, but there were still periodic pauses in self-stimulation which permitted eating, drinking, sleeping, and so forth (Annau, Heffner, and Koob, 1974). When high currents were administered via probes planted in parts of the hypothalamus, the animals pressed continuously at very high rates after being switched to continuous access schedules showing no important decrement in rate for approximately 24 to 48 hr, but they did not continue indefinitely. In one case a rat averaged 30 responses per minute for 20 days (Valenstein and Beer, 1964).

18. *Did animals need a "priming" stimulus to start the behavior?* In other words, was some brain stimulation necessary in a trained animal to create an incentive or drive which then motivated further behavior? With some probe locations this "priming" was clearly necessary; in other cases it was not necessary but very helpful; and in still other cases it caused only moderate improvement in performance (Reid, Hunsicker, Lindsay, Gallistel, and Kent, 1973). Thus in some cases animals performed as if no incentive were needed other than being placed in a permissive environment, which triggered behavior toward the brain stimulus. In other cases where priming was more effective, it was interesting that the priming could often be obtained by stimulating a probe different from the one used for reward (Gallistel, 1969*b*). When two brain reward probes were planted in the same animal, one might be best for priming and the other for rewarding. In this case behavior was optimized by priming with one of the two and rewarding with the other. Furthermore, the rewardingness of a brain stimulus could be considerably enhanced by a different procedure which did not involve brain stimulation at all (Cantor and LoLordo, 1970, 1972). If a normal sensory signal preceded (and thus allowed the animal to anticipate) the brain stimulus by a brief time interval (a fraction of a second or so), this greatly improved the animal's response. The animal preferred signaled to unsignaled brain stimulation in almost all cases. This procedure could even convert a stimulus treated as aversive into one that was positive. This made it seem that one important effect of priming was to "tell" the animal of the availability of brain reward so it could correctly anticipate the outcome of the next behavioral response. It was generally assumed that probe location made the main difference in the need for priming. Priming was necessary (or at least very helpful) with probes in some locations, whereas with probes elsewhere it was not necessary (although priming always causes some improvement in the rate of approach). The anatomical locations that require priming have not yet been differentiated from those that do not; therefore the possibility of individual differences must still be entertained. The most likely answer is that two closely concurrent fiber streams exist, priming being required in one and not the other.

19. *Was an internal drive state required as a precondition for brain reward behaviors?* The first answer is that no deprivation measures were required to cause brain reward behavior. However, the necessity of priming as a prerequisite for brain reward behavior in some cases was possibly an indication that in these cases a drive was needed and that it was supplied as an aftereffect of the same brain stimulation which was rewarding. The rapid approach of other animals to brain pedals after 24 hr with no stimulation and with no deprivation suggested that at least in these cases no drive was required (Scott, 1967; Kornblith and Olds, 1968; Kent and Grossman, 1969).

20. *Did drive manipulations modify brain reward behavior?* Even though drives were unnecessary to provoke brain reward behavior, operations to increase drive often improved performance or caused thresholds to fall (Brady, Boren, Conrad, and Sidman, 1957); and sometimes (but rarely) they had just the opposite effect (Olds, 1958*a*). Food and water deprivation usually caused brain reward thresholds to fall and pedal rates to improve (Brady et al., 1957). However, because these drives made the animals more active, it was difficult to differentiate between the specific and the nonspecific effects of drive. The behavior had a positive feedback character because more pedal behavior (dependent variable) caused more reinforcement (independent variable); or to put it more bluntly, more effect resulted in more of the cause. That there was some specificity was indicated by the fact that deprivation sometimes had the opposite effect. In one experiment animals were maintained on a feeding schedule and tests were made during deprived and sated conditions (Olds, 1958*a*). Some pedal rates were improved during satiation, and others during hunger. In the same experiment animals (males in this case) were castrated and tests were continued for several weeks after castration. Then androgen replacement therapy was used. Some animals were slowed by castration and improved by replacement, whereas others were improved by castration and slowed by replacement therapy. There was a negative correlation between the effect of food and sex drives; in cases where castration improved performance, so did hunger. In cases where testosterone administration improved performance, hunger was inimical to some degree. In other words, most probes responded positively to either hunger or testosterone but not to both. The difference was assumed to be a result of differing probe location, but because there was only one probe per animal the differences could have been individual ones. Individual differences, however, were ruled out in an experiment comparing the effects of hunger and thirst (Gallistel and Beagley, 1971). Given the choice between stimulating one of two different probes, animals chose one of the two when thirsty and the other when hungry. In a different experiment, female rats were used and the self-stimulation rate was observed to covary with the normal estrous cycle (Prescott, 1966). The probe in this case was in the lateral posterior hypothalamus, a location which showed covariation with androgens in males (Olds, 1958*a*).

In some experiments it was shown that the condition of excessive food satiety caused by loading the stomach caused a decrement in self-stimulation behavior (Hoebel, 1968). In this experiment food was injected by means of a tube, which probably caused excessive distention of the stomach. Therefore the "loaded condition" was different from the behaviorally "full" condition of the other experiment. There have been no reports of improved brain reward behavior caused by this procedure, but only a limited range of probe location was reported. In a different kind of experiment, self-stimulation by probes in a region of the midbrain was motivated by a fear-producing stimulus [apparently indicating that in this case the brain stimulus was not as much rewarding as "soothing" (Deutsch and Howarth, 1962)].

21. *Did some brain stimulations cause drive states or drive behaviors?* The answer is yes. Brain stimulation in certain areas often caused one drive or another depending partly on the location of the probe and partly on other factors that are not fully clarified (Hess, 1954; Miller, 1960; Morgane, 1961; Herberg, 1963*a*; Coons, 1964; Mogenson and Stevenson, 1966). Saying the brain stimulation caused a drive means that if the drive object was present the stimulation caused consummatory behavior, and if the object was absent the stimulation caused instrumental behavior. Often this involved some work to get to or at the drive object. Such behaviors were often obtained with probes placed between the medial and lateral hypothalamus (Fig. 9). They were also produced with stimulation in other parts of the hypothalamus or farther afield, but the area between medial and lateral is thought to be most effective. If probes were placed in the anterior part of this longitudinal region, temperature-adjusting and sex responses were most likely to appear (*unpublished observations*). If probes were planted in the anterior part of a

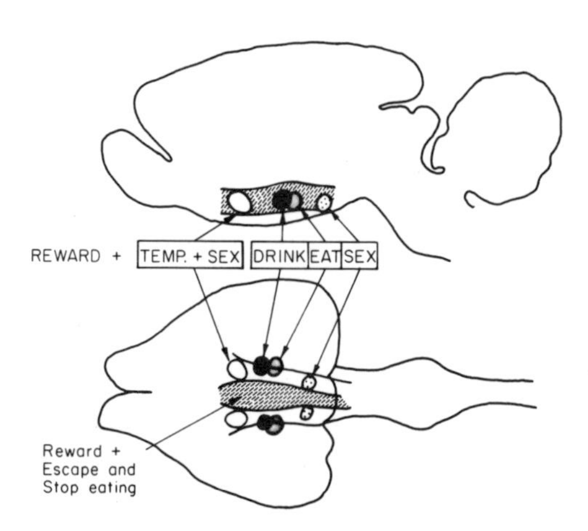

FIG. 9. Array of lateral hypothalamic regions where electrical stimulation causes instrumental and consummatory behaviors related to temperature, drinking, eating, and sex as most likely. The effects are heavily overlapped, but the most likely effect depends on the location of the stimulus.

middle region, food and water responses appeared but water responses were more likely. In the posterior part of the same middle region, food and water responses were still evoked but food responses were more likely (Valenstein, Cox, and Kakolewski, 1970). Probes placed more posteriorly were somewhat more likely to produce sexual behaviors (Herberg, 1963*a*). Because the latter were also sometimes obtained with anteriorly placed probes and because there was much overlap, the idea of localized drive centers was rejected. The idea of an undifferentiated system was also rejected because there was an array of regions from anterior to posterior hypothalamus where temperature, drinking, eating, and sex responses, respectively, were most likely.

Probes placed in a very small medial nucleus near the midline cause oxytocin release and so milk ejection. This can be considered a reproductive drive behavior. The site of stimulation was the paraventricular nucleus of the hypothalamus. Its boundaries were clearly defined and the effects of stimulating this region were well documented. Oxytocin is a fast-acting blood-borne hormone which causes milk ejection through the teats and other reproductive responses in a reflex fashion. Stimulation of the paraventricular nuclei evoked milk ejection in animals with thoracic spinal transections or spinal anesthesia. In estrogenized lactating rabbits, the milk ejection responses were accompanied by augmented uterine contractions (Cross, 1966).

In other experiments the anterior hypothalamus was stimulated thermally, causing temperature drive behaviors (Corbit, 1969, 1970; Adair, Casby, and Stolwijk, 1970; Murgatroyd and Hardy, 1970). When a thermal probe was used to heat or cool the area, it aroused compensatory temperature adjustments. When the area was heated, the animal sought cool stimulation; when it was cooled, the animal performed behaviors to warm the environment.

The "drive centers" defined by electric stimulation were by no means focused. There was no way to place a probe so that a drive effect could be guaranteed on this basis alone. In the best area the ratio of hits was below 100% (possibly as low as one-half or one-third). However, there were focal points where these (rather high) probabilities were achieved. As the probe was moved away from the focus the likelihood of stimulating a drive declined but stayed considerably above zero through all the various parts of the hypothalamus and the related telencephalic and midbrain structures.

22. *Were the drive behaviors evoked by electric stimulation stable?* No. If it was first determined that a given hypothalamic probe could be used for stimulation of a drive behavior, it was usually possible to modify the drive effects of the stimulus by a rather simple kind of "training" procedure (Fig. 10) (Valenstein, Cox, and Kakolewski, 1968; Valenstein, 1973*b*). Suppose the probe evoked eating. If the animal was repeatedly stimulated with interrupted trains (e.g., 1 min on, 5 min off) in the presence of a different drive object, the stimulus eventually appeared to evoke the drive appropriate to

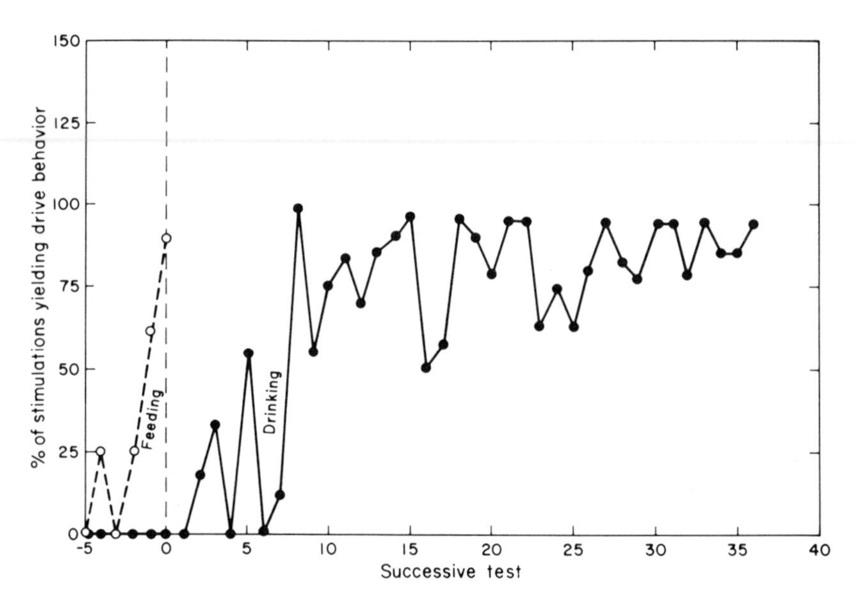

FIG. 10. Valenstein effect. Stimulation caused little drive behavior in early tests, but later it caused eating when both food and water were available. After repeated application of stimulus trains with only water available, the stimulus gradually came to evoke drinking.

the new object. In the end, the rat sometimes still ate during stimulation if given a choice; but in other cases it preferred the new drive object. Because the stimulus did not originally provoke any behavior toward the second drive object, there was evidence of a change in the drive behavior even when the animal preferred to eat. It is sometimes argued that the original eating response to the brain stimulus might itself have been learned in a similar fashion at the beginning of the tests. This had led to serious question of whether the stimulated effect is appropriately called a drive effect at all. Mapping the most likely areas for the different drives into different parts of the hypothalamus, however, was scarcely compatible with the view that all drive effects were learned.

23. *Did some brain stimulations stop specific drive behaviors in the way that satiety stops feeding?* This was a difficult question to answer because aversive stimulation brought many behaviors to a halt without having any specific relation to the drives involved (Krasne, 1962). There were, however, some stimulations that appeared to halt eating behavior in a more specific fashion. The stimulation seemed specific because of special food behaviors that occurred during a poststimulatory "rebound," i.e., during the period just after the stimulation was terminated. The stimulations that had this effect were in the medial hypothalamus, but the exact locations are unknown or in dispute. Possibly the anterior part of the ventromedial nucleus and the adjacent posterior part of the anterior nucleus, or some pathways

in this general area were involved (Wyrwicka and Dobrzecka, 1960; Olds, Allan, and Briese, 1971). When stimulation was applied in these areas in some animals or with some probes it caused hungry animals to stop feeding during the stimulus and the sated animals to begin eating at (or shortly after) the offset of the stimulus. In other words, the electric stimulus caused feeding of a hungry animal to stop, and its offset caused a sated animal to begin eating. Because many brain-stimulated behaviors are replaced by opposed behaviors during a brief period just after cessation of the stimulus, the concept of "rebound" is used. The brain is considered to be replete with "opponent process" systems; electric stimulation is thought to fatigue the stimulated member of an opponent pair, weakening it; and this is supposed to result in a rebound of the opposite character as soon as the stimulus stops. Because of this view, the locations where stimulation stopped eating and rebound evoked it were thought to be more specifically related to this drive system than those locations where stimulation stopped all behaviors without specific rebound effects. The latter stimuli with only general effects were thought to be aversive or inhibitory. The stimuli with specific rebound effects were viewed as possibly activating "satiety" mechanisms. There have been no extensive research programs on "satiety-like" mechanisms for drives other than hunger.

24. *Did the brain "centers" for drives or satiety overlap with those for reward?* In most areas where electric stimulation caused drive behaviors such as eating, drinking, or sex responses, the brain stimulus also provoked brain reward behaviors (Hoebel and Teitelbaum, 1962; Margules and Olds, 1962; Caggiula and Hoebel, 1966; Mogenson and Stevenson, 1966). This was particularly true of the areas in middle and posterior hypothalamus between the medial and lateral areas, and in the lateral area. Stimulation in these areas also produced aversive reactions, but the balance was tipped toward reward. The aversive behaviors were high in threshold and low in rate (and sometimes required that the trains be lengthened). The appetitive behaviors were low in threshold and high in rate. Thus even though there was some *a priori* view that "reward" and "satiety" might be correlated, there was evidence for a correlation of brain reward and brain drive centers. Brain reward behavior, however, was also provoked in other parts of the hypothalamus where drive behaviors were not (or at least where drive effects have not yet been documented). Reward behaviors were also provoked by electric stimulations in the medial hypothalamic centers, e.g., the ventromedial nucleus (Atrens and von Vietinghoff-Riesch, 1972). This was previously thought of as an area where stimulation halted eating (based on experiments with goats mainly). Stimulation here often did not stop eating in the rat. Still there were other parts of the hypothalamus whose stimulation both halted eating and caused rebound eating. Stimulation at least at some of these locations was rewarding. This might suggest a correlation of brain reward centers with both "drive" and "satiety" centers, which points to the obvious fact that

related functions such as reward, drive, and satiety need to interdigitate their mechanisms if they were to interact conjointly to control behavior. Most of the medial hypothalamic nuclei (e.g., ventromedial, dorsomedial, or anterior nucleus) were controversial as members of the "brain reward map." This was because, even though both positive and negative reinforcements were represented, the scale in many medial centers was tipped to the negative. Aversive thresholds were low, and aversive behavior rates high. Self-stimulation thresholds were higher than those in lateral hypothalamus, and rates were lower. It was the slow rates which were especially notable. Nevertheless, there was some reason to believe that stimulation of some medial centers might be better for rewarding maze behaviors and possibly less likely to require priming to elicit reward behavior than stimulation in lateral centers. Moreover, one of the few locations in the brain where there was almost pure positive behavior (rapid behavior to start the stimulus and almost no behavior to shut it off) was the midline, periventricular nucleus of the posterior hypothalamus (Atrens and von Vietinghoff-Riesch, 1972).

That a stimulus should at the same time cause consummatory responses and be pursued as a goal seemed in good accord. Thus the sex, eating, and drinking behaviors caused during a stimulus fitted with the strong goal-directed behaviors aimed at self-stimulation; both effects might derive from a single neuronal mechanism. However, because the stimulus usually also caused instrumental behavior (sometimes hard work) in pursuit of food or water, this made it seem that the stimulus might have a driving or goading character, which might imply a negative state. Therefore it was better to assume that the brain stimulus was affecting a mixed set of elements, both drive and reward ones. It seemed fair to suppose that the different elements were associated in the hypothalamus so they could interact in the control of behavior.

25. *Was the rewarding effect of stimulating the "feeding center" increased by hunger?* The term "feeding center" is used to refer to those locations where electric stimulation caused food-directed behavior. When "reward" probes were planted in areas where eating was also induced, there were paradoxical effects. When animals were "oversatiated" by loading the stomach, reward behavior was reduced (Hoebel, 1968); but when in different experiments the animals were deprived of food for 1 or 2 days, this also curtailed and eventually stopped behavior rewarded by "feeding center" stimulation (*unpublished observation;* Fig. 11). The same animal continued to pedal-press and even increased response rates when the reward was delivered to a different probe, one where sex drive behavior was evoked. Thus the responses augmented during extreme starvation were not the ones rewarded by stimulations of the "feeding center."

26. *Did the animal give up food in order to get "feeding center" stimulation?* No. Animals gave up food as was previously described for some rewarding brain stimulations (Routtenberg and Lindy, 1965; Spies, 1965;

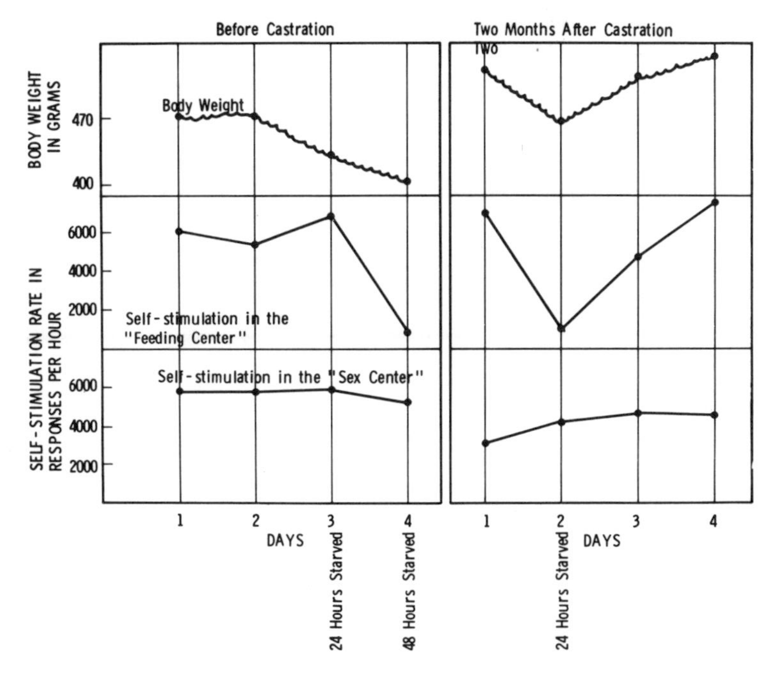

FIG. 11. Self-stimulation in feeding and sex-related areas during food-deprivation and after castration. One probe was said to be in the feeding center because its stimulation caused eating, and the other in the sex center because its stimulation caused ejaculation of motile sperm. The two probes were in the same animal, and during tests alternate 2-min periods were devoted first to one and then to the other probe. Starvation often caused slowing of pedal behavior when the food-related probe was being stimulated, but it did not slow self-stimulation of the sex probe.

Miliaressis and Cardo, 1973), but those which evoked feeding behavior in pretests usually failed in the "self-starvation" tests (*unpublished observations*). In these cases as the animals got hungrier, the brain reward pedal responses became scarcer and the animal gradually returned to eating. Other brain stimulations in hypothalamus and in the ventral tegmental area, however, did cause animals to renounce food and run the danger of starvation. Because the stimulations did not cause eating, however, they would be viewed as being outside of the "feeding center."

27. *Could brain rewards be added to normal rewards?* Yes. In some experiments olfactory bulb stimulation was used as the reward (Phillips and Mogenson, 1969). This was enhanced by simultaneous administration of odors shown to be positive, and curtailed by odors shown to be negative (Phillips, 1970). In other experiments brain stimulation that evoked both drinking and reward behavior was used (Mendelson, 1967; Mogenson and Morgan, 1967). In these cases currents below the "reward threshold" evoked self-stimulation if water was available but not if it was absent. The animals in these cases would self-stimulate and then drink and continue this

cycle of self-administered stimulation alternating (or running concurrently) with normal consummatory behavior. Similar results were also produced with feeding center stimulation and food reward (Coons and Cruce, 1968; Poschel, 1968). Although these experiments and others like them gave the appearance of additivity between the brain reward and peripheral ones, other interpretations (not greatly different) were possible. In the case of the positive odor, it is not clear if this would have been facilitating to any ongoing behavior (and the aversive odor might have slowed behavior generally). In the case of the water behavior, the subthreshold current might have been rewarding by itself, but the simultaneously evoked drive might have been aversive in the absence of water. However, self-stimulation could go on in the presence of water to assuage the induced thirst.

28. *Was the "drive" effect the same as the "priming effect?* No. The animal primed by a prior brain stimulus sought further brain stimulations (Gallistel, 1973), but it did not eat or seek food during this poststimulatory period (Cox, Kakolewski, and Valenstein, 1969). If the probe was in a "drive center" as was quite common, the animal sought the drive object avidly during the duration of the stimulus and switched its attention abruptly away from the drive object during the period when the stimulus was turned off (*unpublished observation*). In the aftereffect of stimulation there was a strong behavior directed toward more stimulation. The drive for food (or another drive object) had disappeared immediately at the offset. Thus the impulse to self-stimulate that decayed gradually after the stimulus was not the same as the drive activated during the stimulus. Furthermore, priming was effective at many sites where there was no sign of any drive being aroused. (Valenstein et al., 1970).

29. *Was the reward effect the same as the priming effect?* In some cases the two could be separated. In one set of experiments a start box connected to a goal box by a simple runway or alley was used. A stimulus applied in the start box was used for priming. A stimulus in the goal box was used for reward. In this test some probes yielded better priming and others better reward [so the animal with two probes gave the best behavior if primed with one and stimulated with the other (Gallistel, 1969*b*)]. Moreover, it was possible to show that the stimulus parameters most effective for priming were different from those most effective for rewarding. Interesting experiments on this have been done with pulse pairs (Deutsch, 1964; Gallistel, Rolls, and Greene, 1969). A repetition rate of pulses (R) was chosen such that R was below threshold but $2R$ was above it. Then pulse pairs were used instead of single pulses and were applied at the repetition rate R. When separation of the two pulses in a pair was sufficient, the effective rate was $2R$; but when the separation was too small, the second pulse became ineffective and the effective rate was R. An abrupt behavior change was expected to occur at the transition, and it was supposed to be possible to test for this. To some degree this expectation was fulfilled. With this method it was pos-

sible to determine for a stimulated effect the "cutoff point" at which the second pulse changed from effective to ineffective. This was taken to be a measure of the "refractory period" or some such parameter of the underlying neuronal elements. If two stimulated phenomena had the same cutoff point, it indicated similar underlying neurons. These were, of course, not necessarily identical; many neurons in the brain have similar refractory periods so, even at best, the method was not very strong. If two stimulated phenomena had different cutoff points, it indicated different underlying elements. Brain reward and brain stimulated "drives" had the same cutoff point, 0.6 msec (Rolls, 1973). The priming effect had a different one, 0.8 msec (Gallistel, Rolls, and Greene, 1969). Since this was also the cutoff point for a set of simultaneously stimulated neurons thought to be involved in "arousal," it was considered possible that priming and arousal might have something in common (Rolls, 1971*a*). Even a differentiation of two effects by this method, however, did not imply two totally different mechanisms; it is possible to imagine several ways in which a partly common mechanism would be differentiated. Suppose, for example, that stimulation was applied to an axon. It would fire the axon and its terminals in the forward direction and the soma-dendrite input mechanism in a backward direction. Now imagine that the axon could be fired at a high rate but the soma-dendrite mechanism could not. The second pulse in a pair might then be effective for the axons but ineffective for the dendrite. What difference could this make? One answer is that the axon alone might support continued brain reward within a bout of behavior, but sustained interest or renewed behavior after several minutes of waiting might require a short-term memory. This might necessitate activating the dendrites during the initial reward period in order to cause connections to form between them and other coactive sensory traces.

30. *Were the rewarding effects of a brain stimulus simple or a compound?* If priming were an essential component of the reward stimulus then the answer would be: compound. The animal would need to be primed by one effect of the stimulus and rewarded by a different one. The two fiber sets implied by the pulse pair experiments might suggest this kind of complexity. The fact that animals run mazes without priming puts a dent in this supposition, but there are other possibilities that need to be considered. The drive might not be needed during the pursuit behavior but only during the consummatory endpoint. Some experiments (Mendelson, 1966) appeared to show that the animal would run a maze without a drive if the drive was supplied along with the reward at the end of the maze. In this experiment probes in a drive center were used to present the "drive" (electrical drive) in the goal box. It is not clear to me that the "drive" stimulus was not itself an added reward, but other experiments have pointed in the same direction. Reward may therefore be complex in much the same way pain is supposed to be. One theory of pain is that it always depends on a pattern of stimulation (Melzak and Wall, 1965). Nonintense stimulation of the skin surrounding a

point stimulus may suppress pain, while punctate stimulation, which appears to make up but a small part of the larger stimulus, is painful. This has led to a theory that pain is not simple. It requires one kind of stimulation uncounteracted by another kind. There seems reason why rewarding stimulation might also be compound. The notion that a drive and a reward need to go together to make reinforcement fits with food behavior. Almost any food can be made aversive if the animal is pretreated with sufficient excess of it. It seems possible, therefore, that a brain stimulus might activate more than one component of the pattern of neural events required to "key" the reward lock. At least it seems likely that a combination of neuronal processes might be required to trigger the reward process.

If the effect were complex, the complexity might be on the afferent side of the "reward neurons," and thus the brain reward stimulus might still be simple. In other words, a hunger plus a gustatory signal would need to be conjoined to cause normal activation of a reward neuron, but the activated reward neuron would not require further complementary conditions.

31. *Was there any indication of a common denominator such as the term "pleasure" implies?* The fact that stimulation in the lateral hypothalamus could be "converted" from drive to drive by training procedures (Valenstein et al., 1970) suggested that the main import of the stimulus might be its common denominator properties. It is equally likely, however, that the stimulus affected several drives which could be further sensitized by their appropriate targets. It seems possible that the stimulus caused rather specific drives, which then became pathologically channeled toward false goals by the regular association between the brain drive stimulus and the particular goal object. If there were a common denominator, its stimulation might be purely positive. That purely positive reinforcement caused by brain stimulation was rare mitigated the likelihood of such a system. However, this might be explained by arguing that positive and negative common denominator neurons were mixed (so as to act reciprocally). In such a case stimulation would be ambivalent even though the actual neurons involved were not. In any event the question of whether there is some common denominator of positive reinforcement (or possibly even a common denominator between positive and negative reinforcement) (Olds and Olds, 1962, 1964; Stein, 1964*c*, 1965) is unanswered. It deserves further study.

32. *Was there a focal center where lesions abolished reward behavior?* The answer was not clear, but probably there was not. Lesions of specific telencephalic areas such as the septal area or the amygdaloid complex had small effects if any on brain reward behavior evoked by hypothalamic stimulation (Ward, 1960, 1961). Lesions along the main path to the hypothalamus failed to stop olfactory bulb self-stimulation (Valenstein and Campbell, 1966), although there were alternate pathways (Routtenberg and Sloan, 1974). Procaine applied in the hypothalamus stopped olfactory bulb-evoked reward behavior (Nakajima and Iwasaki, 1973). Lesions anteriorly placed in

the hypothalamus did not stop pedal behavior reinforced by more posterior stimulation (Olds and Olds, 1969). These anterior lesions did, however, block maze behavior reinforced by the same stimulus (Olds and Hogberg, 1964). This seemed to indicate that a path from hypothalamus to cortex might be necessary if the behavior to be reinforced were so complex that it needed the "higher centers." Pointing in this same direction were experiments in which all of the brain anterior and dorsal to the thalamus was removed (Fig. 12) (Huston and Borbely, 1974), including neocortex, paleocortex, and basal ganglia. Many behaviors did not occur at all in these animals. The animals were "rewarded" with brain stimulation for performing rather simple behaviors, and the frequency of these was substantially and appropriately modified by brain reward. Thus the telencephalon was dispensable as far as the reinforcing effects of brain stimulation were concerned even though complex behaviors could not be trained by reinforcement without it. The most interesting feature of the animals without telencephalons was that there was no extinction of the reinforced behaviors. Withdrawal of the reinforcing

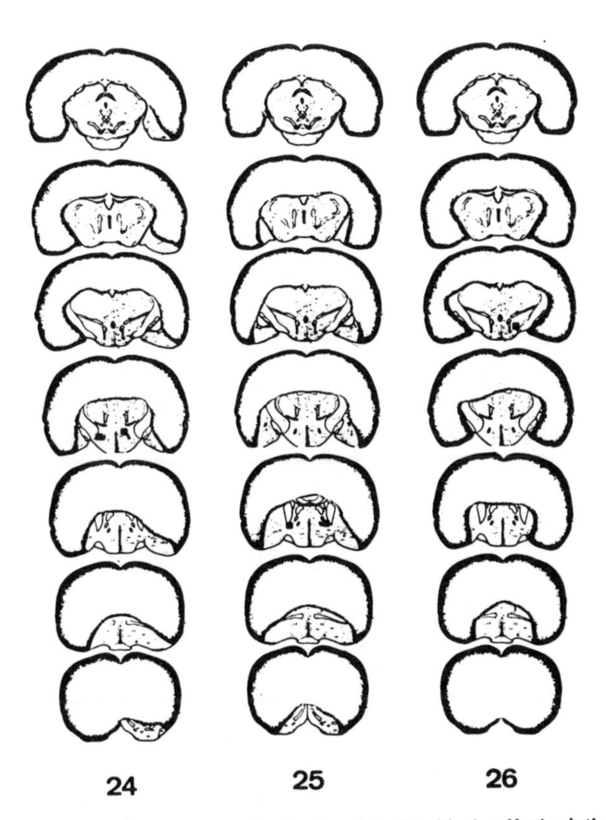

FIG. 12. Large telencephalic lesions in three brains that failed to block self-stimulation but did block its extinction. (From Huston and Borbely, 1974.)

stimulus did not cause the behavior to disappear or its frequency to be reduced. The only way the behavior could be stopped was by changing the stimulus contingencies so as to reward the animal for doing incompatible things. Thus the upper part of the brain was required for complicated performances and for extinction of even simple ones.

Even though electrical stimulation in the middle part of the medial forebrain bundle was still reinforcing after anterior hypothalamic lesions in the same bundle, still there was some reduction in rates (Fig. 13) (Boyd and Gardner, 1967; Olds and Olds, 1969). Sometimes this was quite pronounced; but usually after several weeks for recovery, the rates came back up to approximately two-thirds of original levels. Lesions placed above the hypothalamus on pathways up to the thalamus had similar effects, reducing the rates at first but permitting substantial recovery. Posterior lesions placed on the medial forebrain bundle path toward the midbrain were the most effective, but even in these cases there was usually substantial recovery (up to 50% of former levels or even higher several weeks after surgery). These experiments appeared to imply that lesions in all three zones might have abolished the behavior altogether, but no such experiments were reported.

Damage to the locus coeruleus, which is the origin of the main norepinephrine path to telencephalon, caused similar (or possibly even more severe) damage to brain reward behavior (M. E. Olds, *private communication;* L. J. Ellman, *private communication*). Also poisons applied in the ventricles which damaged all the forebrain catecholamine pathways were extremely effective in blocking brain reward behavior (M. E. Olds, *private communication*).

33. *What were the best parameters for the electric stimulus?* Often it did not seem to matter. Sine wave trains of alternating current and square wave trains of pulses were used. Negative pulses were more effective than positive ones—as is generally the case with electrical stimulation of nerve or muscle (Wetzel, Howell, and Bearie, 1969). Increases in frequency added to the effectiveness of a train. As this occurred when the duration was fixed, it

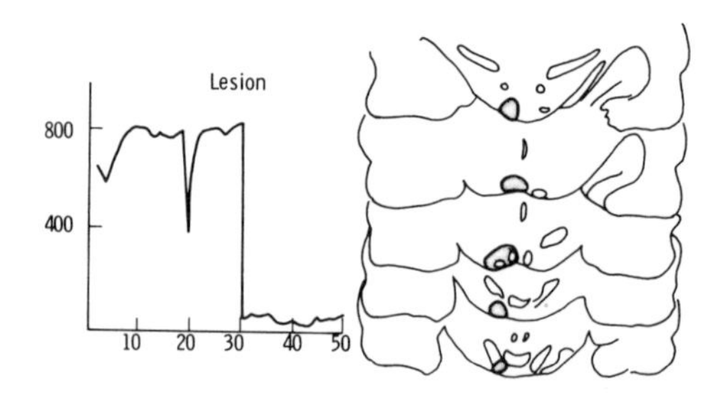

FIG. 13. Lesion in the medial forebrain bundle that caused a nearly complete cessation of self-stimulation via a nearby probe placed on the same side anterior to the lesions. Pedal rate in responses per test are on the ordinate. Successive days of testing are on the abscissa (Boyd and Gardner, 1967).

appeared to indicate only that more stimulations were more effective than fewer (Ward, 1959; Keesey, 1962). When frequencies became too high, however, the effectiveness did not increase further; it appeared likely that alternate pulses were rendered ineffective by the refractory periods of the cells involved. In square wave studies, lengthening the duration of the pulses was not so effective a way of adding to the amount of stimulation as was augmenting the frequency or the peak amplitude. It took approximately two or three times as much charge added by lengthening the pulses to get the same increase in self-stimulation rate as by increasing the amplitude. Thus to get the most behavior for the least charge, very brief pulses were by far the most effective. However, the mixed nature of the response often observed with short pulses of very large amplitude suggested that the cost of this procedure was to stimulate a very broad swath of brain tissue and thus a loss of stimulus localization (*unpublished observations*). As opposed to increasing the duration of the pulses, which was relatively ineffective, doubling the frequency often had quite the same effect as doubling the amplitude. This seemed to indicate that doubling the number of stimuli applied to a small area or doubling the area had quite similar effects.

The probe size and stimulus parameters interacted; and the larger the probe, the larger the minimum effective amplitude (*unpublished observations*). This was logically attributable to the fact that current density rather than current *per se* was the effective stimulus. Thus with probes of approximately 60 μ diameter, sine wave currents of about 5 μA (rms) were sometimes effective stimuli. With probes of 400 μ diameter, currents under 200 μA were never effective.

The "size" of the stimulus was best varied by increasing the frequency, amplitude, or duration. Frequency was rarely the method chosen because it became confused in the region between 500 and 2,000 Hz (as indicated above). Increases in the amplitude of the stimulus caused three kinds of change depending on the location of the probe. One was a steady increase in rate of pedal-pressing for each increase in current level up to a ceiling, with no decline in rates at very high stimulus levels (Olds et al., 1960). A second was an increase up to a point with later decrease on further addition of current (Reynolds, 1958; Keesey, 1962). A third was an "undulation"—small increases augmented pedal rates, further increases would bring them down, still further increases in current would cause rates to go higher again (Olds, et al., 1960). These three effects were interpreted in terms of the layered or homogeneous composition of the stimulated area. If the area surrounding the tip was relatively homogeneous, more stimulation caused more effect. If there was a border between a positive reinforcement area and a counteracting area, small currents could be positive and larger currents would engage the countersystem. If a positive reinforcement area was transected by a narrow pathway of counteracting elements, the undulating curves would be explained.

When "trials to criterion" in a maze or discrimination problem were used as the measure of learning rate, animals learned just as fast to low-intensity as to high-intensity stimuli, even though they ran much faster to the high-intensity ones (Keesey, 1966). Theories about possible confusion from high-intensity signals were introduced as a possible explanation. Although this seems likely, it is surprising that things would be so well balanced between rising reinforcement and rising confusion that there would be neither improvement nor decline in learning rate as the intensity was increased. A second possibility was that the learning rate itself had some sort of asymptote. This did not appear to be the answer either, as animals learned faster if food reward was used.

The effect of train duration on brain reward behavior turned out to be complicated. At the long end of the continuum I have observed animals to self-administer trains in the cingulate cortex that lasted 5 to 15 min. At the other extreme, in search of a minimum effective train, I once used a single pulse of 2.4 msec duration; it served as a reward for a skilled rat with a hypothalamic probe. The animal had a pedal rate of two to four per second, and it was likely the self-administered train rather than the individual pulses that sustained the behavior.

Different brain locations had different optimal stimulus durations (*unpublished observations*); different electric current intensities also had different optimal durations. To support self-stimulation, septal area probes required longer trains than those in the hypothalamus; and in either location, weaker stimulations needed to be longer than strong ones.

As indicated above in the discussion of aversive countereffects, animals self-selected trains that were shorter than those shown to be maximally effective in other situations (Keesey, 1964). This led to the conclusion that even though several short trains were more rewarding than a long one, a long one was still more rewarding than a single short one. Support for the view that a repeatedly interrupted train should be more rewarding than the same amount of stimulation applied continuously came from experiments showing that the onset of the train was probably more rewarding than its continuation (Poschel, 1963; Deutsch and Albertson, 1974). Other experiments supported the complementary view, however, that aversive side effects apparently built up over time (Bower and Miller, 1958). Most likely adaptation to both continued trains and aversive countereffects were involved.

One interesting argument was that the added effectiveness of long trains came not from added reward value but from added priming power. An experiment aimed to demonstrate this seemed to show that trains of approximately 0.3 sec (64 pulses at 200/sec) were maximally rewarding, but that the priming power was augmented by increasing the number of 0.3-sec trains to 10 or more delivered at 1/sec (Gallistel, 1969*a*). The cutoff of the rewarding effect at 0.3 msec ran counter to the common sense notion that more rewards are more rewarding than fewer (even for rats). From my experience with experiments of this kind, I would not expect this finding to hold up under several changed conditions. With less intense stimulation, I would expect to see a considerable lengthening of the 0.3-sec period during which added stimulation had added reward value. Similarly, with other probe locations I would also expect a substantial lengthening of this period. Furthermore, by using another mode of testing that would eliminate the priming altogether, having one trial an hour or one trial a day, I would expect a much longer series of rewards to be much more effective than a 0.3-sec train. Thus I have come to three tentative conclusions regarding the problems and controversies related to extending the duration of the stimulus trains. First, with some probe locations the onset of the train may be more rewarding than its continuation; but with other locations the opposite might be true. Second, in some cases there may be aversive effects that are slow in onset and that attenuate the rewarding effects of extended trains. Third, the argument that extending trains beyond 0.3 sec adds to "priming" but not to "reward" may be true only for a limited set of conditions.

34. *Could one guess either by the animals' responses or by the nature of the stimuli that these would be rewarding?* In some cases, as already indicated, this might be possible. For example, when the stimulus produced a consummatory sex (Herberg, 1963*a*) or food (Coons, 1964) behavior, this might be guessed to be rewarding. However, when the stimulus caused the animal to brave a painful foot shock on the way to food it would not be guessed that the stimulus itself was rewarding. In a different (and possibly unrelated) kind of experiment, a cold animal pressed a pedal to heat the hypothalamus (Corbit, 1973). To me this seemed the only case where it was obvious that the animal was pressing a pedal to counteract the brain effects of a drive.

35. *Were there any relations of brain reward to sleep?* Yes, some rewarding brain stimulations put animals to sleep, although this was not usual (Angyan, 1974). The more usual rewarding stimulations (which did not put animals to sleep) were related by experiments to paradoxical sleep (Steiner and Ellman, 1972). This is the kind of sleep with rapid eye movements, twitches, and an awake-looking EEG that is thought to be related to dreams in humans. Mammals normally devote a certain proportion of their sleep time to this kind of sleep. If they are deprived of paradoxical sleep by special experimental procedures, they later make up for the loss by spending a larger part of the sleep in this state. The deprivation also causes a moderate increase in feeding, sexual behavior, and brain reward behavior. Animals deprived of paradoxical sleep but permitted to self-stimulate are interesting. The brain reward behavior seems to compensate for the shortage of paradoxical sleep so that such animals do not spend sleep time making up the loss.

Other reports indicate daily rhythms in self-stimulation behavior (Olds, 1958*b*; Terman and Terman, 1970). These suggest a relation of the behavior to sleep and waking cycles. Besides these more or less direct (but poorly understood) connections to sleep and paradoxical sleep, there is a pharmacological connection that is discussed in more detail later. A neuronal messenger substance, serotonin, which is possibly involved as a "sleep hormone," opposes brain reward behavior under some circumstances and promotes it under others (possibly probe location makes the main difference). From the evidence, therefore, I would guess that some brain reward behavior is related to the main sleep system, but most is not. That which is not, however, may have an important relation to paradoxical sleep, because such sleep may be tied into the brain's drive-reward system.

D. Summary

Brain reward behavior occurred when fibers of the olfactory brain and the brain's catecholamine sytems were stimulated. The main point of intersection of these two systems was in the hypothalamus; at least this was the area where the greatest concentrations of these two kinds of fibers were located. All parts of the hypothalamus yielded reward behavior, but in the lateral parts (which handle most of the input-output messages) positive effects were most unambiguous. An in-between area (between medial and lateral hypothalamus) yielded very ambiguous effects, including aversive and drive components. That is, the animal escaped from these stimulations as well as approaching them, and the stimulations also caused instrumental and consummatory responses in pursuit of normal rewards. Some very medial areas of hypothalamus near the ventricle yielded predominantly positive effects like the far lateral areas. Even in the predominantly positive areas, negative countereffects were detected by careful analytical methods. In the mixed in-between areas of reward-aversive-and-drive effects, there was a vague map with temperature, drinking, eating, and sex behaviors arrayed from front to back. However, these behaviors could be changed to some degree from one to the other by a simple "training" procedure (i.e., stimulating the animal in the presence of the to-be-pursued goal object). Self-starting behavior that required no drive and no priming was evoked with some probes, and these were also the best for motivating complicated maze behaviors. In other cases the behavior appeared to need priming (prior brain stimulation) to get it going.

Four problems arising from the brain stimulation studies were: (1) What neurons caused the rewarding effects? (2) Why did training cause drive behaviors to change? (3) What caused the aversive countereffects (or the responding to interrupt stimulus trains) in the predominantly positive areas? (4) What made the difference between stimulations which required priming and those that did not?

Lesions

A wide range of hypothalamic lesions and pathologies affect drive and reinforcement behaviors. The lesion methods have been sharpened by the use of quite small knife cuts to sever fibers. With these cuts and with electrolytic methods, some lesions caused obesity and others a loss of eating and drinking behaviors. In other experiments male sex behavior, female sex behavior, and temperature regulation were impaired or abolished. The cuts and lesions severed input-output paths from widely dispersed areas. Therefore the brain structures involved in the various effects are still unknown. Nevertheless, the studies have been extensive, particularly in relation to obesity and starvation, and the character of these effects has been clarified to some degree.

Experiments aimed at finding specific sites where tissue damage caused these effects were done mostly with rats. There is some indication that in this regard rats may be only a rough model for other mammals. There are differences even between male and female rats. Nevertheless, the rat work is taken as giving some idea of the locus and character of the effects for the "general mammal."

A. Overeating and Obesity Caused by Hypothalamic Damage

It has been known for a long time that lesions at the base of the brain cause animals and humans to become obese. The difficulty was originally ascribed to the pituitary and to a fault in the metabolic system under its control. Later research opposed this view to some degree, although still later research caused a partial revival. The opposed researchers showed (1) that the lesions did not have to affect the pituitary to be effective (Hetherington and Ranson, 1942*a,b*); and (2) that overeating was more important than faulty utilization of food as the most obvious culprit (Brobeck, Tepperman, and Long, 1943). Both overeating and the excessive laying down of fat deposits are now supposed to be twin (and somewhat independent) culprits (Bernardis, Chlouverakis, Schnatz, and Frohman, 1974). Research emphasis, at least, makes overeating a main one.

The anatomical focus of this effect has not been pinpointed with certainty even in the rat. Large lesions (which destroyed 2 or 3 mm^3 of the 8 mm^3 of hypothalamic tissue) placed in many different parts of the hypothalamus caused animals to become obese. There were some large lesions that did not have the effect, and likely a small minority that had the opposite effect, but the majority were effective in causing hypothalamic obesity (Hetherington, 1944). Smaller lesions of about 1 mm^3 were used to further localize the critical tissues. When these were placed bilaterally, there turned out to be a large number of different locations in the medial hypothalamus and in the midlateral parts of the hypothalamus where lesions caused obesity to some degree. Almost two-thirds of the points tested in a map of the hypothalamus yielded these effects (Anand and Brobeck, 1951).

From these studies the focus was thought to be the ventromedial nucleus, which is a very prominent member of the medial group of hypothalamic nuclei. It is almost at the bottom of the hypothalamus and about halfway from the front to the back. It is because of this central location in relation to the effective lesions that it has been accepted as a focus. It has seemed possible to many that, instead of the ventromedial nucleus, some set of fibers easily damaged by lesions in this general vicinity might be an alternate candidate for the focus.

Other experiments added some weight to the view that a fiber bundle was mainly involved. These demonstrated that the effect could be achieved without destroying neuron cell bodies. It was only necessary to make a knife cut between the medial and lateral sectors of the hypothalamus (Albert and Storlien, 1969; Gold, 1970). If these knife cuts were placed in anterior or posterior sectors they failed, but if placed in a middle sector they appeared to have quite similar effects to the medial lesions (Paxinos and Bindra, 1972). Because this seemed a likely method to destroy important input or output pathways of the ventromedial nucleus, it did not by itself upset the generally accepted view that the ventromedial nucleus was the focus. However, one set of knife-cut studies was a little surprising. Instead of cutting between medial and lateral, the cut was made in the heart of the ventromedial nucleus, cutting it in two, or even along its medial edge. This left either one-half of the nucleus or most of it still attached to the lateral area. Still it caused the full measure of obesity (Sclafani, Berner, and Maul, 1973). This made it seem that something still more medially placed than the ventromedial nucleus might be involved—possibly the special cells along the wall of the ventricle, or transport systems coming from the ventricle or from the blood. Substantial (but milder) obesity was also caused when the knife-cut lesions were placed some distance out into the lateral hypothalamus (Sclafani et al., 1973). Thus it appeared that a connecting system traversing a rather long distance between the ventricular wall and the wheel-shaped neurons of the lateral hypothalamus might be involved. Although these studies caused some doubt about ventromedial hypothalamic involvement, they did not cause any revolution. It was still some medial part of the middle hypothalamus that seemed to be involved.

A much newer method of selectively poisoning a pathway that is more tangentially related to this part of the hypothalamus has, however, led to second thoughts (Ahlskog and Hoebel, 1972). These experiments are discussed later. Although they suggest that there may be no tightly bounded satiety center in this part of the hypothalamus, they do not eliminate this region as a candidate for some specially important role in the effect.

What kind of effect is involved? To find out if it was really a fault in metabolism, rats with these lesions were prevented from overeating (Brobeck et al., 1943). Their diet was matched to that of an unlesioned group to see if they would become obese on the same diet. They did not. This indicated that the lesions did not by themselves cause the rats to become obese and that they did cause overeating. The experiments might be thought to show that the lesions did not by themselves modify the proportion of food that got converted to fat deposits. This is mistaken. Dieted (nonobese) animals with these lesions had a disproportionate amount of their weight in fat (Bernardis et al., 1974). The excessive fat was produced by an over-rapid conversion of glucose to fat. This by itself would cause overeating. The generally accepted view, however, is that even if there is a more direct effect on fat stores there is also an independent effect on eating.

What kind of overeating was it? The picture is clouded to some degree. As the animals recovered from anesthesia during the hours after electrolytic surgery, they appeared at first to have a very high hunger drive. They ate ravenously (Brobeck et al., 1943). Animals almost choked to death trying to get more food into their mouths. I do not know how long this voracious feeding lasted. My impression is that it disappeared in a day or two, after which the animal settled into a long "dynamic" period which lasted for several months. During this time there was regular day-to-day overeating. If food was available around the clock, the animals spent a great deal of time eating. It was not that meals lasted too long but rather that they started too soon. A normal rat waits between meals for a period determined by the previous meal size; the lesioned rats started eating again too soon (Le Magnen, Devos, Gaudilliere, Louis-Sylvestre, and Tallon, 1973). Thus their body weight rose. The rate of weight gain was substantially above that of normal controls (Brobeck et al., 1943). When the animals reached a weight of two or three times that of controls after a month or two, the weight gain leveled off and eating slowed. The animals became "static" obese animals. The word "static" was used because the weight gain was stabilized. Because the dynamic phase of weight gain terminated in this static condition, it became attractive to suppose that one effect of the lesion was to cause something like a thermostat to be reset at a new and much higher level.

Fitting with this interpretation of a changed level of "regulation" was evidence that the animal would "defend" the new high level against experimental manipulations which caused body weight to go temporarily higher or lower than the new "set point" (Hoebel and Teitelbaum, 1966).

The voracious behavior immediately after the lesion, the overeating which came during the longer later period, and the high stabilized weight in the third period could all be taken to indicate a heightened hunger drive. Several experiments appeared to counter this supposition. Obese animals, when briefly deprived of food, were much less tolerant of quinine-adulterated foods than normal animals (Teitelbaum, 1955). Moreover, after they had become "static," these animals gave up sooner if work was required for food (Miller, Bailey, and Stevenson, 1950). In other experiments normal and lesioned rats were given foods mixed with a non-nutritive ingredient. At some mixture levels, normal rats made up the nutritional deficit by eating more. Obese rats, apparently responding to the worse taste, often ate less (Teitelbaum, 1955). Because of the failure to tolerate unappetizing foods, to work for food, and to compensate for nutritional deficiencies, the view arose that there was a lowering of the hunger drive side by side with the resetting upward of the "hungerstat." However, in many experiments animals with the obesity-causing lesions were kept nonobese by limited diet; in these cases there were good indications of heightened rather than lowered hunger drive (Kent and Peters, 1973; Singh, 1973; Wampler, 1973). Moreover, these lesioned but nonobese rats were induced by hunger to accept nonpalatable (quinine-adulterated) foods much as normal rats were (Franklin and Herberg, 1974). Thus modification of the hungerstat upward was accompanied by increased drive, which could be demonstrated if animals were not allowed to overeat. While the cause of the overeating may have been the over-rapid conversion of blood glucose to fats (which thus required eating to replenish the blood glucose), the main symptom was that the animals did not wait a normal interval between meals.

Besides augmenting the food drive, these lesions also increased the level of a less-focused drive that might be called "irritability." The animals became excessively reactive to all the signals of their world, and showed a mixture of fear and aggression in circumstances where this seemed inappropriate. This was first observed in cats (Wheatley, 1944). Thus animals with medial lesions appeared to be both hungrier and more irritable. While the two effects could have been related, it is hard to guess whether they were.

B. Starvation Caused by Hypothalamic Damage

Damage in a small set of lateral hypothalamic locations caused an opposite pathology (Anand and Brobeck, 1951). The animals refrained from eating and drinking; they starved to death unless remedial steps were taken. Tubing a liquid diet into the stomach kept them alive. This was first observed incidentally in experiments on hypothalamic obesity, and it was amply verified in later experiments. Lesions had this effect if they removed the lateral half of the lateral hypothalamus at the level of the middle sector. Milder effects having similar initial appearance were caused by just lowering a lesion probe into the area and then withdrawing it—without passing the electric current usually used to make a lesion (Morrison and Mayer, 1957). Complete effects could also be induced by knife cuts that severed the lateral hypothalamus from other still more laterally placed structures (Grossman, 1971; Grossman and Grossman, 1971; Sclafani et al., 1973). Among these still more laterally placed structures, two parts of the extrapyramidal system (globus pallidus and substantia nigra) have attracted the most attention, although connections of the lateral areas to other basal ganglia (including the caudate nucleus and the amygdala) or even to the neocortex could not be ruled out as the ones whose cutting caused the effect.

A comparison of obesity and starvation-inducing knife cuts was interesting. In different experiments bilateral cuts extending from the top to the bottom of the hypothalamus were made at different distances from the midline (in the rat the hypothalamus extends just over 2 mm from the midline). Cuts 0.5 mm from the midline (shaving the edge of the third ventricle, which occupies the medial-most 0.25 mm) caused obesity; cuts 1 mm from the midline between medial and lateral hypothalamus had the same effect. Cuts 1.5 mm lateral in the middle part of the lateral area were ambiguous. There were initial undereating reactions followed by overeating of appetizing foods. In some cases there was simultaneous undereating of unappetizing foods and overeating of normal or positive ones (Sclafani et al., 1973). Cuts 2.2 mm from the midline at the lateral edge of the lateral area caused the full syndrome: undereating and starvation; this was the maximum point. Cuts 0.3 mm more lateral caused much milder undereating. Thus medial and lateral cuts had opposed effects (Grossman and Grossman, 1971). The medial effect extended so close to the midline as to suggest involvement of the ventricular wall. Cuts quite close together in the 1.5-mm region had radically different effects; and the lateral effect dropped off sharply at the lateral edge (even though lesions at 2.2 and 2.5 mm severed many of the same pathways).

What fibers would be severed by the 2.2-mm cut and spared by the 2.5-mm cut? One group was those connecting the substantia nigra and caudate nucleus of the extrapyramidal system (Oltmans and Harvey, 1972). This made it interesting that "poisoning" the ascending "dopamine" fibers in this bundle caused many of the effects of lateral hypothalamic lesions, i.e., loss of instrumental and consummatory responses, particularly those related to eating (Ungerstedt, 1971*b*). These were different fibers from the set whose poisoning caused obesity, but like them they did not really involve the hypothalamus as their main origin or target. Because this dopamine bundle is one important member of the catecholamine neuron systems and because they may be a set of drive or reward fibers, they are discussed again later in a special section on the catecholamines.

What behaviors and controls were lost with these lesions, knife cuts, and poisonings? The answer is multifold. First, temporarily after the lesion there was a general loss of appetitive behavior and possibly a loss of all instrumental behavior. The behaviors temporarily blocked included eating and drinking (Teitelbaum and Epstein, 1962), male sex responses (Hitt, Hendricks, Ginsberg, and Lewis, 1970; Hitt, Bryon, and Modianos, 1973; Modianos, Flexman, and Hitt, 1973), behavioral thermoregulation (Satinoff and Shan, 1971), and even operant escape and avoidance behaviors (Balinska, Romaniuk, and Wyrwicka, 1964; Appel, Sheard, and Freedman, 1968; Coscina and Balagura, 1970; Schwartz and Teitelbaum, 1974). Furthermore, there was a pronounced sensorimotor defect that also made feeding and other operant behaviors difficult (Marshall and Teitelbaum, 1974). During the same temporary period there was a pronounced aversive reaction to food and water when placed in the mouth (Teitelbaum and Epstein, 1962). Animals responded with manifestations of distaste or disgust. The food was not swallowed but wiped from the mouth with the paws and there were other signs that food or water in the mouth was aversive. Because of this aversion it was not sufficient to place liquid diet in the mouth, for the animal rejected it. Some additional method was required to get the nutrients into the stomach. However, even when the lesions were sufficient to cause death by starvation, time and appropriate remedial procedures could bring about considerable recovery (Fig. 14). This was prompted first by tubing liquid diets. After several days of tube feeding, animals began to accept highly palatable foods by mouth. At first these needed to be supplemented by tube feeding. After another period of time, several days to several weeks, animals would keep themselves alive eating palatable foods if they were provided. Still, they needed water tubed into the stomach, or liquid diets that served to hydrate the animals by normal means. At some time after this they would eat regular food and drink enough water during eating to stave off dehydration. The loss of voluntary or instrumental behavior and the changed affective reactions to food were thus relatively short-lasting.

There were other more specific deficits that did not repair with time. One was a failure to respond to internal water shortages by drinking; a second was a failure to respond to internal glucose shortages by eating; possibly also there was a failure to respond to similar sodium shortages appropriately (Epstein, 1971). Recovered animals would drink to relieve dryness of the mouth and this could keep them alive; but they did not drink on the basis of dehydration of cells or body fluids. Thus if the animals were offered water separately when there was no food to cause the mouth to become dry, they would not drink, and if water was available only at these times they would die of dehydration. Similarly, they ate in response to many factors, but when glucose in the blood (glucose available to the brain) was sharply reduced by insulin, they did not meet this deficit by eating (as normal rats do). When sodium shortages were induced by special procedures, animals with similar but possibly not identical lesions failed to meet the challenge as normal rats do (Wolf, 1964). Thus there were specific sources of ingestion behavior that were inoperative; all could have involved brain cells that failed to detect local shortages in the brain itself.

Besides these, there was also a change in the "hungerstat" settings so the

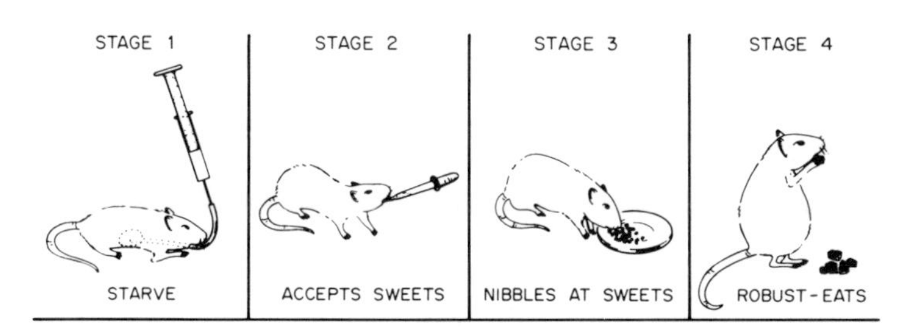

FIG. 14. Successive stages of recovery from lateral hypothalamic damage (Teitelbaum and Epstein, 1962).

animal regulated its body weight at a new and unnaturally low level (Powley and Keesey, 1970). If body weight was artificially lowered by experimental manipulations before the brain damage, there was sometimes no initial period of food rejection (even though similar lateral lesions always caused this initial failure to eat in animals that were not prestarved).

Thus lateral lesions damaged several mechanisms involved in normal food and water ingestion: (1) instrumental behavior; (2) hedonic properties of food; (3) specific remedial responses to water, glucose, and possibly NaCl deficits; and (4) the target level for body weight. The loss of instrumental behavior and the modification of hedonic properties was temporary; the animal recovered from these in several days. The loss of responses to cellular water, glucose, and NaCl deficits lasted; but animals eating normal diets on the basis of taste and other factors, and drinking on the basis of dryness of the mouth, compensated adequately for these lasting defects. Thus to the unsophisticated observer, the animals appeared completely recovered after a month or two had passed from the time of the lesioning.

Because medial and lateral lesions caused opposite changes in body weight targets (setting them higher and lower, respectively), the question of how the two would interact was interesting. In one set of experiments medial lesions were made at first, causing obesity; lateral ones were made later, and these caused starvation as they would have done if they had been made alone (Anand and Brobeck, 1951). This led to the view that the lateral mechanism was needed for eating; and the medical sector did nothing by itself but only acted on the lateral sector as a brake when energy stores became excessive.

Other cases involving more complete medial lesions changed the picture, turning it half-way about, by showing that the medial sector might act by itself, countering eating by some other path not directed to the lateral sector (Ellison, Sorenson, and Jacobs, 1970). These showed that aversive reactions to food depended on the medial area even when there was no lateral sector for it to act upon. Lateral lesions alone caused cessation of feeding and ejection of food from the mouth as if it were aversive. Medial plus lateral disconnections caused cessation of feeding, but food placed in the mouth was not ejected; there was no aversive reaction in this case. Thus the aversive reaction exhibited in animals without lateral areas depended in some way on the medial area. Hence it had some action even after the lateral area was gone.

These data at first suggested a dual control. Some mechanism passing through the lateral hypothalamus (e.g., the nigrostriatal system) might promote instrumental and consummatory reactions of a positive character directed toward the goals of the basic drives. Some mechanism passing through the medial hypothalamus might mediate aversive reactions toward food during periods when hormonal, metabolic, or visceral conditions made positive reactions inappropriate. Other studies suggested that there were at least two other controls that also acted against the positive reactions. These were revealed by lesions in the caudate nucleus and the amygdala.

Lesions in the caudate nucleus, when reasonably complete, caused positive instrumental reactions to be aimed at inappropriate (nonsense) targets. In cats, lesions which removed all of the caudate nucleus turned many stimuli into targets or "magnets." The animal behaved as if imprinted on things put before it, and would endlessly follow a tin can, a ball of string, or an experimenter's hand (Villablanca, 1974). They did not, however, eat these things or even mouth them as if trying to eat them. This looked like a release phenomenon and made it reasonable to guess that the caudate nucleus in normal behavior checked positive instrumental reactions when targets were inappropriate. The caudate nucleus exchanges messages with substantia nigra through the nigrostriatal system. Neuropharmacological experiments suggest that the two may be reciprocal inhibitors. Because the lateral lesions which damaged the substantia nigra end of the same system caused a deficiency of positive reactions and the caudate lesions caused excesses of these, it was tempting to imagine an opponent process mechanism with the substantia nigra end promoting and the caudate end opposing positive instrumental actions toward things. Other lesion studies pointed to the amygdala as still another opponent.

The amygdala exchanges messages with the hypothalamus through two well-known fiber systems, the stria terminalis and a larger system of smaller fibers. It is known to have both excitor and inhibitor actions on medial centers of the hypothalamus (Murphy and Renaud, 1969); its actions on lateral systems are not well documented, and it has no known action on the substantia nigra. Lesions in the amygdala caused consummatory reactions to inappropriate objects. Rats with these lesions failed to avoid novel foods—which were treated as dangerous by unlesioned animals (Rolls, E. T., and Rolls, B. J., 1973). They also consumed foods previously associated with poisoning that are also avoided by normal rats (Rolls and Rolls, 1973).

Aside from these rather subtle defects, there was also an immediately obvious set of abnormal behaviors. Animals with these lesions repeatedly commenced consummatory responses with inappropriate objects; both feeding and sex responses were frequently misdirected (Klüver and Bucy, 1937). There was also a loss of aversive reactions to dangerous objects. The facet

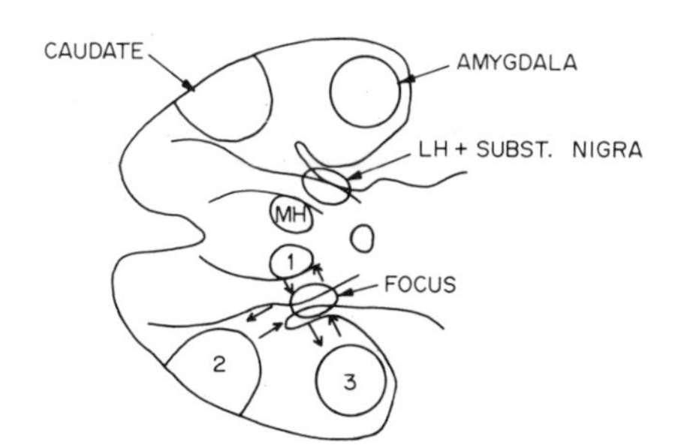

FIG. 15. Positive focus and its three opponents as indicated by lesions. Focus = lateral hypothalamus (LH) and substantia nigra; here lesions cause a temporary loss of appetitive behavior. Its three opponents are: (1) medial hypothalamus (MH), (2) caudate, and (3) amygdala.

of this behavior that marked it off from that caused by the other lesions was the repeated misdirection of consummatory reactions. These animals actually tried to eat inedible things and often tried to mate with inappropriate (even inanimate) objects.

The medial hypothalamus, caudate nucleus, and amygdala thus appeared to comprise three separate sources opposing positive reactions. The medial hypothalamus opposed positive reactions to food during periods when the visceral state said no; the caudate nucleus opposed positive reactions of an instrumental character directed at nonsense objects; and the amygdala opposed positive reactions of a consummatory character directed at inappropriate objects. At the hypothalamic level these three counterinfluences appeared to be acting against a single mechanism that promoted instrumental and consummatory reactions of a positive nature, a mechanism that could be destroyed or damaged by lesions in the lateral area, particularly if these damaged the substantia nigra end of the nigrostriatal bundle. While this would suggest three negative influences acting against a single positive one (Fig. 15), the course of recovery from lateral hypothalamic lesions suggested that the lateral hypothalamic area might have one or more allies working on its positive side.

What other structures might be on the positive side? Experiments on the course of recovery from lateral hypothalamic lesions suggested the cortex itself. Cortex manipulations could dramatically modify the course of recovery. The normal course of recovery (which progressed from loss of all instrumental behavior, through eating palatable foods but needing water tubed into the stomach, to eating more or less normally and looking robust) took approximately 4 to 8 weeks (Teitelbaum and Epstein, 1962). After this, newly learned adaptive mechanisms, or redundant ones that recovered after the first traumatic period, served to make the animals appear normal in spite of losing important controls.

These backup mechanisms ("learned," "recovered," or "unwrapped") were more precarious than would be guessed from watching the recovered behavior; and they depended in some unexplained way on the cortex (Teitelbaum, 1971). Their borderline character and their relation to the cortex were demonstrated by experiments involving a bizarre cortical manipulation that has had a vogue because of its supposed "temporary" character. The manipulation is to apply excessive potassium to an area of the cortical surface. This causes waves of unnatural electrical activity to sweep slowly and repeatedly across the cortex for a period lasting several hours. Neuronal activity is silenced by this "spreading depression." As a consequence, temporary feeding aberrations occurred even in normal animals; but in the rats recovered after lateral hypothalamic lesions, these "temporary" cortical depressions had much more enduring effects. The hard-won recovery that had taken 1 to 2 months to accomplish was set back almost to its beginnings. It required the full range of therapeutic procedures and time to be reinstated. This is, so far as I know, the only reported behavioral effect of spreading depression that outlasts the electrocortical phenomenon and then lasts not just for hours but for days, weeks, and likely even months. This new and puzzling finding does not, of course, answer the question of how recovery occurs, but it does tell that recovery is precarious when it is complete and that it depends in some way on relations of hypothalamus and cortex.

To me this seems to fit the idea that the cortex itself may be one main partner of the hypothalamus in the emotional control of behavior. If the hypothalamus is putting together an "affective package" (i.e., a set of signals making some things taste good and some bad), it seems likely that the cortex is a prime source of data for these computations, and a prime target for the emotional message after it has been computed.

The reacquisition of positive food responses after hypothalamic lesions and the connection of this to the cortex may be related to another set of findings. Experience in the normal animal has a profound influence on the "taste" of food (insofar as this term may be defined by behavioral reactions). Interestingly, both the hypothalamus and its outposts toward the cortex are needed for these effects of experience on taste.

C. Experience and the Taste of Food

Observational studies on humans and other animals and experiments with rats all indicate that food does not "carry its flavor on its sleeve." The hedonic character of the taste changes after experience; i.e., the taste of things is rarely determinate at first encounter. Furthermore, after many encounters, things that have "tasted good" for a substantial period can change and begin to "taste bad." The reason for this instability in the taste of things appears to be twofold. The first is that tastes are rarely positive when they are new (Rolls and Rolls, 1973). The second is that foods closely correlated with illness (at least with certain types of sickness) are changed to negative (Fig. 16) (Garcia and Ervin, 1968).

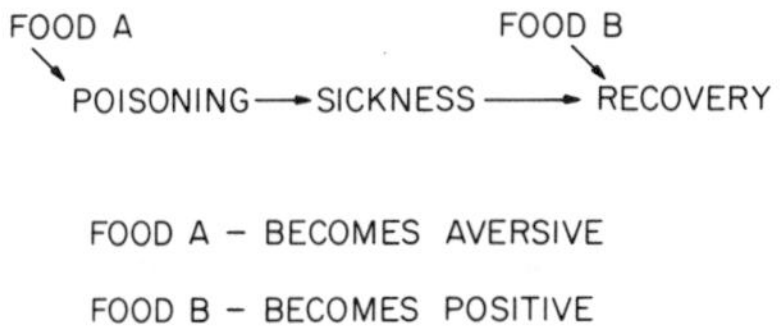

FOOD A ↘ POISONING → SICKNESS → RECOVERY ↖ FOOD B

FOOD A – BECOMES AVERSIVE

FOOD B – BECOMES POSITIVE

FIG. 16. Garcia effect.

This does not mean that experience can make "anything" taste good; but experience is an important component in this determination. By itself this of course comes as no great surprise. What is interesting is the repeatable set of details surrounding the behavioral mechanisms that produce these effects in rats. From the present point of view, it is even more interesting to observe the way these mechanisms interact with the hypothalamic mechanisms we have been discussing.

The function of these mechanisms is to make dangerous foods taste bad. There is both a distrust of novel foods and a negative reaction to poisons. This mode of speaking does scant justice to the way the "intrinsic" taste of things seems to be modified. When a rat first encounters a food with a novel taste, it nibbles and then responds with surprise and apparent distaste (Rolls and Rolls, 1973). The food is then treated as negative for a period of time (amounting, I believe, to several days). After this the food is responded to as good, middle, or bad, depending on its other characteristics; but in the beginning the food is treated as if it had a bad taste until (1) it is tested in small amounts, and (2) a time has passed.

The other side of this coin is that if the animal gets sick during this waiting period, the food ends up tasting bad (Garcia and Ervin, 1968). Furthermore, if the food has been acceptable and has been treated as hedonically positive, one sickness can cause a 180° reversal of this evaluation even if this occurs after its ingestion.

There are two features of this acquired negative reaction to food which are quite surprising to psychologists who have studied other kinds of "learning." One is that it works especially with taste stimuli. In most learning experiments it does not much matter whether the conditioned stimulus is an auditory, visual, or somatic signal. If any one of these is paired with shock, the animal learns to fear it. In the taste experiments, it is not the way the food looks or its tactual qualities, but only the gustatory and olfactory properties that make up its "taste" that become aversive when the animal gets sick. The animal does not learn to avoid the places where he ate the meal or the sounds that accompanied the meal, but only to avoid foods that taste that way. Moreover, after training, the animal does not respond to the taste as if it were a signal of impending danger but rather as if it were intrinsically negative, distasteful, and disgusting.

The second interesting character different from what would be expected by the psychologist of normal learning is the time scale involved. The time between eating and getting sick can be several hours. Even though this long time intervenes, the animal can learn in just one trial. In Pavlov's experiment, if the bell and the food were separated by an hour or so, one would not call that an association of these two stimuli, but rather a dissociation. I do not believe any other circumstance is known where an animal or a human being woud learn to associate things separated by such long periods of time.

Both the restriction of this taste aversion learning to gustatory signals and the association of stimuli separated by hours from one another make this a special phenomenon. The learning mechanisms involved in most rat learning experiments are likely not involved here at all.

Perhaps it is even wrong to speak of learning. This is perhaps the basic way a drive like hunger gets converted into a set of well-targeted homing reactions so that the animal starting with ill-defined drives ends up with particular object pursuit patterns.

Damage to the lateral hypothalamus (Roth, Schwartz, and Teitelbaum, 1973) or to the amygdala (Rolls and Rolls, 1973) modified this set of mechanisms for establishing the hedonic quality of food. Lateral hypothalamic lesions created animals that first responded to everything with distaste, and later could not learn to respond with appropriate distaste after poisoning. On the contrary, amygdala lesions from the beginning caused a failure of several different distaste reactions—based on novelty, inappropriate objects, or poisoning. This left the possibility that amygdala was a home of distaste reactions, and lateral hypothalamus one of its suppressors or opponents. It is not quite this simple, however, because the loss of learned distaste reactions after lateral hypothalamic lesions suggested that in one way or another this "distaste-suppressing" region was necessary in distaste learning. The amygdala at least could be considered a home of negative definitions of inappropriate objects.

D. Other Drives

The effects of hypothalamic lesions were not restricted to feeding behavior, although this was by far the best studied. The lateral lesions which caused temporary loss of positive and instrumental reactions toward food at the same time caused the loss of other positive and instrumental reactions. Those directed to get water (Teitelbaum and Epstein, 1962), to correct the temperature of the environment (Satinoff and Shan, 1971), or to avoid danger (Balinska, 1968) were all absent during this period. The reactions involved in male sexual behavior were also gone (Hitt et al., 1970). It seems likely, therefore, that the whole repertory of operant, instrumental, or voluntary behavior was abolished, at least temporarily. Moreover, the permanent damage to defenses against glucose shortage were matched by permanent losses of defenses against water and sodium shortages (Epstein, 1971). Lateral hypothalamic damage, at least in the middle or posterior part, had a broad spectrum of effects, and no single drive was the common denominator.

The medial lesions that caused overeating caused a concomitant increase in irritability, aggression, and in some cases drinking. These lesions also caused a moderate decline in sexual behavior (Paxinos and Bindra, 1973). The multidrive effects weighed against the argument for specific drive centers anatomically differentiated. Some facets of the data, however, weighed against a total lack of specificity. First, some of the different effects could be caused separately. Sometimes even though the experimenter could not give rules for separating the effects, he often observed one of the results without the other (Satinoff and Shan, 1971). Second, the different effects had different optimum loci. The best knife cuts to cause obesity and irritability were those just lateral to the anterior part of the ventromedial nucleus and the posterior part of the anterior hypothalamic area (Paxinos and Bindra, 1972). The best area for drinking excesses (diabetes insipidus) was more ventral and possibly more lateral (Sclafani et al., 1973). Other neurons at the "source" of one part of the drinking deficiency were discovered in the front part of the lateral hypothalamus (i.e., the lateral preoptic area). These were not related to feeding and were related to only one of the causes of drinking (Epstein, 1971).

Sexual behavior was maximally affected by lesions in the anterior hypothalamic complex (Lisk, 1968; Singer, 1968; Hitt et al., 1973), lesions which also abolished automatic temperature regulatory behaviors (Hamilton and Brobeck, 1964; Anderson, Gale, Hökfelt, and Larsson, 1965). Medial lesions in one anterior hypothalamic area caused impairment of female sex behavior; and those in another area, which stands just one step farther forward, caused impairment of male sex behavior (Singer, 1968). The latter was also damaged by lesions in two neighboring regions (i.e., the olfactory tubercle, which is still farther forward, and the nearby part of the lateral hypothalamus). Anterior lateral lesions impaired male sex behavior without having general effects against instrumental behavior such as were caused by more posterior lesions in the medial forebrain bundle (Hitt, Bryon, and Modianos, 1973). As can be deduced from earlier statements, posterior medial forebrain bundle lesions also damaged or abolished male sex behavior, but in this case it was a general effect (Paxinos and Bindra, 1973).

Automatic mechanisms of temperature regulation were maximally impaired by about the same medial preoptic lesions that had maximum negative influence on male sex behavior (Anderson et al., 1965). It is interesting that operant behaviors to regulate the temperature of the environment survived these lesions (Satinoff and Rutstein, 1970). As I said earlier, these depended on the integrity of the lateral hypothalamic pathway, as did other instrumental and operant behaviors. The separation of the two kinds of mechanism seems to indicate that although some steps of the temperature control process may be housed in the "preoptic temperature center," there must also be some temperature driven system that survives lesions in this area. Interestingly, the anterior lesions that interfered with automatic temperature regulation had main side effects related to eating and drinking (Hamilton, 1963; Hamilton and Brobeck, 1964). Warm temperatures normally depress food intake, and cold temperatures usually raise it; after the anterior lesions, however, they no longer did. These lesions also caused a failure to drink similar to that which occurred after lateral hypothalamic lesions; the animals drank in response to a dry mouth but did not drink on the basis of dehydration alone (Epstein, 1971). Similar (but not of course the same) lesions in dog and goat caused an even greater loss of drinking behavior (Anderson and McCann, 1956; Anderson, Gale, and Sundsten, 1964).

The lesion studies thus suggested a way to divide the hypothalamus into clusters (Fig. 17) with different behavior control functions. From this point of view, the hypothalamus was divided into three medial clusters: an anterior one related to temperature and sex mechanisms; a middle one related to feeding, drinking, irritability, and aggression; and a posterior sector with no set of well-demonstrated drive relations. The anterior and middle clusters were each shown to have special relations to adjacent lateral areas (in the sense that the medial and lateral lesions had effects related to the same general cluster of drive behaviors). Each medial sector apparently needed the adjacent parts and all the more posterior parts of the medial forebrain bundle. The geometry suggested that critical input-output fiber systems between the medial clusters and lower brain levels arched bidirectionally through the medial forebrain bundle. Thus posterior, middle, and anterior lateral lesions all damaged sex behavior, whereas only middle and posterior lesions damaged eating behavior. The integrity of the lateral hypothalamic pathway needed to be preserved between the posterior boundary of the diencephalon and the particular cluster in order to preserve the drive behavior involved.

Besides having relations to different drives, the anterior and middle clusters differed in another way. The middle seemed to be a "stop" part of a start-stop system related to feeding; the anterior cluster seemed to be only part (or the focal part) of a start-and-go system related to other drives. The anterior cluster, particularly in its relation to sex behavior, had but one side to its picture. Lateral or medial sector lesions could damage the drive by causing a behavioral deficit, but there was no way to cause an excessive performance of sex behaviors. The drives of the middle sector, however, were subject to

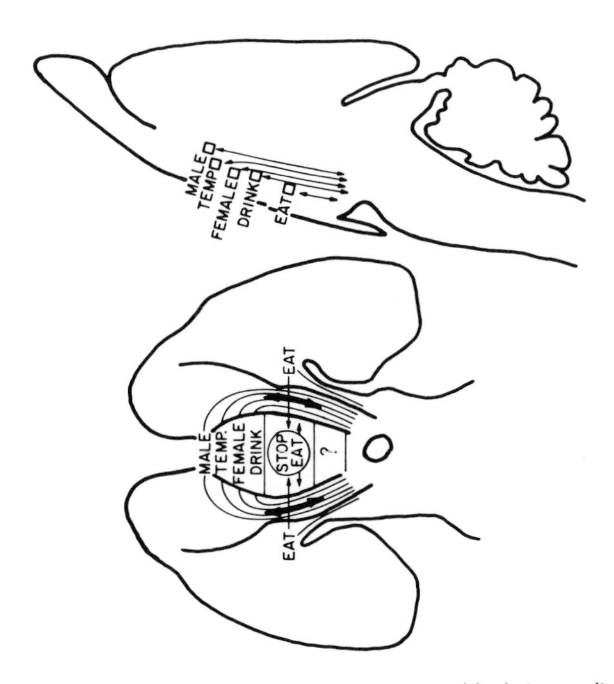

FIG. 17. Drive clusters in the hypothalamus suggested by lesions studies.

both excess and deficit pathologies. At least eating illustrated this bidirectionality. It is possible that the character of the drive had something to do with whether it had bidirectional "centers" and whether it was centered in the anterior or middle cluster. Sex and temperature "drives" are stimulus-aroused to a large degree. Food and water drives are often aroused by internal deficit states. Possibly the drives that depend on internal conditions need both start and stop mechanisms, and are accordingly tied to the middle cluster, whereas the stimulus-aroused drives need only start and go mechanisms and are therefore tied to the anterior cluster.

Why were clusters placed medially? Hormone-transport mechanisms near the ventricle might be "the reason." The main blood-borne messengers related to food drives are thought to be those which stop or attenuate feeding. The ones in the sex system, on the contrary, facilitate or trigger sex behavior. This makes it possibly appropriate that the stop part of the food start-stop system should be placed medially to receive the chemical "stop" message; by the same token the start part of the sex drive mechanism might also be appropriately placed in a medial area.

Catecholamines

A. Clinical, Anatomical, and Biochemical Studies Relating Amines to Behavior

The best known neurotransmitter, acetylcholine, has important relations to the hypothalamus, as have other less well-known transmitters such as gamma-aminobutyric acid (GABA). Of paramount importance in the hypothalamus, however, are the amine transmitters. These include norepinephrine, dopamine, and serotonin. The behavioral and autonomic controls exercised by the "visceral brain" and the hormone systems appear inextricably linked to the amine transmitter systems. Therefore these receive major attention here.

The amine transmitter systems are different from that of acetylcholine. Their action time is much slower in onset and more enduring (Bloom, 1974). Acetylcholine transmitter action starts in less than a millisecond, and its action is complete in several milliseconds. Norepinephrine starts in hundreds of milliseconds, and its action endures for seconds. Norepinephrine can be carried in the blood like a hormone. There its half-life of approximately 1 min is in almost the same order of magnitude as that of some hormones. The amines thus form a bridge between the faster neurotransmitters and the slower hormones. The long time constants are of interest because drives and rewards involve processes that need to be stabilized for periods of seconds, minutes, or hours, and drive cycles extend even to days.

The study of the brain amines was greatly stimulated by the discovery of a family of drugs useful in schizophrenia. Actually there were three families: the rauwolfia alkaloids (best exemplified in reserpine), the phenothiazines (of which chlorpromazine is the most important), and the butyrophenones (Shepherd, Lader, and Rodknight, 1968). The latter two families are in wide use. Their main action is to block norepinephrine and dopamine receptors in the brain (Snyder, 1974). Reserpine causes all the amines to be discharged from their storage sites (synaptic vesicles), making a temporary surfeit of unbound amine, but this is oxidized and in the end there is a substantial depletion (Bruecke, Hornykiewicz, and Sigg, 1969). These drugs focused the quest for an understanding of schizophrenia on the amines and provided a set of tools for the manipulation of amines in the brain.

The counteraction of agitated psychotic behavior by drugs which blocked the action of catecholamines was matched by antidepressive actions of drugs synergistically related to the amines (Loomer, Saunders, and Kline, 1957). Of these, amphetamine was most interesting and best studied, even though it has a poor antidepressant record (Stein, 1964*a,b*). It is interesting because of its direct positive actions on general activity levels, its special actions on drive behaviors, and its well-documented synergism with the catecholamine transmitters (Snyder, 1974). Other chemicals which counteract the degrading enzyme showed much more clinical promise (Bruecke et al., 1969). These "monoamine oxidase inhibitors" were effective antidepressant drugs, but they had side effects that curtailed their use.

Catecholamines were thus apparently implicated in schizophrenia and depression. Anticatechol drugs were effective in the former; proacting drugs were active in the latter. This made the study of brain catecholamines a matter of considerable interest.

Scientific study of the brain's amine systems was greatly facilitated by discovery of a neuroanatomical method. The method of Falck and Hillarp (Falck, Hillarp, Thieme, and Thorpe, 1962) made it possible to stain these systems so they could be clearly seen in the brain and to some degree even separated from one another. This is something that has not been possible to such a degree for any other transmitter system. The organization and arrangement of the amine systems that emerged from using this method were quite unexpected.

The cell bodies occur in small clusters in lower parts of the brain and the axons are broadcast from these to supply endings in the whole brain (Fuxe, 1965; Ungerstedt, 1971*c;* Lindvall and Björklund, 1974). In the rat, which is best studied, this focalization of cell bodies and broadcast of axons is carried to an extreme degree (Fig. 18), but even in higher animals it occurs to a considerable extent (Nobin and Björklund, 1973). The norepinephrine fibers start farthest back and go farthest forward. These fibers have their origin in the medulla and the midbrain. The axons of the norepinephrine system point down to the cord, up to the cerebellum, forward to the midbrain, and to all of the forebrain. Ascending fibers are grouped into at least two bundles. The dorsal bundle converges in the lateral hypothalamus or just above it and then diverges to thalamus, paleocortex, and neocortex. The ventral bundle converges on the hypothalamus and ends there, comprising a main source of neural control over hormonal function. There are other norepinephrine bundles, but these two are the best described.

The serotonin fibers start farther forward in the midbrain (the best-known system of these comes from a medial nucleus, the raphe). They converge on the lateral hypothalamus and then diverge. It is not clear whether they innervate paleocortex or neocortex to as great a degree as the norepinephrine fibers do.

The dopamine fibers start still farther forward—at the boundary of midbrain and diencephalon, in ventral "limbic" midbrain areas, in substantia nigra, and in medial hypothalamus. The bundles from ventral midbrain and substantia nigra converge on the lateral hypothalamus and then run well-known (and relatively short) courses to olfactory tubercle and caudate

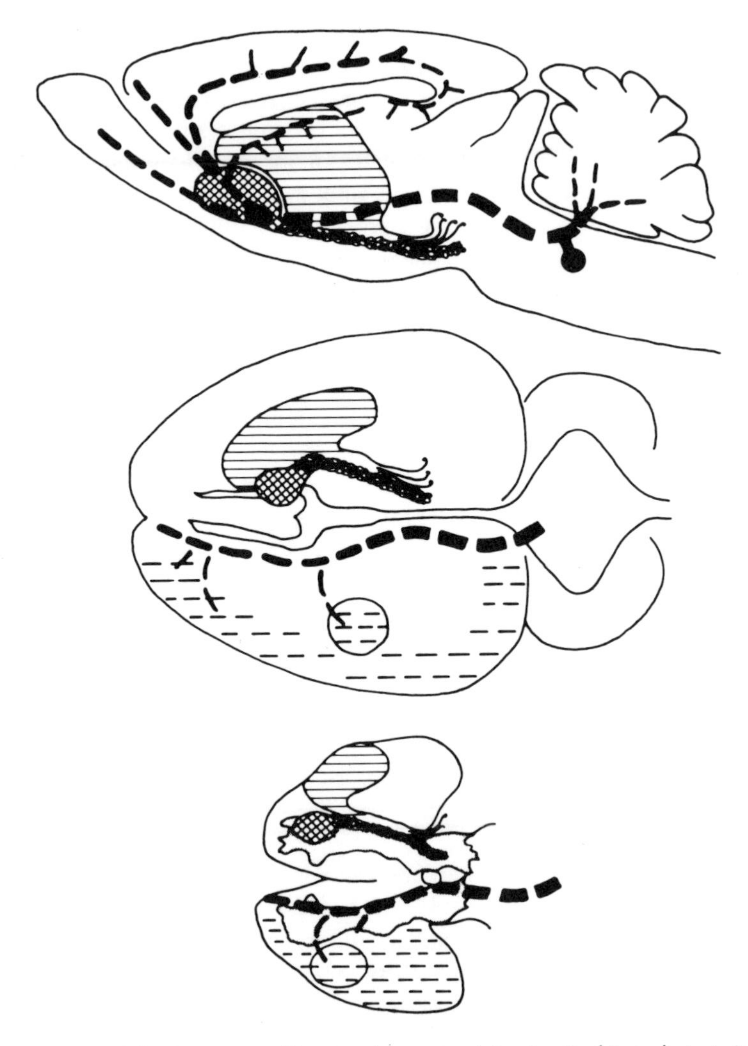

FIG. 18. Three catecholamine systems. The dorsal norepinephrine bundle (dashes) starts in the locus coeruleus at the boundary of the medulla and runs to cerebellum, hippocampus, and cortex. The meso-limbic dopamine system (scrambled lines and cross-hatching) starts in the ventral midbrain and runs to lower parts of the paleocortical-olfactory system. The nigrostriatal dopamine system (straight lines and single hatching) starts in the substantia nigra and runs to the caudate nucleus. One or both of the last two may run beyond their known targets because dopamine is found in the cortex. The raphe serotonin system is not shown; it starts between the source of the dorsal bundle and that of the dopamine systems and runs much of its course near the norepinephrine system.

nucleus, respectively (both of these are just in front of the hypothalamus). They probably also go beyond because dopamine is found in cortex along with norepinephrine.

Thus it is something like a set of Chinese boxes: norepinephrine starting first and going farthest, serotonin starting next and stopping sooner, dopamine starting last and stopping first. All three systems of fibers are very concentrated in parts of the lateral hypothalamus (in or near the medial forebrain bundle). There they leave many endings, and from there they emerge to send their widely broadcast axons. Why they come together before diverging (which is unusual) is not clear. The most surprising thing, however, is the small number of cells, and the small size of the clusters in relation to the extremely wide ramification of these long, minute, and multiple dividing axons. Each of the neurons involved, if it functions like an ordinary neuron, exerts from an area deep in the brain an influence on other neurons distributed throughout the whole brain.

The small size of the axons had caused them to be more or less invisible to older neuroanatomical methods. The amine pathways therefore are long point-to-point fibers that had never been "seen" before. It is the only known case of a relatively small cluster of neurons sending axons to more or less all other parts of the brain.

Chemical and neurophysiological studies show the amines to have seven or eight special properties. First, two of them (dopamine and norepinephrine) have a common substrate, tyrosine (de la Torre, 1972); moreover, one (dopamine) is the normal precursor of the other (norepinephrine). Second, these differ from acetylcholine in the mode of inactivation. The acetylcholine messages are limited in time by degradation. This takes the form of hydrolysis under the influence of an enzyme, acetylcholinesterase (Krnjevic, 1974). Acetylocholine supplies are then replenished by acetylating choline under the control of a different enzyme, cholinacetylase. The amines were originally thought to be inactivated by degradation (oxidation in this case). Excessive supplies are degraded by this process under the influence of the monoamine oxidase enzyme, but this is not the route of inactivation. When amines are secreted by nerve terminals the messages are limited in time by reuptake of the amine back into nerve terminals where it is thought to be repackaged into vesicles for reuse [or oxidized if supplies are excessive (Iversen, 1967)]. Reuptake apparently also allows these neurons to replenish their stores from "free" amines in the interstitial fluid, possibly permitting them to borrow excesses from their neighbors. Third, monoamine oxidase provides a negative feedback mechanism to limit the brain supplies of the catecholamines so that the brain contents remain within narrow limits. Fourth, all three of the amines convey their message by causing a second messenger to be released inside the target cell; this is cyclic adenosine monophosphate (AMP) (Siggins, Hoffer, and Bloom, 1969). This second messenger is a common step between the amines and the peptide hormones. All use it to activate their targets. Fifth, the amines usually have inhibitory effects when piped directly into the nervous system (Phillis, 1970). Sixth, the same amine when circulating in the brain's vascular system often appears to excite the animal and to cause acceleration of the same neurons that are suppressed by direct chemical stimulation. Seventh, a "blood-brain" barrier separates the amines in the bloodstream from the brain amines. Eighth, as already mentioned, the onset and offset of the effect is slow when these are compared with the onset of acetylcholine.

Thus a considerable list of properties fits the catecholamines for special functions (Fig. 19): (1) the common substrate (tyrosine) between dopamine and norepinephrine, and the precursor role of dopamine to norepinephrine; (2) the reuptake mechanism which apparently permits the monoamine terminals to compete for scarce supplies; (3) the monoamine oxidase which provides a negative feedback on available supplies (a preplanned scarcity); (4) the "second messenger" cyclic AMP, which forms a common step in the

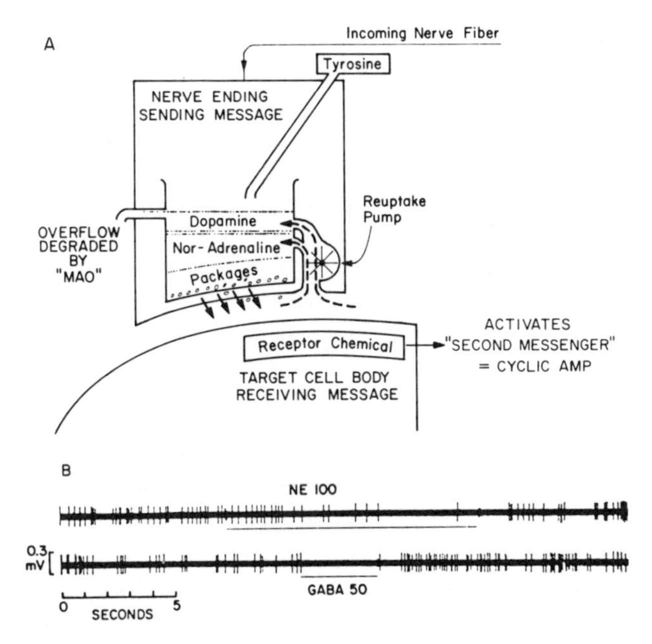

FIG. 19. Special properties of catecholamine systems. A: Nerve endings. Tyrosine is the common substrate of dopamine and norepinephrine (Nor-Adrenaline), and dopamine is the direct precursor of norepinephrine (other endings use dopamine without converting it to norepinephrine). Whichever catecholamine is used is packaged in inactive "capsules" or packages. These are released from endings and the substance released from them by the incoming nerve message. They act on a receptor chemical in the target cell, and this in turn acts through a second messenger (cyclic AMP), which is a common denominator between functions of amine transmitters and peptide hormones. After use, the catecholamine is recovered by the reuptake pump for reuse. Monoamine oxidase (MAO) forms a negative feedback system to keep supplies in a brain area at a relatively constant level. B: Iontophoretic application of catecholamine on neurons causes inhibitory actions with slow onset and long duration (Segal and Bloom, 1974a). NE, norepinephrine.

action of catecholamine and peptide hormones (some of which may also be central nervous system transmitters); (5) the deceleratory or inhibitory modulation; (6) the sometimes opposed action of the same chemicals when they circulate as hormones; (7) the blood-brain barrier to separate circulating from brain amines; and (8) the slow onset and long duration of action. Although it is by no means clear what special functions they mediate, their properties would fit them for controlling behavioral priorities. This is because the repeating theme is competition for an "artificially" limited resource, and all the time constants involved are in the order of magnitude of behavioral episodes rather than of neurophysiological events.

B. Catecholamine Depressor Drugs and Brain Reward

The chemicals which depress the actions of the amine systems, particularly the catecholamines, fall into three classes (Bowman, Rand, and West, 1968). First there are chemicals which act as if they blocked the receptor mechanism so the chemical message carried by the amine would not be received. These include chlorpromazine itself, as well as haloperidol, which is its equal in counteracting psychotic agitation (Snyder, 1974). Both of these most likely have other actions, but blocking amine receptors is thought to be the main one. These drugs blocked electrically stimulated reward behavior in low doses (chlorpromazine, 2 mg/kg; Olds, Killam, and Bach y Rita, 1956). At these doses the animals appeared behaviorally alert; there was no obvious soporific effect. The counteraction of brain reward behavior in these cases was not as informative as it might seem. This is because a number of other behaviors were simultaneously suppressed or mitigated in much the same way (Chance and Silverman, 1964; Cook, 1964). Feeding, drinking, and sexual behavior were curtailed if work was required for these goals; however, patients treated by these drugs sometimes became obese (Lewis, 1965). The deficit was not even limited to positive responses. Behaviors motivated to avoid noxious stimulation before it happened were depressed by the same doses that depressed self-stimulation (Cook, 1964). However, in some cases escape behaviors that occurred after the noxious stimulation was applied survived (Olds, Hogberg, and Olds, 1964). This at least proved that behavioral capability still existed. Chlorpromazine and haloperidol thus abolished or at least curtailed a variety of behaviors with foresightful or anticipatory character. These were behaviors that would be considered voluntary or purposeful if they were performed by humans. If there was a general loss of voluntary or purposive behavior, this at first would suggest that the loss of brain reward behavior was not by itself surprising or interesting. On second thought, however, one might argue that the brain reward system evidenced in self-stimulation experiments forms the brain's substrate of purposive behavior; and thus it might still be the specific target of these drugs. Many studies make this supposition appealing (even though it is still unproved).

Another family of drugs is made up of those that block the peripheral actions of the catecholamines. The "alpha blockers" usually counter exciter actions, and the "beta blockers" usually counter inhibitory ones (Lewis, 1965). Neither of these blocks either self-stimulation or psychotic agitation when applied systemically. However, this was to be expected because they do not cross the blood-brain barrier. The alpha blockers do bring self-stimulation to a halt if applied in the ventricles of the brain (Wise, Berger, and Stein, 1973). The relative lack of vogue of these drugs in psychiatry and brain research probably derives from their failure to cross the blood-brain barrier. It is interesting and a little surprising that although most of the brain actions of the amines are supposed to be inhibitor actions, self-stimulation and many other central actions are blocked by the drug that usually blocks exciter action in the periphery.

Besides the blockers, the next main class of amine action depressors is the inhibitors of synthesis. Alpha-methyl-*p*-tyrosine blocks the conversion of tyrosine to dopamine, thereby blocking the normal route of formation for both catecholamines (Cooper, Bloom, and Roth, 1974). The conversion of tyrosine to dopamine is called the "rate-limiting step" because there is a scarcity of the enzyme that causes the transformation. This scarcity is possibly used by the organism as part of a feedback mechanism to maintain a relatively stable level of these two amines in the brain. As far as I know, the synthesis blockers have no fame as psychoactive drugs. (I do not know why.) They are effective in blocking brain reward behavior (at least alpha-methyl-*p*-tyrosine is) (Poschel and Ninteman, 1966; Black and Cooper, 1970; Gibson, McGeer, and McGeer, 1970; Cooper, Black, and Paolino, 1971). Disulfiram and diethyldithiocarbamate are drugs which block the formation of norepinephrine from dopamine. For some reason they make the animal quite sick. They also block brain reward behavior but incompletely (Wise and Stein, 1969; Roll, 1970).

The third class of amine depressors is the depleters. These act by releasing amines from stores. The released amines are soon degraded by oxidation. This is the process blocked by the monoamine oxidase inhibitors. The releasers have mixed effects (Stein, 1966). The two drugs best known as releasers are reserpine and tetrabenazine. They were mainly negative with respect to brain reward behavior. There was, however, a brief initial period of behavior acceleration when tetrabenazine was used; this lasted only a few minutes. It was followed by a suppression that lasted for hours. Reserpine caused a much longer-lasting depression of behavior and caused the animal to respond to drugs and other things in a strange way for an even longer period, days to weeks (Olds et al., 1956). Reserpine was originally the favored drug for use against psychotic agitation. Eventually it gave way to chlorpromazine (Lewis, 1965). I would guess that long-lasting side effects were the main problem, but I am not sure. So far as I know, tetrabenazine is not used for treatment of disease. The main effect of both drugs on brain reward behavior was to depress it.

However, this effect could be temporarily reversed (Stein, 1966). Both drugs had a strong initial positive effect if used in combination with a monoamine oxidase inhibitor. The latter prevented degradation of the freed amnes, keeping them unbound but undegraded. So long as it lasted, this appeared to have a very positive effect on brain reward behavior. If the amines packaged and ready in vesicles inside of nerve terminals were required to make brain stimulation rewarding, then getting them out of the vesicles should have damaged rather than improved this effect. If the amines were already released, and if this was all there was to reward, then why was the animal still stimulating its brain? Several answers seemed possible. One was that the freed amines were taken up into other fibers and re-released by stimulation (but if the drug prevented the packaged pool from existing, this did not fit). Another was that the animal—being confused as the noncontingent "drug-reward" gradually replaced the contingent electrical reward—was unable to learn that the link between responding and reward had been broken, and thus perseverated in what had now become a "superstitious response." A third was that the free amines brought receptors to near threshold; and brain stimulation, causing still further amine secretion, pushed them over. The "superstitious" explanation was not wholly unlikely; after extinction, free rewards sometimes cause rewarded behaviors to recur. However, I think another possibility must also be seriously entertained: that the amines are only part of the story, and possibly released amines plus stimulation of other brain fibers are required for reward.

C. Catecholamine Synergists and Brain Reward

The positive relation of the brain catecholamines to brain reward behavior was further attested to by studies of drugs that augmented or promoted the actions of the amines. Clinically these counteracted psychotic depression, and in animal studies they promoted brain reward behaviors. However, the case was far from completely clear. There are several classes of proacting drugs.

The first class is the "releasers." The activating releasers include amphetamine, relatives of amphetamine, and alpha-methyl-*m*-tyrosine. All had direct positive actions on brain reward behavior (Stein, 1964*a,b;* 1966; Crow, 1970). These drugs release catecholamines from their binding sites, much as the "depleters" do, making them free and therefore active (Trendelenberg, 1959; Snyder, 1974). For some reason the released amines in this case are not as totally depleted and degraded as is the case when depleters such as reserpine are used. Thus these releasers act as if they were depleters plus monoamine oxidase inhibitors rolled into one. They probably also have other actions that add to the effect. Amphetamine, for example, mimics the action of the catecholamines to some degree, and also prevents reuptake, thus keeping the amines free; it may also be a monoamine oxidase inhibitor, albeit a poor one (Lewis, 1964; Snyder, 1974). Amphetamine is used clinically for temporary relief in depressed or somnolent conditions (Lewis, 1964), but its benefits are brief and there is a pronounced negative aftereffect (Goodman and Gilman, 1955).

Its positive effects on brain reward behavior are mixed and there is a troubling lack of specificity. In many kinds of behavior experiments amphetamine augments "slow" behaviors and depresses "fast" ones (Dews, 1958). Brain reward behavior is no exception to this rule.

Nevertheless, it seems possible that some special relation exists. One of the main signs pointing in this direction came from experiments in which undrugged rats did not at first show any brain reward behavior, even though the probes were correctly placed (Olds, 1972). In most experiments there were a number of animals that failed to stimulate their brains. In some cases this was due to gross misplacement of the brain probes, but in others the probes were not obviously misplaced. It was originally thought that small differences in location (too small to be analyzed) were of paramount importance. However, amphetamine treatment dispelled this view to some degree. When probes were in the right general area, amphetamine regularly caused brain reward behavior to occur even in cases where there had been no prior sign of it (Fig. 20). When probes were grossly misplaced, there was

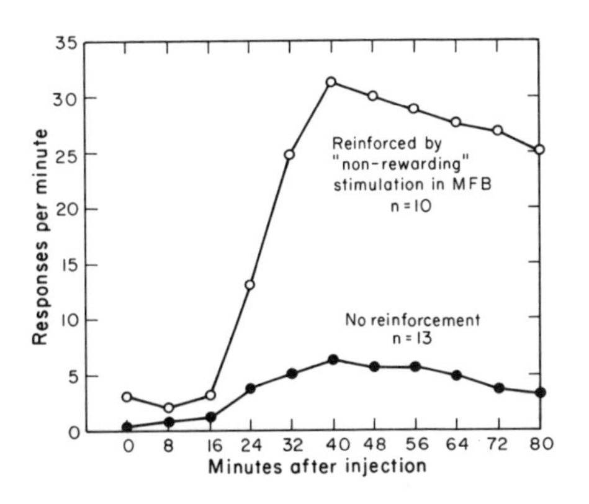

FIG. 20. Interaction of amphetamine with previously "unrewarding" hypothalamic stimulation (Olds, 1972). n, number. MFB, medial forebrain bundle.

no such effect. Animals started responding only when responses were followed by stimulations in the appropriate parts of the brain. Amphetamine has a reputation for enhancing previously learned behaviors (extinguished ones, for example) over other random behaviors, but this was not a previously learned behavior. Thus it looked as if some deficiency specially related to brain reward was compensated for by amphetamine. If so, then amphetamine might have a specific relation to brain reward behavior. Another argument pointing in the same direction was that the general effect of amphetamine on behavior had certain similarities to the effect of the rewarding brain stimulation.

used as procatecholamine drugs. L-DOPA is a precursor that is turned to dopamine in the brain and can then be converted to norepinephrine. This route of dopamine production bypasses blockade of the step from tyrosine to dopamine. A different drug, which is sometimes called DOPS, is considered a precursor of norepinephrine but not of dopamine. L-DOPA is used directly in treatment of Parkinson's disease and has seemed to promote sex behavior as a side effect. I do not know whether these two compounds work on brain reward behavior by themselves. L-DOPA and DOPS both counteract the suppressive effects of alpha-methyl-*p*-tyrosine (which blocks the formation of catecholamines by preventing conversion of tyrosine to dopamine). L-DOPA, which bypasses this blocade for both dopamine and norepinephrine, is more effective than DOPS, which supposedly permits only norepinephrine to be made (Stinus and Thierry, 1973).

The data on procatecholamine drugs thus showed all of them to support brain reward behavior singly or in combination (Fig. 21). However, they suggested a theory that leaves many questions unanswered: It was that free amines outside the synaptic vesicles and even outside of the axon terminals promote both self-stimulation behavior and relief from psychotic depressions.

D. Amine Pathways and Brain Reward

The study of the amine pathways has greatly added to the table of facts and ideas relating brain reward, psychiatric drugs, and the amines. Using the method of Falck and Hillarp (Falck et al., 1962), first Fuxe (1965), then Ungerstedt (1971*c*), and finally Lindvall and Björklund (1974) mapped the amine fiber pathways in the brain. These maps, which have successively completed and corrected one another—and which have at times looked more clear-cut than they do at present (Jacobowitz and Palkovits, 1974)—have proved an important interlacing of the catecholamine and brain reward maps. Even before these pathway maps were related to brain reward behavior, a link of this phenomenon to catecholamine systems was championed on pharmacological grounds (Stein, 1964*a*). The maps therefore almost immediately raised the possibility that all the effects of stimulating lateral hypothalamus might be resulting from stimulation applied to one or several of these bundles (Dresse, 1966; Stein, 1968; Crow and Arbuthnott, 1972).

A strong argument has been made in favor of the "dorsal norepinephrine bundle" as one reward system (Crow et al., 1972; Ritter and Stein, 1973). This originates at a site just below the cerebellum, a small cluster of cells, most of them contained in a cell group named the locus coeruleus (Ungerstedt, 1971*c*). This sends norepinephrine-containing fibers into the cerebellum, the hippocampus, the neocortex, and likely to all other parts of the forebrain. Even though the broadcast of these fibers covers almost the whole brain, they are gathered together in tightly packed bundles (where special effects from stimulating them might be expected) only in clearly demarcated regions of passage, regions which include a dorsal part of the medial forebrain bundle. Besides the dorsal norepinephrine bundle, an equally strong argument has added two dopamine bundles (Dresse, 1966; Routtenberg and Malsbury, 1969; Crow, 1971; German and Bowden, 1974). One of these originates in the ventral tegmental area and sends a focused bundle to the olfactory tubercle and other ventral parts of the olfactory cortical system. The other originates in the dorsal part of the substantia nigra and sends a focused bundle to the caudate nucleus, which is a main part of the subcortical motor system. Both collect heavily in the lateral hypothalamus, and both probably send fibers beyond their targets in a more broadcast fashion. The one norepinephrine bundle and the two dopamine bundles thus provided a common theme, matching much of the brain reward map. They also pointed the way to the discovery of new locations where electrical stimulation would cause brain reward behavior (Dresse, 1966; Crow et al., 1972; Farber, Steiner, and Ellmann, 1972; Ritter and Stein, 1973). Although not established as a fact, the view that these norepinephrine and dopamine elements widely broadcast in the brain make up important "reward systems" is a very strong hypothesis.

Mapping studies (Fig. 22) showed that electrical stimulation in or near the locus coeruleus itself caused brain reward behavior (Crow et al., 1972; Ritter and Stein, 1973). In this case there were some special characteristics.

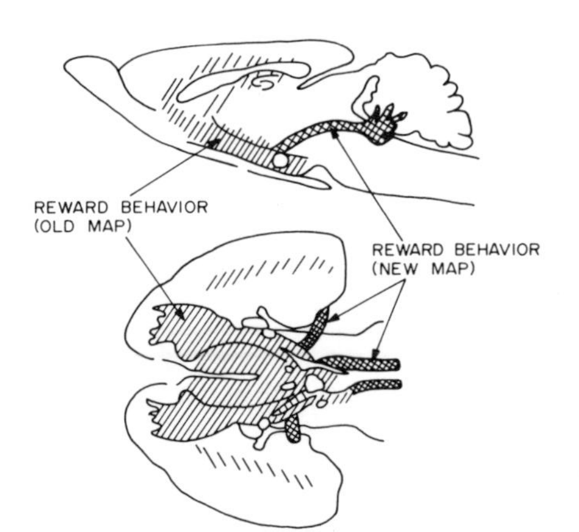

FIG. 22. New reward maps tracked self-stimulation to the origin of the dorsal norepinephrine bundle under the cerebellum, and to the substantia nigra at the front of the midbrain (Dresse, 1966; Routtenberg and Malsbury, 1969; Crow et al., 1972; Ritter and Stein, 1973).

The behavior was both slower, more regular, slightly less frenzied, and somewhat more difficult to train. Other stimulations along the course of the ascending "dorsal bundle" have also been shown to cause brain reward behavior (Crow, 1972*a;* Farber et al., 1972). In both the origins and the course, it is still possible that some other nearby close running systems might be at the root of the phenomena (Lindvall and Björklund, 1974), e.g., some visceral or gustatory afferent system. Still, because the effective sites do follow its course, the most likely hypothesis points to the dorsal norepinephrine bundle (Crow, 1972*a;* Ritter and Stein, 1973).

Other maps pointed with almost equal force to the centers where the two dopamine systems originate (Dresse, 1966; Routtenberg and Malsbury, 1969). Some argument was made in these cases that norepinephrine bundles might run to or through these areas and that the dopamine bundles might not be involved (Lindvall and Björklund, 1974). It seems somewhat more likely, however, that stimulation affecting dopamine bundles, even where they were separated from norepinephrine ones, also yielded brain reward behavior (German and Bowden, 1974).

Lesion studies (Fig. 23) showed that brain reward behavior in many cases could be abolished or depressed by lesions in the sources of the dorsal norepinephrine bundle (M. E. Olds, *private communication;* L. J. Ellman, *private communication*). This supported a catecholamine theory of brain reward. However, its force was mitigated to some degree by the ease with which these deficits could be repaired. Amphetamine "replacement therapy" served to make these animals behave as if there were no brain damage. The animals with locus coeruleus lesions behaved in much the same way as other animals that seemed to lack an innate predisposition to brain reward behavior (Olds, 1970). Both groups of animals responded to amphetamine application with responses that made them look in all ways like intact animals with no lack of disposition at all. If amphetamine substituted for free catecholamines, one wonders what fibers were being stimulated by these animals that made them press the pedal. The most likely answer would be that a few remaining nor-

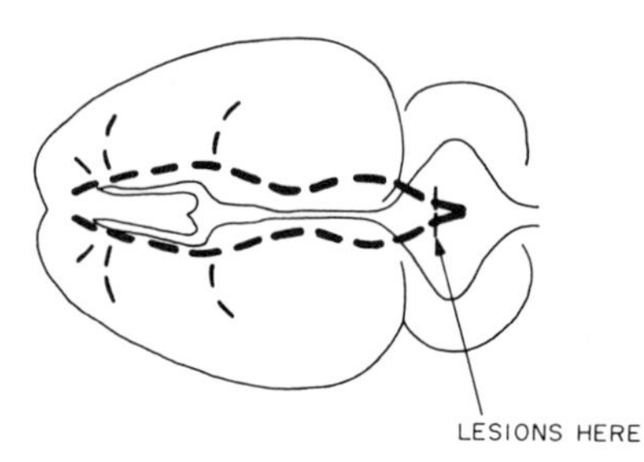

FIG. 23. Lesions in the locus coeruleus at the source of the dorsal norepinephrine bundle abolished or weakened brain reward. This could often be restored to a considerable degree by administration of amphetamine (M. E. Olds, *private communication;* S. J. Ellman, *private communication*).

epinephrine fibers (or dopamine fibers) were potentiated by amphetamine so their effects would be sufficient to provoke behavior. The data still leave another possibility that cannot yet be entirely ruled out. This is that free norepinephrine (or amphetamine as a substitute) is a prerequisite to brain reward behavior, but that stimulation of some other fiber systems is also involved. That is, the combination of the two stimulations would be necessary, or stimulation of either one against a background of the other. The possibility that stimulation of two systems at the same time is necessary for brain reward has been raised many times by Deutsch and his followers (Deutsch, 1960; Gallistel, 1973).

Other, quite different lesion studies have added to a growing body of suggestive evidence correlating the norepinephrine fiber system with reward behavior. Substantial damage was done to that branch of the dorsal norepinephrine system entering the cerebellum. This produced a dramatic example of the previously documented finding that catecholamine neurons regrow and proliferate after damage to their axons in a way that may be an order of magnitude better than other neurons. When half the cerebellar projection of these neurons was cut, it caused a doubling of the catecholamine endings in cerebellum rather than the reduction that might seem the obvious outcome. At the same time, another branch of the dorsal norepinephrine

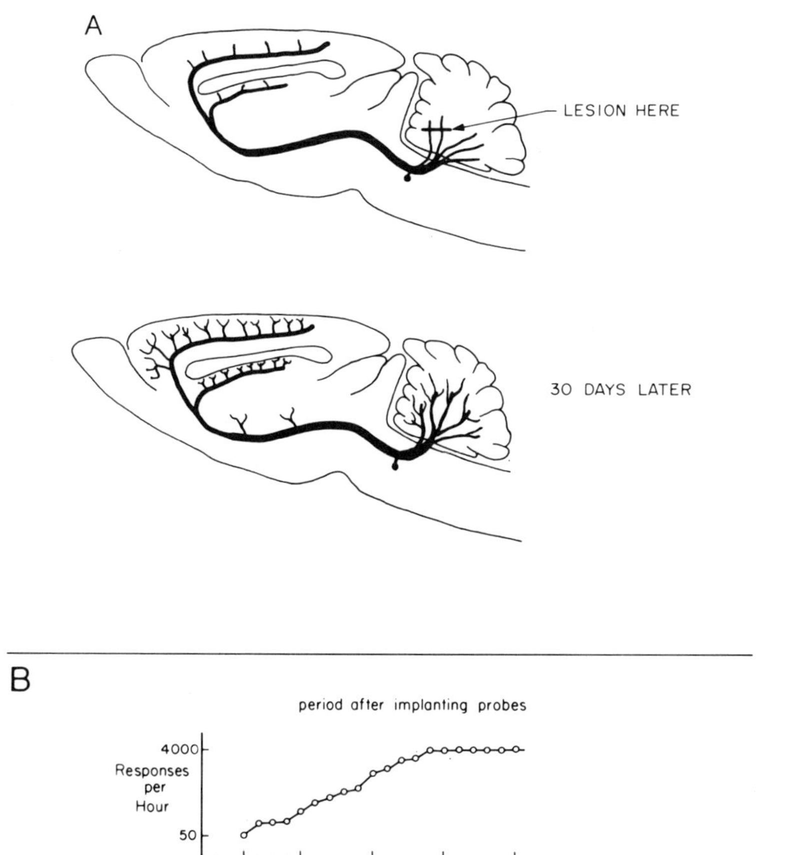

FIG. 24. A. Regrowth and proliferation of catecholamine pathways. B. Improvement of self-stimulation behavior caused over a 2- to 3-week period after damage to a part of the dorsal norepinephrine bundle (Olds, 1958*d*; Pickel et al., 1974*b*).

system which supplies the hippocampus was studied. In the hippocampus, which is supplied by a different branch of the same dorsal norepinephrine system, there was an even larger (as much as sixfold) increase in norepinephrine endings (Pickel et al., 1974*b*). This seemed to imply a very large increase in all endings of the norepinephrine bundle when it was damaged anywhere. The change took 2 to 4 weeks to become complete.

It was the time course of the change that provided a surprisingly good match for a similarly timed improvement in self-stimulation behavior (Fig. 24). It has long been known (though not published except in symposium discussions) that self-stimulation behavior improves from the time of implantation, and that this improvement continues for about 2 to 4 weeks from the date of surgery (Olds, 1958*d*). Because the improvement occurred, regardless of whether the animal was stimulated, it appeared to be a consequence of surgery. It was baffling because the results of surgery were thought to be over much sooner. Because probe implantation into a self-stimulation would damage a norepinephrine bundle if the norepinephrine theory of reward were correct, this suggests that the timed improvement might well be due to the regrowth and proliferation caused by this damage.

E. Poisoning the Catecholamine and Serotonin Pathways

The catecholamine view of brain reward and drive behavior was advanced by a special method to poison pathways selectively, either all at once or one at a time. For the catecholamine-containing neurons, the poisoning was done by applying 6-hydroxydopamine (6-HDA). When this was applied in the ventricles or in the cisterna magna together with a monoamine oxidase inhibitor, a large proportion of the catecholamine terminals in the forebrain was destroyed (Bloom, Algeri, Groppetti, Revuelta, and Costa, 1969; Burkard, Jalfre, and Blum, 1969; Uretsky and Iverson, 1970; Breese and Traylor, 1971). One way this could be assayed was by utilizing the fact that the catecholamine content of the forebrain was greatly depressed. For example, after pretreatment with pargylene (50 mg/kg), 200 μg 6-HDA in the ventricles of the rat caused more than 90% of the forebrain's dopamine and norepinephrine to be depleted (Stricker and Zigmond, 1974). Thus a method was provided to study the relation of these to reward and drive behaviors.

When this method was used, brain reward behavior was greatly reduced, abolished altogether in most cases (Breese, Howard, and Leahy, 1971; Antelman, Lippa, and Fisher, 1972). The brain reward behavior attenuated by this means could be restored either by the use of amphetamine or by ventricular application of norepinephrine (M. E. Olds, *private communication*). This provided another example of the apparent restoration of aminergic function by providing for free amines in the brain fluids even though a majority of the norepinephrine axonal systems was supposedly damaged. It must be supposed either that the epinephrine worked even without its fibers (in which case some other fibers must have been supporting the self-stimulation) or that cells undamaged by 6-HDA were sufficiently numerous to support brain reward behavior when replenished by exogenous amine, or that rapid regrowth and reuptake was the cause of the success of this kind of "replacement therapy."

Besides its relevance for brain reward theories, the method of amine pathway poisoning also had important implications tying other motivational behaviors to the catecholamine-containing neurons and axons (Fig. 25). When 6-HDA was applied to one of the special amine pathways, either at its source or along its course, the damage was restricted (Ungerstedt, 1970, 1971*b*). Much of the bundle (including many of its distant endings) together with many of the other neuronal structures near the injection site were damaged to some degree. Even though the chemical apparently damaged more than just the catecholamine elements, the method was still considered to have an important element of specificity (although this is not fully proved); at least different sites of application (i.e., application to different catecholamine bundles) caused different pathological conditions.

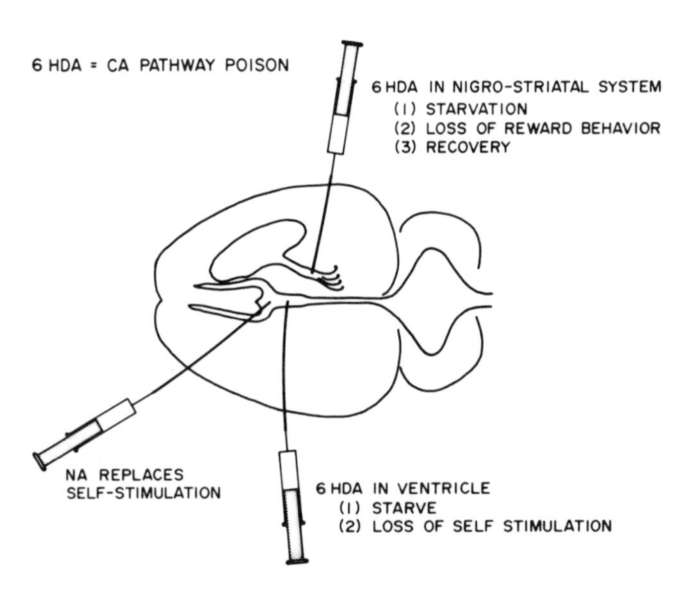

FIG. 25. 6-HDA poisoned the catecholamine (CA) pathways and affected motivated behavior. In the nigrostriatal pathway it caused the "lateral hypothalamic syndrome" (Ungerstedt, 1970, 1971*b*); in the ventricle it had much the same effect (Stricker and Zigmond, 1974) and also blocked self-stimulation (Breese et al., 1971). Self-stimulation blocked this way could often be restored by ventricular administration of norepinephrine (NA) (M. E. Olds, *private communication*).

When applied to the ventral norepinephrine bundle, the one that carries norepinephrine mainly toward the medial hypothalamus, 6-HDA caused many of the symptoms of the medial hypothalamic obesity syndrome (Ahlskog and Hoebel, 1973). Animals overate and became obese (Fig. 26).

When 6-HDA was applied to the nigrostriatal pathway—the one that carries dopamine mainly from the substantia nigra to the caudate nucleus of the extrapyramidal system—this caused what looked like "hypothalamic starvation." At first, animals refused food and ejected it from the mouth (Ungerstedt, 1971*a,b,c,* 1974*a,b*). They died of starvation if they were not force-fed. After recovery there was a lasting loss of response to dehydration and to cellular glucose deficits (Marshall and Teitelbaum, 1973). Like animals with lateral hypothalamic lesions, these animals retained or recovered their ability to modulate food intake in response to heat stress (Marshall and Teitelbaum, 1973) and were sufficiently recovered to regulate body weight and to appear to be normal feeders and drinkers in spite of the loss of response to special hunger and thirst stimuli. Also like animals with lateral hypothalamic lesions, they lost the ability to generate new aversions to food when foods were correlated with later sickness. Furthermore, there was a pronounced sensorimotor defect that also made feeding (and other operant behavior) difficult; at least this appeared in the early stages. In all these

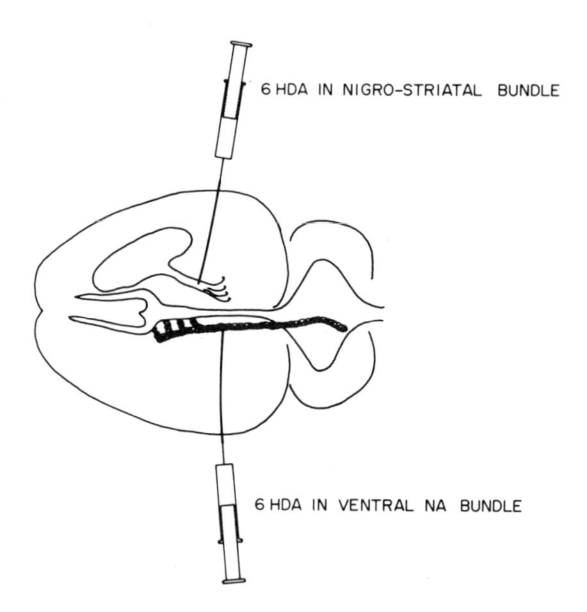

FIG. 26. Opposite effects of poisoning two catecholamine pathways. In the nigrostriatal pathway the lesions caused starvation and loss of voluntary behaviors; in the ventral norepinephrine (NA) bundle it caused overeating and obesity (Ahlskog and Hoebel, 1973).

respects, the pathology engendered by application of 6-HDA to the substantia nigra matched the pathology engendered by other lesions in or near the lateral hypothalamus. This was possibly not very surprising as there were lesions in or near the lateral hypothalamus caused by this method.

It was more surprising to find that many of the same symptoms could be produced by 6-HDA plus pargylene applied in the ventricles in a fashion that did very little obvious biological damage (Stricker and Zigmond, 1974). This caused temporary failure to eat and drink, and sensorimotor defects also occurred. After recovery there was a loss of responses to glucose deficiency and dehydration. However, in this case there was no loss of the ability to form new aversions when food was correlated with later sickness. Several things were surprising about this syndrome. First, because ventral bundle poisoning resulted in obesity, and nigrostriatal poisoning caused starvation, there was no way to guess in advance what the ventricular poison would do. If it poisoned the system closest to the ventricle, it should have caused obesity; instead it caused starvation. (The nigral pathway is the farthest from the ventricle.) This appeared to indicate a distant action of the chemical.

Another set of interesting findings came from studies in which pretreatments were used to direct the ventricular 6-HDA especially toward dopamine or norepinephrine systems (Stricker and Zigmond, 1974). If dopamine systems were mainly damaged there was a severe "lateral hypothalamic" syndrome, but all cases recovered. If norepinephrine was mainly damaged there was a much less severe syndrome and full recovery. If both systems were damaged in an exacerbated way (caused by pretreatment with a monoamine oxidase inhibitor) total failure of recovery occurred in about half the animals, although the others survived. In all cases, however, there was evidently permanent loss of response to glucose shortage and cellular dehydration. It was surprising that the "learning" of aversions based on sickness survived, apparently indicating that this did not depend on catecholamine systems. However, 6-HDA in the ventricles caused considerable impairment of another kind of aversive learning (Cooper, Breese, Howard, and Grant, 1972*a*). It was surprising that a type of aversive learning normally associated with the lateral hypothalamus syndrome was spared by ventricular 6-HDA, whereas a kind of aversive learning normally spared by lateral lesions was damaged.

Besides the effect on eating and drinking and avoidance learning, the ventricular 6-HDA augmented irritability and aggression (Nakamura and Thoenen, 1972; Coscina, Seggie, Godse, and Stancer, 1973). Moreover, 6-HDA poisoning of the dopamine pathway that travels from the ventral midbrain to the ventral aspects of the olfactory cortical system in cats caused some effects of lateral hypothalamic lesions, reducing eating and drinking to some degree but particularly in this case causing the sensorimotor aspects of the defect (Frigyesi, Ige, Iulo, and Schwartz, 1971). This was surprising because these would be thought to be related mainly to the nigrostriatal system.

In other experiments a different but similarly acting poison was applied in the ventricle to damage the serotonin fiber systems. The chemical in this case was 5,7-dihydroxytryptamine. It caused a major depletion of telencephalic serotonin levels. The main behavioral effect in this case was an increased irritability—as would be expected reasoning from other lesions causing similar depletion of serotonin (Ellison and Bresler, 1974).

F. Ventricular Injection

The amphetamine studies and studies with catecholamine precursors have been well supplemented by direct application of catecholamines in the lateral ventricles in such a way as to bypass the "blood-brain barrier" and make a direct test of some of the amine hypotheses (Wise and Stein, 1969).

When brain reward behavior was blocked by disulfiram, which prevented the conversion of dopamine to norepinephrine, the animals often became quite sick or sedated. For this or other more specific causes, brain reward behavior was suppressed or at least attenuated. Direct ventricular application of norepinephrine counteracted these effects to some degree, causing the behavior to return to near-normal rates. Ventricular application of dopamine and serotonin failed to have this effect. These experiments were criticized on the theory that "sedating effects" of the synthesis inhibitors might have

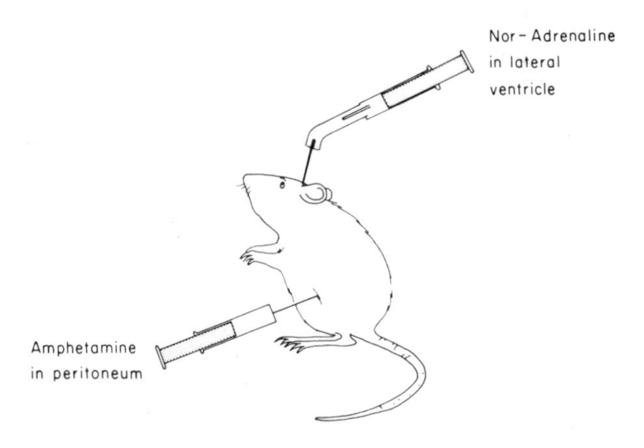

FIG. 27. Norepinephrine (Nor-Adrenaline) administered in the ventricles like amphetamine applied intraperitoneally caused an improvement in self-stimulation behavior if rates were low to begin with (Wise et al., 1973).

been counteracted by the centrally administered norepinephrine, and this could have been a main source of the effect (Roll, 1970). Therefore further evidence was needed on centrally administered catecholamines.

In a later experiment aimed to answer this objection, norepinephrine was administered in the ventricles of animals with no antecedent treatment (Wise et al., 1973). In these experiments a well-trained animal was used. During a period when there was very slow brain reward behavior owing to a near-threshold brain reward stimulus, *l*-norepinephrine was administered in the ventricles. Locke's solution and *d*-norepinephrine (which is a relatively ineffective "isomer") were used for control. When 10 μg norepinephrine were administered in the ventricle, there was a prompt acceleration of brain reward behavior (Fig. 27). It appeared to commence within seconds of the chemical application in the ventricles. It reached a maximum about 24 min after application and was still present after 32 min. The rapid onset of the effect appeared to suggest some direct excitatory action of the drug on neural mechanisms along the ventricular wall—possibly, for example, an inhibitory action on the parts of the septal area that lie adjacent to the ventricle near the site of injection. Nevertheless, these experiments left little doubt that norepinephrine applied in the ventricle had a specific or nonspecific positive relation to brain reward behavior when applied in 5- or 10-μg quantities.

Saline and *d*-norepinephrine, used as control solutions, had minor excitatory effects. The *l*-norepinephrine was substantially more effective.

In these same experiments, serotonin was observed to have a negative effect on brain reward behavior when directly applied in 5- and 10-μg quantities. This agreed with data from other experiments in which *p*-chlorophenylalanine (PCPA; used to block serotonin production) caused augmentation in self-stimulation behavior, and 5-hydroxytryptophan (5-HTP; a precursor of serotonin) reduced it; but there was other opposed evidence to be discussed later. These experiments bolstered the view of Stein that brain reward behavior is both dependent on norepinephrine and countered by serotonin.

In other experiments of similar type, the positive action of exogenous norepinephrine applied in the ventricles was confirmed (Olds, 1974). Doses of 10, 20, 30, and 40 μg were applied in 2 to 7 μl of artificial cerebrospinal fluid. All doses augmented brain reward behavior under some conditions. The low (10 μg) dose was particularly effective. The largest effect was obtained when electrical stimulation was at or near threshold levels. Although this study confirmed the positive action of norepinephrine, it failed to confirm the negative actions of serotonin. Instead, like norepinephrine, serotonin had some positive effects at low doses, but the data were ambiguous. The effects with dopamine in the same experiment were even more equivocal; it may have had positive effects, but this was far from clear. The active isomer of norepinephrine is *l*-norepinephrine. In this experiment the inactive *d*-isomer was used as control. It also had some possible positive effects, but these were even less than those of serotonin or dopamine. In other experiments ventricular applications of *d*- and *l*-amphetamine were also made (M. E. Olds, *private communication*). In this case the *d*-isomer is more effective in norepinephrine systems. When 100 to 300 μg *d*-amphetamine was applied by this route, it had much the same effect as 1 to 3 mg/kg applied systemically; i.e., it augmented brain reward behavior, particularly when this was slow by virtue of threshold stimulus levels. In this case as peripherally *d*-amphetamine was far more effective than *l*-amphetamine. Thus while leaving some questions surrounding serotonin and dopamine, these studies confirmed the role of ventricular norepinephrine in promoting brain reward behavior. Norepinephrine and amphetamine applied centrally had much the same effects as amphetamine applied systemically.

Because the direct application findings were the most convincing evidence in favor of the catecholamine theories of brain reward behavior, it is important to keep the record straight by placing mitigating evidence alongside the positive facts. Detracting are several possibilities. One is that the amines applied in the ventricle suppress inhibitory systems along the ventricular wall. Norepinephrine at least has a mainly suppressive effect when applied directly in the brain. The septal area, caudate nucleus, hippocampus, and medial hypothalamus are all systems which line the ventricular wall, and all have substantial records as behavioral inhibitors. Thus norepinephrine could have its effect on brain reward behavior by suppressing these inhibitors. Second, the difference in findings between studies which show serotonin to be negative and those which show it to be positive in relation to brain reward behavior must be taken for now as evidence that small differences in method may reverse the main direction of these experiments. Finally, when telencephalic catecholamine systems have been greatly damaged by poisons, ventricular catecholamines still promote reward behavior. This leaves open the possibility that stimulation of noncatecholamine systems in some way is involved. As things stand, I do not see the mitigating evidence as sufficient to counteract the amine theory of brain reward. The theory, however, is nothing more than a good (but not yet compelling) hypothesis.

G. Direct Chemical Stimulation in Hypothalamus

Besides application in the ventricle, drugs and neurohumors have been applied in medial and lateral hypothalamus and similarly at other locations. The most dramatic effects were obtained with acetylcholine agonists (and angiotensin) on drinking. Carbamylcholine, which mimics some actions of acetylcholine but is much less easily inactivated, was used in most of these tests. When it was applied in small quantities in the hypothalamus, it caused animals to drink (Grossman, 1960). This at first caused the view that some "cholinergic drinking mechanism" was housed in the hypothalamus. Later studies showed that the chemical had similar effects when injected in many different brain regions (Fisher and Coury, 1962). Moreover, best effects were achieved in the "anterior hippocampal commissure," an area with no synapses—a place very near the ventricles and particularly near to one periventricular apparatus called the subfornical organ (Fisher, 1969). Later it was found that similar effects were induced by applying angiotensin, the hormone-like substance of the kidney which plays a role in hypovolemic drinking (Epstein, Fitzsimmons, and Rolls, 1970). While this substance had pronunced effects in the preoptic area (and possibly even activated the vasopressin-releasing neurosecretory cells in the supraoptic area) it has now been shown to cause drinking mainly by direct action on the subfornical organ (Simpson and Routtenberg, 1973). This is one of the "circumventricular organs" (specialized parts of the ventricular wall with neurosecretory activity, which may function as blood-brain "windows" for movement of messages both ways). While the action of angiotensin at this point very likely plays some role in drinking, the mechanism of action is unknown. It is now generally assumed that the actions of carbamylcholine and other acetylcholine agonists on drinking are also caused by action at the subfornical organ. At least it no longer seems likely that acetylcholine by itself is some sort of drinking hormone acting on a specially coded hypothalamic drive system.

Similar experiments with norepinephrine and feeding fared better. There was a relatively delimited set of locations where direct application of norepinephrine caused the satiated animal to eat (Booth, 1967). When these points were mapped, the results looked partly like a map of locations where electrical stimulation caused animals to eat, but also partly like a map of places where electrical stimulation caused animals to stop eating. Some of the locations were quite close to those areas where knife cuts, electrolytic lesions, or chemical blockers caused eating. This pointed to a possible depressive effect of the exogenous norepinephrine on a satiety mechanism (Coons and Quartermain, 1970). However, the chemical effects in areas where electrical stimulation caused eating pointed in the other direction. The case for norepinephrine as a special proeating hormone had many good arguments against it. First, amphetamine caused animals to undereat (Magour, Cooper, and Faehndrich, 1974); by this it would be guessed that catecholamines opposed eating. The same supposition was fostered by the obesity-inducing effects of chlorpromazine (Lewis, 1965). Furthermore, the 6-HDA experiments appeared to indicate a dopamine system (lateral) that promoted feeding and a norepinephrine (medial) system that suppressed it. Thus pharmacology and 6-HDA studies pointed to mixed actions of the catecholamines with norepinephrine as a mainly antifeeding substance.

In other experiments aimed at unraveling the problem further, alpha- and beta-norepinephrine receptors were blocked separately by appropriate drugs, and isoproterenol, which stimulates the beta receptor only, was also used (Margules, 1970*a,b*). The conclusion from these studies was that the alpha action of norepinephrine mediated the cessation of feeding caused by excessive stomach or vascular loads, and the beta action mediated cessation of feeding caused by aversive taste factors. These suppositions were in harmony with the negative action of amphetamine on food intake and the positive action of chlorpromazine. They also fit well with the later discovery that 6-HDA lesions of the ventral bundle caused overeating (Ahlskog and Hoebel, 1973). It was troubling nevertheless that smaller quantities of norepinephrine applied unilaterally in about the same region (perifornical area of medial forebrain bundle) should have had opposite effects (Leibowitz, 1974). One possibility was that amine fibers themselves were actually suppressed when amines were applied along their axonal course. Some other studies of quite a different nature seemed to make this a likely answer.

In experiments that occupied me for several years, unilateral applications of a variety of chemicals in the medial forebrain bundle were made (Olds, Yuwiler, Olds, and Yun, 1964). I became convinced that most direct chemical stimulation studies used far too much fluid. When I used even 0.1 μl of a control solution (neutral saline or artificial cerebrospinal fluid) animals would bar-press to "self-inject" these supposedly inert solutions. This led me to suppose a mechanical stimulating action of even these small amounts. When the quantities were reduced to 0.01 μl this action disappeared. In a series of studies, therefore, arrangements were made by a special system of devices (Fig. 28) to apply 0.003 μl after each pedal response. Under these conditions inert control solutions were not active, but "chelators" (i.e., substances which acted by withdrawing ionic calcium from brain fluids) caused a great deal of activity when applied in or near the medial forebrain bundle. Citrate, phosphate, pyrophosphate, ethylenediaminetetraacetate, bitartrate, and creatinine sulfate all had this kind of action, and it appeared that the threshold concentrations in each case agreed with the affinity for calcium. Thus it was fair to assume that these substances acted by withdraw-

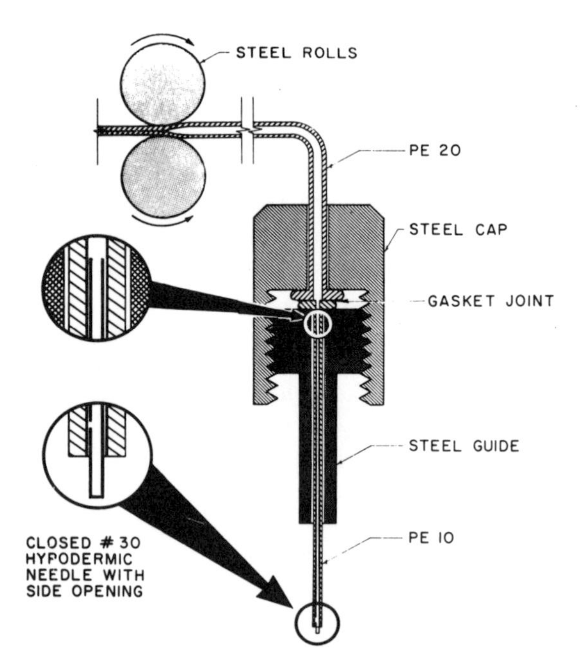

FIG. 28. Device for automatic application of very small quantities of various neurohumors in the hypothalamus (Olds et al., 1964).

ing ionic calcium from the hypothalamic fluids. These experiments were originally arranged to test for rewarding effects of chemical injections, but they failed in this. Animals pressed pedals which caused injections of chemicals into the hypothalamus, but it turned out that the pedal responding was secondary to behavioral excitation caused by the applied chemicals. Special methods to dissociate the two kinds of effect (e.g., maze tests) that worked with electrical stimulations did not work with the chemical injections. The problem appeared to be that the chemical stimulation could not be brought under full control. The animals could inject a stimulating chemical, but there was no way for the experimenter to stop its action (to prevent negative aftereffects or to require the animals to press again to get "more"). However, the experiments did serve to divide chemicals (and mixtures) into those whose application in the hypothalamic reward areas caused activation (measured by pedal behavior) and those whose application had no effect. In one series of tests, the dose was kept constant at 3 nl of fluid per pedal response, and the concentrations of various chemicals were varied from 1 to 200 mmoles/liter. Acetylcholine, norepinephrine, epinephrine, and serotonin were used to determine if any of these would activate the hypothalamus. No activating effects were observed. These same substances were then applied again mixed with activating solutions of pyrophosphate. In mixtures all the supposed neurohumors suppressed the action of the "chelator." However, there were substantial differences in concentration required. Epinephrine and norepinephrine were effective in the smallest concentrations (12 mmoles/liter). These were followed by serotonin (75 mmoles/liter) and then GABA and acetylcholine (more than 150 mmoles/liter). Because the threshold for the acetylcholine effect was high, its negative action was possibly caused by excesses and depolarization block. The negative action of epinephrine and norepinephrine in much smaller quantities was more likely due to some direct "inhibitory" action. In view of the later discovery of positive actions of norepinephrine applied ventricularly and the many pharmacological indications of norepinephrine as a requisite for brain reward behavior, these negative actions (suppressive of all behavior) were surprising. To me the most likely explanation was that the directly applied norepinephrine had as its main action an unnatural inhibitory influence on the fibers of the medial forebrain bundle, this being just the opposite of the main excitatory action of electrical stimulation.

Later in the course of this same series of experiments, some positive actions related to transmitter and hormone systems were observed. Carbamylcholine and acetylcarnetine—both of which supposedly mimic acetylcholine action to some degree but are less vulnerable to the degrading action of cholinesterase—were found to cause brief episodes of behavioral activation when applied directly in medial forebrain bundle regions. These cholinergic substances were not as active as the chelators, however.

The most active substance used was testosterone sulfate (Olds, 1964).

This substance was active in 3 mmole/liter quantities. Estrone sulfate and even cholesterol sulfate were tried as control substances; they appeared to have some positive action. These compounds were not stable, however, and so fair tests could not be made. The possibility remained, nevertheless, that steroid hormones might have general excitatory actions when applied along fiber bundles or, as would be even more interesting, special excitatory actions in the hypothalamus.

These studies did not answer the question I started with: a chemical code for reward in the brain. They did, however, make it clear that direct application of catecholamines in the brain (even when applied with careful attention to osmolarity, pH, and ultrasmall quantities with similarly small quantities of carrier solution) could yield outcomes strangely at odds with pharmacological evidence. Most likely, directly applied chemicals act in an unphysiological fashion on passing fibers rather than acting on the appropriate subsynaptic targets.

H. Dopamine

Is brain reward behavior supported mainly by norepinephrine or dopamine pathways? Are both required or can either system sustain the behavior acting alone? Most evidence appears to point to the last possibility; but the issue is still in doubt. Neuroanatomical data supported the view that dopamine plays a role equally important as that of norepinephrine in brain reward behavior. Electrical stimulation applied to the area compacta of the substantia nigra (the origina of the nigrostriatal pathway) and stimulation applied to the ventral tegmental area of Tsai (the origin of the mesolimbic dopamine pathway) both caused high rates of brain reward behavior with very low thresholds (Routtenberg and Malesbury, 1969). Of these, the ventral tegmental area has passing norepinephrine fibers, but there is no similar report yet for the substantia nigra. Furthermore, stimulation along the lateral edges of the hypothalamus in an area mainly devoted to the dopamine pathways caused intense brain reward behavior. These observations were best interpreted by assuming that the dopamine pathways, like norepinephrine ones, marked brain regions where electrical stimulation was rewarding. In a third dopamine system the cell bodies are medially placed in the hypothalamus. This system is most likely involved in hypothalamic regulation of hormone systems; its involvement in reward behavior is much less clear. It is similar in this regard to the ventral norepinephrine system, which is also involved in hormonal control. Of the two dopamine systems that were implicated by the correlation of their brain maps with behavioral reward maps, the mesolimbic system connects two poorly understood sectors of the olfactory-visceral brain, and the nigrostriatal pathway makes up part of the extrapyramidal motor system. The nigrostriatal system consists of the substantia nigra, the caudate nucleus, and the pathway between. It is a bidirectional pathway that may carry inhibitory messages in both directions. That is, the dopamine bundle from the substantia nigra is thought to have mainly inhibitory actions in the caudate nucleus, and this is reciprocated by a bundle containing a different inhibitory transmitter (GABA). Both paths most likely have offshoots to the globus pallidus, which is another part of the extrapyramidal motor system. Because lesions in the substantia nigra or lesions cutting the pathway caused a temporary loss of purposive behavior, and lesions in the caudate nucleus caused excessive behavior of a "targeted" type, it was tempting to assume that this pair of opponents was a major force in accelerating or decelerating behaviors of this type. The loss of operant behavior caused by poisoning the dopamine path and the positive reinforcement caused by its stimulation pointed to the substantia nigra as the positive factor in the pair. The excesses of pursuit behavior caused by caudate lesions were matched by experiments in which caudate stimulation brought targeted behavior to a halt (Buchwald, Wyers, Lamprecht, and Heuser, 1961). Because pursuit reactions survived and were even exaggerated after caudate lesions, the substantia nigra might be considered the control center for these behaviors. However, if these behaviors recovered after substantia nigra influences were severed by lateral hypothalamic or 6-HDA lesions, this would indicate that there were other co-acting centers. Functions of this type have regularly turned out to be diffusely and redundantly localized. Attention should be turned to the globus pallidus, which is a target for offshoots of both ascending and descending aspects of the nigrostriatal pathway. It might be an integrator of the caudate and nigral effects. Even if this were true, however, there would probably be alternative stations where such integrations might also be carried out. The cortex (particularly frontal and motor cortex) and midline thalamus would come to my mind next because of their close ties to the extrapyramidal motor systems. The nearby amygdala and its "periamygdaloid cortex" also deserve candidacy because of their apparent involvement in the "motivationally meaningful" aspects of behavior (Klüver and Bucy, 1937; Olds, 1955; Weiskrantz, 1956; Schwartzbaum, 1965). For all of this, I believe that the caudate-substantia nigra "opponent system" (and possibly the globus pallidus between) may well turn out to be "first" among a set of "coequal" control systems for this kind of behavior.

Pharmacological studies point to dopamine as well as norepinephrine as having some special relation to brain reward. Amphetamine pointed in two directions: directly to norepinephrine in some cases and directly to dopamine in others (Taylor and Snyder, 1970, 1971; Svensson, 1971; Scheel-Kruger, 1972).

Studies appeared to show *d*-amphetamine 10 times more effective than *l*-amphetamine in relation to norepinephrine functions but the two equally effective on dopamine ones; but later studies blurred or reversed this (Taylor and Snyder, 1970, 1971; Snyder, *private communication*). Behaviorally, it was shown that the *d*-isomer was about 10 times as effective as the *l*-isomer in producing locomotor activity (or exploratory behavior). This was therefore assumed to represent a norepinephrine action of amphetamine, but *d*-amphetamine was only two times as effective as *l*-amphetamine in producing "stereotyped behavior." This was supposed to be to some degree (although not entirely) a dopamine action of amphetamine. Other experiments applied this method to brain reward behavior (Phillips and Fibiger, 1973). The *d*-isomer was seven to 10 times as effective as the *l*-isomer if probes were planted in the lateral hypothalamus, but the isomers were equally active if the brain reward probe was planted in the substantia nigra. This seemed to make the point that either of the two amines could play a major role depending on the probe location.

Other pharmacological experiments linking brain reward behavior and dopamine have been performed with apomorphine, which stimulates dopamine receptors (Andén, Rubenson, Fuxe, and Hökfelt, 1967; Ernst, 1967). Probes were planted in the "mesolimbic" dopamine system (at both ends), in the substantia nigra, in the lateral hypothalamus, and in the locus coeruleus of the dorsal norepinephrine system (Broekkamp and van Rossum, 1974). Apomorphine (0.2 mg/kg) consistently facilitated self-stimulation in some cases but inhibited it in others. This variability did not seem to be a function of the probe location; it appeared within each set of brain probes. The effect of the drug, however, was highly reproducible for individual animals (each of which had only one probe). Those animals that bar-pressed under the influence of the drug did not extinguish when the current was reduced to zero, indicating that pedal-pressing in this case had become a stereotyped behavior. The authors concluded that the apomorphine stimulation of the dopamine receptors was in this case just a different way to give the brain reward, and the question of whether an individual animal pedal-pressed depended on the chance contiguities that occurred at the onset of this rewarding condition.

An indirect link of dopamine and brain reward was also made by drugs which caused repetitive behaviors more directly. Drugs such as morphine, cocaine, and amphetamine (all of which have some reinforcing properties) were able to generate stereotyped behavior (Fog, 1969, 1970). The actual form of the behavior depended on the species and the behavioral situation (Randrup and Munkvad, 1970). In higher species with a complex behavioral repertoire the stereotyped behaviors differed from individual to individual. The stereotyped behavior of an individual, however, was reproducible during repeated injections (Ellinwood, 1971; Nymark, 1972; Rostrosen, Wallach, Angrist, and Gershon, 1972). One view was that the actual behavior that occurred depended on its chance occurrence at the onset of the drug action or on its previous reinforcement in a particular situation (Skinner, 1948; Ellinwood, 1971; Broekkamp and van Rossum, 1974). Due to the sustained performance of the behavior during the sustained reinforcing effect of the drug, this behavior was then thought to be repeated in a stereotyped and "superstitious" manner. By pharmacological and 6-HDA studies these stereotyped behaviors were linked to dopamine (as opposed to norepinephrine). For example, they were almost equally caused by *d*- or *l*-amphetamine (Taylor and Snyder, 1970, 1971), and they were modified by 6-HDA lesions and other lesions in the nigral or mesolimbic dopamine bundles (Randrup and Munkvad, 1970; Simpson and Iverson, 1971; McKenzie, 1972; Iverson, 1974; Neill, Boggan, and Grossman, 1974).

It is a similarity in character that relates this stereotyped behavior to brain reward (Ellinwood, cited in Snyder, 1972). Both often involved a compulsive repetition with the actual specification of what is to be repeated varying not only from species to species but from animal to animal. In rats amphetamine often induced sniffing or licking. In cats and chimps it was sometimes looking from side to side. In humans it was sometimes expressed as purposeless (paranoid) thought process (Angrist, Shopsin, and Gershon, 1971). It could be a single activity performed repeatedly or a small repertoire of behavior so performed. It dominated behavior. It was nondistractable, driven, rapid, and repetitious. It had no observable significance. The difference of amphetamine-induced stereotypy from brain reward behavior is that it was aimless, whereas we assumed there was an aim to get the brain reward. In other words, self-stimulation was arranged so the compulsion inducer came at the end of the behavior sequence. If we grant amphetamine as having some rewarding side effects, these came before, during, and after the compulsive behavior. Thus self-stimulation makes sense in a way that amphetamine compulsions do not. Still, because there were situations where animals sustained superstitious responses in the presence of sustained rewards, the two kinds of behavior could be close relatives. This seemed particularly likely when dopamine pathway were at the self-stimulation site.

I. Serotonin

5-Hydroxytryptamine (serotonin) is a close relative of the catecholamines. It occurs in the blood (where it is carried in platelets) and in the stomach (where it has hormone-like actions involved in stomach motility). It is distributed through the brain in uneven fashion, suggesting that it is a transmitter in some systems (Lewis, 1965). It is stained by the fluorescence method and this shows that most serotonin-containing cell bodies are located in the midbrain along the midline; the axons of these traverse the medial forebrain bundle and terminate in the paleocortex and other telancephalic structures (Dahlström and Fuxe, 1964). Experiments point to a likely involvement of serotonin as a neurohumor or neurotransmitter in a system whose mainly inhibitory actions are involved in pain suppression (Tenen, 1967; Harvey and Lints, 1971) and sleep (Jouvet, 1974). Reserpine, the best-known catecholamine depletor, is also a serotonin depletor (Lewis, 1965). Furthermore, serotonin is degraded by monoamine oxidase much as the catecholamines. Thus the monoamine oxidase inhibitors favor serotonin as well as the catecholamines (Lewis, 1965). The actions of serotonin were thus at first hard to separate pharmacologically from those of the other amines. Several methods are now available. PCPA prevents the formation of serotonin in much the same way as alpha-methyl-*p*-tyrosine prevents the formation of the catecholamines (Koe and Weissman, 1966); and 5-hydroxytryptophan bypasses the PCPA block permitting a restoration of the serotonin supplies (Harvey and Lints, 1971).

Proserotonin drugs have been known to antagonize brain reward behavior (Bose, Bailey, Thea, and Pradhan, 1974); and antiserotonin drugs have increased pedal-pressing rates for brain rewards (Poschel and Ninteman, 1971). This has formed the basis for a mainstream conviction that serotonin is a naturally occurring antibrain-reward compound—mediating the aversive effects of negative things according to one view (Wise et al., 1973)—a view supported by the fact that direct application of serotonin in the ventricles can attenuate brain reward behavior (Wise et al., 1973). Nevertheless, there is a strong countercurrent of opinion suggesting that serotonin might be the mediator in one self-stimulation system while being an opponent force in another. This argument is that serotonin and the serotonin neurons are endogenous analgesic and soporific factors involved in sleep (Jouvet, 1974) and in the attenuation of pain (Tenen, 1967; Harvey and Lints, 1971; Yunger and Harvey, 1973). Such a system might simultaneously attenuate aversive and euphoric states. If self-stimulation of some catecholamine system induced a euphoric condition, serotonin agonists might attenuate this self-stimulation. If self-stimulation at some (possibly serotonergic) sites was mainly effective by inhibiting aversive conditions, serotonin agonists might well facilitate this behavior. The finding that some brain reward stimulation retards escape-avoidance responses (Routtenberg and Olds, 1963) would fit this view. The finding that some brain reward behavior is promoted by aversive drive (Deutsch and Howarth, 1962) also fits to some degree. The latter sites were in the dorsal midbrain in a location where they might well have had special effects on serotonin fiber systems. The finding that some self-stimulation behavior induces sleep (Angyan, 1974) also fits. Further support comes from pharmacological studies which show positive effects of serotonin agonists on self-stimulation (Poschel and Ninteman, 1968) and negative effects of serotonin antagonists (Stark, Boyd, and Fuller, 1964; Margules, 1969; Gibson et al., 1970; Stark, Fuller, Hartley, Schaffer, and Turk, 1970). In accord with the latter view, some recent studies have pointed to self-stimulation behavior induced by probes near the midbrain midline and thus possibly near or in serotonin cell or fiber systems. Indicating the possible independence of this behavior from catecholamines was the fact that it was highly resistant to ventricular 6-HDA (Olds, 1975). Correlated studies showed that other self-stimulation behavior which was slowed or halted by 6-HDA could be positively affected not only by ventricular application of norepinephrine but also by ventricular application of serotonin (Olds, 1974). This might indicate that the medial forebrain bundle brain probes involved were stimulating mixed fiber systems, getting some of their rewarding effects from catecholamine fibers and some from serotonin fibers. Thus evidence exists for serotonin's positive and negative relation to brain reward behavior. The negative evidence is still perhaps the strongest, but it is not yet strong enough to settle the issue.

J. Acetylcholine

Acetylcholine has two modes of action (Lewis, 1965). The faster action, exhibited at the neuromyal junction, is called a "nicotinic" action because the drug nicotine mimics this effect. This fast action is opposed by a number of drugs such as curare. The slower action is exhibited at the parasympathetic effectors (and in "slow postsynaptic potentials" elsewhere). It is called a "muscarinic" action because it is mimicked by the drug muscarine. It is also mimicked by pilocarpine. This slow action is opposed by a number of drugs such as scopolamine and atropine. Brain reward behavior is antagonized by pharmacological manipulations which increase or prolong the muscarinic actions in the central nervous system (Stark and Boyd, 1963). While there is a general muscarinic antagonism *vis-a-vis* operant behavior (Pfeiffer and Jenny, 1967), the same arguments which suggest a specifically positive role for amphetamine may be used to suggest that there is some special antagonism of muscarinic drugs and brain reward behavior. Physostigmine, which prevents the inactivation of acetylcholine in the brain, slows or stops self-stimulation. Atropine can counter this effect. Control studies with drugs which do not cross the blood-brain barrier show that it is the central not the peripheral actions of acetylcholine that are involved.

Nicotine, on the contrary, augments brain reward behavior (Olds and Domino, 1969; Newman, 1972), and this action can be countered by the antinicotinic drug mecamylamine. Because it has a generally positive action on operant behavior (Morrison, 1967), there is a question if this nicotinic effect is special to brain reward behavior; however, this question gets about the same answer given for muscarinic effects and amphetamine.

The interesting counterbalance of adrenergic and nicotinic agonists supporting operant behavior and muscarinic agonists opposing it with equal force may be an accident of the different numbers of synapses of different kinds involved in positive reinforcement. A more daring notion might point to "reward" neurons with a particular character. If there were adrenergic reward neurons in the brain, and if these were excited by nicotinic actions and countered by muscarinic ones, this would fit. It would make some sense of the fact that many maps of catecholamine cell bodies match with maps of acetylcholinesterase, which may indicate a sensitivity to acetylcholine of the neurons involved (Jacobowitz and Palkovits, 1974; Palkovits and Jacobowitz, (1974). It would also make reward systems somewhat like the sympathetic fibers exciting from the superior cervical ganglion. These are adrenergic. They are excited by nicotinic actions of acetylcholine and are both excited and suppressed by slower muscarinic actions. The suppression is mediated through a dopaminergic interneuron (Libet and Owman, 1974). It would be surprising if central reward neurons were very similar to peripheral sympathetic ones because naively one would associate sympathetic activity with aversive conditions. Nature, however, repeatedly makes do with mechanisms at hand and turns things to new uses.

Single Unit Studies

A. Units and Feeding

Neurons in the hypothalamic "feeding centers" often seemed ready to fire in any pattern hoped for by the investigator. Reciprocal inhibitory relations between the medial and lateral hypothalamus were observed in numerous experiments, but positive action of medial stimulation on lateral unit activity, and negative actions of lateral stimulations on lateral units, were also well documented.

In one set of studies medial unit spikes were accelerated and lateral ones decelerated by intravenous glucose infusions. In hungry animals ventromedial units first fired at a slower frequency than lateral ones; glucose infusion then reversed this (Anand, Chhina, Sharma, Dua, and Singh, 1964; Chhina, Anand, Singh, and Rao, 1971). In other experiments the spontaneous accelerations and decelerations of medial and lateral units were observed (Oomura, Oomura, Yamamoto, and Naka, 1967). Then ether and electrical stimulation were used to modify this activity. Each acceleration of medial activity was accompanied by a deceleration of lateral activity and vice versa. Furthermore, medial stimulation suppressed lateral activity, and lateral stimulation suppressed medial activity.

A harmonious view of medial-lateral opponent process emerged from these studies. It was rudely countered by experiments from other groups. Medial stimulation accelerated some lateral units and decelerated others; those accelerated were in larger numbers (Van Atta and Sutin, 1971). Lateral stimulation failed to inhibit medial units, although these could be decelerated by amygdaloid stimulation (Murphy and Renaud, 1969). Lateral stimulation suppressed the activity of the majority of nearby units in the same lateral area (Ito, 1972).

The reason for these widely divergent reports was apparently that different kinds of neurons resided in the same place and possibly were recorded selectively in different experiments. The diversity was shown by iontophoretic studies used to seek neurons activated by direct application of glucose through micropipettes (Oomura, Ono, Ooyama, and Wayner, 1969). In these, 0.4 M glucose was mixed with 0.4 M NaCl so that the NaCl would "transport" the glucose. Nearly half the units recorded from the ventromedial hypothalamus were accelerated and none decelerated by this method of glucose application. In the lateral area, approximately one-third were accelerated and a similar proportion slowed. No similar effects were observed in recordings from neurons in thalamus and cortex. The theory of a glucose receptor in the hypothalamus thus received some support. The findings, however, should be viewed with some caution because at least in one study glucose placed in the ventricle of the brain had no effect on eating (Epstein, 1960).

In other experiments neuronal activity in the hypothalamus was recorded before and during feeding behavior (Fig. 29) (Hamburg, 1971). Neurons of the "feeding" center were spontaneously active in hungry, food-seeking rats. This might signify a correlation of their activity with hunger drive; however, no test was made to determine if the activity would disappear at low drive levels. When hungry animals were given access to a dish of food they began eating, and at this time the neuron activity was considerably and abruptly decelerated. The animals could be induced to contend for food

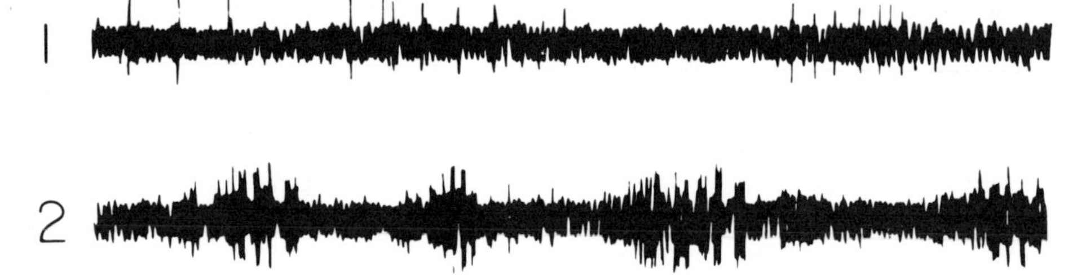

FIG. 29. Silencing of lateral hypothalamic spikes during feeding (Hamburg, 1971). The two traces are recordings from the same probe. Spikes appeared at about 20/sec in trace 1, made while the animal was hungry and awaiting food. These spikes disappeared in trace 2, made while the animal was eating. The bursts in trace 2 are "chewing artifacts" not neuron action potentials. Traces are approximately 1 sec in duration.

while still eating by attempting to withdraw the food while the animal was chewing. The animal would struggle to retain the dish while continuing to eat. During these episodes of simultaneous instrumental and consummatory behavior the hypothalamic units began again to discharge at brisk rates. Thus the suppression was correlated with the cessation of instrumental activities rather than with the rewarding stimuli or the consumatory activity.

Further evidence for a correlation of this family of large lateral hypothalamic units with the preconsummatory phase of feeding behavior came from conditioning experiments. Units which yielded small responses or none at all to auditory signals prior to conditioning were markedly changed by a Pavlovian experiment in which the signal was correlated with food presentation 1 sec after each onset. After 10 or 20 trials of pairing, each auditory signal caused a substantial acceleration of many of these units (Linseman and Olds, 1973; Olds, 1973). The acceleration had a latency of approximately 40 msec (Fig. 30), indicating that it was a rather direct response (not fed

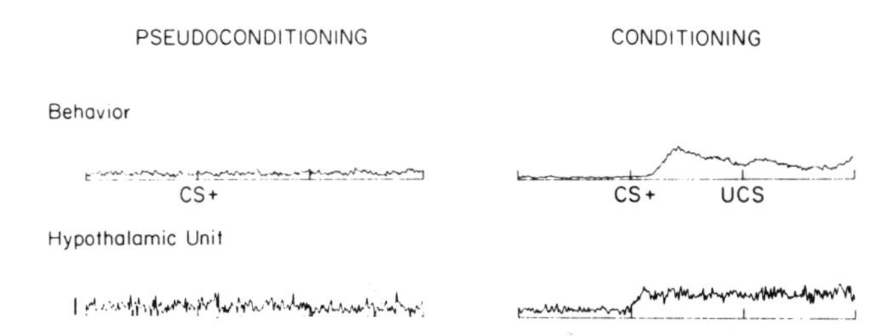

FIG. 30. Behavior and hypothalamic unit response before and after conditioning. The upper traces portray the average output of a detector attached to the head that measured head movements in arbitrary units. The lower traces represent the spike frequency of a lateral hypothalamic unit; the *vertical bar* (far left) represents a rate of 5 spikes/sec. The traces represent 3 sec. At the end of the first second a tone (CS+) was started which continued to the end. During conditioning a pellet dispenser (UCS) was triggered at the end of 2 sec. Prior to conditioning (pseudoconditioning) the tone caused very minor changes in the unit and behavior responses. After conditioning it caused a substantial behavior response with a 170 msec latency and a large unit response with a 20- to 40-msec latency (Linseman and Olds, 1973).

back from the newly learned behavior). Thus these supposed "drive" units were silenced during feeding behavior (when drive was still high) and were triggered into action by conditioned stimuli related to food. The fact that they were active during instrumental pursuit and accelerated by stimuli that heightened pursuit behavior suggested that they might be involved in controlling the instrumental phase of high drive behavior. The kinds of element that would be triggered during the instrumental but not the consummatory phases of drive behavior was not fully clarified.

B. Units and Drinking

Neurons that responded to water shortages and governed at least some compensatory responses were studied by Hayward and Vincent (1970). Neurons were recorded from the lateral preoptic area and the nearby suproptic nucleus, which contains vasopressin secreting cells. Thirst was triggered by piping hyperosmotic solutions into the carotid body. This activated a family of supposed osmodetectors in the preoptic area, and secondarily the vasopressin-containing neurons. Vasopressin acts through the kidney to preserve water. Both the osmodetectors and the vasopressin neurons were then slowed during drinking (Vincent, Arnauld, and Bioulac, 1972). The slowing was immediate, not waiting for digestive absorption of water to compensate for the deficit. The neurons were thus activated by drive inducing manipulations and slowed by rewarding ones.

Angiotensin is a hormone-like substance secreted from the kidney when the volume of body fluids is low. It acts on the brain to cause drinking. Direct application onto supraoptic neurons by iontophoresis caused them to fire (Nicoll and Barker, 1971). As the substance appeared to have its action on drinking at a different brain location (Simpson and Routtenberg, 1973), its action on the supraoptic nucleus might be to suppress water secretion.

C. Units and Reproductive Behavior

The mechanisms of reproduction involve many interactions of brain activity and hormone activity. Ovulation (bursting of the follicle and discharge of the egg) is caused by luteinizing hormone from the pituitary, and this in turn by a releasing factor from the brain. Because the causal chain passes through the brain and because ovulation is a clearly defined episode occurring during a critical period on the afternoon of the third day of the 4- or 5-day estrous cycle of the rat, it has been a target for studies aimed to unravel the interaction of brain and hormone activity. Neuronal activity during the critical period has been recorded in several laboratories. An accleration of activity occurred in a number of related brain centers: the amygdala, nucleus of the stria terminalis which links amygdala and hypothalamus, septal area, anterior hypothalamic-medial preoptic sex centers, and in deeper centers where the neurosecretory cells are thought to reside—the arcuate and ventromedial nuclei of the hypothalamus (Kawakami, Terasawa, and Ibuki, 1970). From these data it was thought that activity from the amygdala and septal area might converge on the preoptic area where it would start activity in trigger cells projecting to the neurosecretory cells in the arcuate region. Because much the same activity occurred even when hippocampal stimulation prevented ovulation (Gallo, Johnson, Goldman, Whitmoyer, and Sawyer, 1971) and because preoptic area stimulation both excited and inhibited neurons in the arcuate region (Haller and Barraclough, 1970), the hypothesis was treated with some caution but not abandoned. Some support for it came from experiments in which preoptic neurons were antidromically activated by stimulation in the arcuate region. These showed the fibers from the preoptic area to be slow-conducting, like neurosecretory neurons, but they were not generally thought to be neurosecretory neurons (Dyer and Cross, 1972).

Further tests were made by removing other brain influences first and hormonal factors second to find which of these activated the preoptic area neurons and if these neurons were themselves sufficient to trigger ovulation through the arcuate region. First, the preoptic-arcuate system was severed from the rest of the brain (Cross and Dyer, 1970*a,b*). Because preoptic neurons were accelerated during the critical period after this, the idea that other brain inputs were required to activate the preoptic area was eliminated. Ovariectomy stopped this neuronal activity (Cross and Dyer, 1972) showing that hormonal conditions were likely responsible for this (and that preoptic neurons might be hormone detectors). Surprisingly, the preoptic activity did not suffice to cause ovulation after the severing of other brain inputs (Cross and Dyer, 1971*b*), suggesting that some cofactor from other brain areas was required, possibly converging with preoptic axons at the arcuate level. Dopamine applied during the first hour after surgery compensated for the loss, suggesting a relation of the dopamine neuron system to the missing cofactor (Dyer, *unpublished observations,* cited in Cross, 1973).

Direct application of progesterone and estrogen intravenously caused biphasic and even triphasic effects on preoptic neuronal activity, but the main trend was for the gonadal hormones to suppress or slow these neurons (Lincoln, 1967; Alcaraz, Guzman-Flores, Salas, and Beyer, 1969; Chhina and Anand, 1969). Although this seemed at odds with the rise of activity during the critical period of ovulation (Dyer, Pritchett, and Cross, 1972), detailed study of the changes in hormone level resolved the difficulty (Brown-Grant, Exley, and Naftolin, 1970). Estrogens peaked prior to the critical period and fell rapidly, decreasing by half or more before the onset of this period. If estrogens suppressed preoptic neuron activity, this rapid decline could activate them by a release mechanism.

The interactions of brain and hormones in male sex behavior were less well studied. In this case the behavior is triggered by special signals from the female and by other arousing signals. These are synergistic with circulating male sex hormone, triggering its production, and profiting by the heightened levels which sensitize the animal to these signals. Unit activity recorded in the preoptic area became coupled to arousing signals and to the brain's arousal system when circulating androgens were present, and this correlation was attenuated by their absence (Pfaff and Gregory, 1971*a,b*). Fitting their supposed relevance to male sex behavior, these neurons were sometimes responsive to olfactory signals emanating from the estrous female. These and other scattered data did not provide a neuronal analysis of male sex behavior, but they did indicate the direction of current studies.

The best-studied units of a brain hormone system were the oxytocin neurosecretory cells. These are located in the paraventricular nucleus of the hypothalamus. They eject oxytocin into the blood, which causes milk ejection at the nipple (with several seconds required to transport the hormone from the brain to the teat). The hormone also causes other reproductive responses in male and female. The neurosecretory neurons have been monitored with microelectrodes. They were identified by antidromic stimulation from the neural lobe of the pituitary (Moss, Dyball, and Cross, 1972*a*). This electrical stimulation fired the paraventricular neurosecretory cells antidromically and at the same time caused milk ejection. When 50 pulses/sec was applied for approximately 15 sec, the ejection occurred at about the end of the train. In other tests the firing patterns of these neurons were correlated with milk ejection when it was caused by suckling (Lincoln and Wakerley, 1973). Milk ejection occurred periodically in lactating rats even when they were anesthetized if the pups were left nursing. The neurosecretory cells of the paraventricular nucleus anticipated and apparently caused these milk ejection episodes. They yielded explosive bursts firing at 50/sec for approximately 2 sec followed by 15 sec of total silence and then milk ejection (Fig. 31).

The hypothesis of a causal relation of the paraventricular events and the milk ejection was furthered by the fact that knife cuts separating these cells from the rest of the brain depressed their firing and reduced oxytocin secretions to zero (Dyball and Dyer, 1971). These neurons showed normal accelerations and decelerations of rate during the long intervals between milk ejections as if they were participating in normal neuronal processes at this time. Because 100 spikes per minute during these periods was not correlated

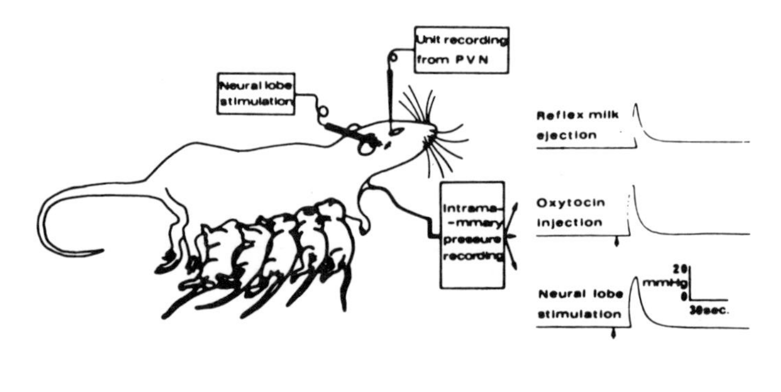

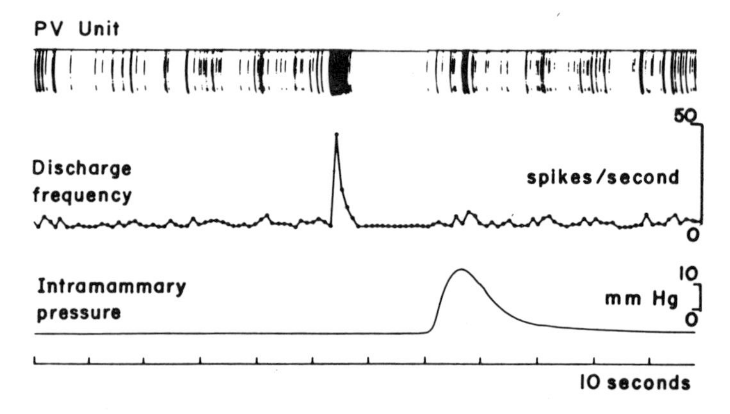

FIG. 31. Firing patterns of oxytocin neurosecretory cells correlated with milk ejection responses noted by Lincoln and Wakerly (1973) in the laboratory of Cross (Cross, 1973). Top: Intramammary pressure was similar during reflex milk ejection or during that caused by oxytocin injection or by stimulation of oxytocin axons in the neural lobe. Bottom: The tracings show (1) a digital portrayal of each unit spike, (2) a tracing indicating frequency of firing by its amplitude, and (3) the mammary response. When pups suckled there were periodic bursts of oxytocin neurons, followed by silence and then milk ejection. The burst and the silence may both have been required to cause the peptide secretion. PVN = paraventricular neurosecretory cells. (From Cross, 1973.)

with any sign of hormone secretion, but 100 spikes per 2 sec followed by 7 sec of silence was regularly followed by milk ejection, a special kind of neuronal activity correlated with neurosecretion seemed possible. Either a critical rate was needed to yield output, or a different pattern of neuronal activity was correlated with the neurosecretory message.

In other studies (Cross, Moss, and Urban, 1971; Moss, Urban, and Cross, 1972*b*) these cells were shown to be excited by acetylcholine and glutamate as are many cells in the central nervous system. They were decelerated by norepinephrine and GABA, again in harmony with other neuronal populations. There was an interdigitated family of non-neurosecretory elements, however, that looked by several tests to be opponents or counterneurons. These were activated by surgical interventions that silenced their neurosecretory neighbors (Cross and Dyer, 1971*a;* Dyball and Dyer, 1971); they were also activated by norepinephrine and suppressed by acetylcholine (Moss et al., 1972*b*), which is most unusual for such a family of neurons. It seemed possible, therefore, that these counterelements might be reciprocal inhibitors of the neurosecretory neurons. Other experiments established the possibility (but far from proof) of positive feedback of neurosecretory elements on themselves (Moss et al., 1972*a*). These showed that the neurosecretory cells were activated by iontophoretic application of oxytocin, the same peptide hormone which they produced, transported, and ejected.

D. Temperature

In temperature regulation there are two problems and two effector systems. One is related to the temperature of the environment, the other to the internal or core temperature of the body. The animal normally adjusts core temperature by means of "vegetative" adjustments: shivering, perspiring, constricting or dilating vessels, and so forth. The animal usually adjusts environmental temperature by moving, although other "operant" responses may be used. Lesions in the preoptic area severely damaged the automatic adjusting system, but behavioral temperature adjustment still occurred. This means that both detectors and effectors sufficient to mediate the operant system survived.

The demonstrated brain responses to peripheral temperature detectors, however, were in the preoptic area. Units in the preoptic area of dogs responded to environmental temperature changes before any central temperature change had resulted (Witt and Wang, 1968). Besides these peripheral effects, local heating or cooling in the brain also excited or decelerated unit spikes recorded from some areas, including the preoptic, anterior hypothalamic, and even the posterior and tuberal area of the hypothalamus. Such experiments have been carried out in cats (Nakayama, Eisenman, and Hardy, 1961; Nakayama, Hammel, Hardy, and Eisenman, 1963), dogs (Hardy,

Hellon, and Sutherland, 1964; Cunningham, Stolwijk, Murakami, and Hardy, 1967), and rabbits (Hellon, 1967; Cabanac, Stolwijk, and Hardy, 1968). Approximately 10% of the elements in the anterior hypothalamic and preoptic area region responded to local heating or cooling. The most common response was for these units to increase their rate of firing linearly during warming. However, there were units that responded only to cooling; and some responded to both warming and cooling. The temperature-sensitive units of the posterior hypothalamic areas were more apt to respond to cooling than those of the anterior and preoptic areas. In the preoptic area some of the temperature-sensitive units were also sensitive to environmental temperature changes; others were specialized to central or peripheral changes (Hellon, 1970). Tests for effects of peripheral temperature changes on units outside the preoptic, anterior hypothalamic region have not been made.

E. Stress

The stress reaction initiated by pain or damage or negative stimulation causes a chain of hormonal events. The hypothalamic releasing factor (CRF) is the first member of the chain. Its only known action is on the pituitary to trigger adrenocorticotropic hormone (ACTH) release. ACTH or one of its fractional components probably acts back on the brain to trigger fear behavior (de Wied, 1974) and maybe even to curtail (Motta, Fraschini, and Martini, 1969) or enhance (Steiner et al., 1969) further ACTH secretion. ACTH also acts on the adrenal cortex to provoke secretion of a cortical steroid such as cortisol. The latter has numerous actions on the bodily stress mechanisms, and it also acts directly on the brain. It attenuates the fear reactions (which are promoted by ACTH) and inhibits ACTH secretion (de Wied, 1974). The possibility of direct brain actions of both ACTH and cortisol has been demonstrated by iontophoretic methods (Ruf and Steiner, 1967; Steiner et al., 1969). Several hundred units were recorded from hypothalamus and midbrain. Of these approximately 17% were suppressed by iontophoretic application of a cortisol substitute (dexamethasone-21-phosphate). Approximately 1% were accelerated, and the rest were unaffected. About half the cortisol-sensitive units were excited by acetylcholine and decelerated by norepinephrine. The most interesting outcome of these studies was from application of ACTH to some of the same cells. Four out of six cells tested (that were inhibited by the cortisol substitute) were excited by ACTH. These experiments therefore left the impression of either a special family of cells excited by ACTH and suppressed by cortisol, or of generally excitatory and inhibitory effects of these two substances.

Other evidence appeared to support the idea of a generally excitatory action of ACTH and of a generally decelerating role of cortisol. ACTH injections in rats under urethane anesthesia, for example, induced a rise in multiunit activity in the arcuate nucleus (Sawyer, Kawakami, Meyerson, Whitmoyer, and Lilley, 1968). ACTH also augmented firing activity of units widely scattered in the hypothalamus (Van Delft and Kitay, 1972). (However, there was no obvious diminution of activity caused by hypophysectomy, possibly because this caused a balanced loss of both ACTH and cortisol.) Adrenalectomy (depleting cortisol) increased the firing rate in anterior hypothalamus (Dafny and Feldman, 1970) but not in posterior hypothalamus (of rats under urethane). Aversive stimulation caused 80% of units in the posterior hypothalamus to respond with accelerations or decelerations. Adrenalectomy increased the ratio of excited to inhibited units. This made it tempting to suppose that the same stimulus could have both excitatory and inhibitory pathways to the same elements, and that cortisol could switch it from one to the other. Animals with hypothalamic islands in which most units fired fast were used in other experiments (Feldman and Sarne, 1970). In these, cortisol usually caused an initial reduction in firing frequency of most cells in the island. Although there was some counterevidence suggesting excitatory actions of cortisol, the consensus was that cortisol treatment had a general or specialized suppressive influence, and ACTH an effect in the excitatory direction.

F. Recordings and Brain Reward

The most common stimulation site in these experiments was the part of the lateral hypothalamus that contains the axons of the medial forebrain bundle. These axons come from many sources: several olfactory forebrain structures, several brainstem monoamine systems, local path neurons, medial hypothalamic neurons, and the brainstem sources of ascending periventricular and mammillary peduncle fibers. A single stimulus could well influence some elements from each of these fiber systems (and most likely there are others I have failed to mention). The stimulus would not only activate the somadendritic sources of these fibers (antidromically) but would influence the targets of these fibers (orthodromically) and the targets of fiber collaterals by an antidromic and then orthodromic route.

Although there are interesting arguments that brain reward behavior depends on simultaneous stimulation of a mixed set of fibers, even the proponents of such views would hardly argue that all the medial forebrain bundle axons participated in the causation of the reward behavior. It is the fact that more tracts are being stimulated than are needed for the effect that makes determination of neuronal correlates of brain reward a difficult and as yet unsolved puzzle.

The electrical brain reward stimulus has many direct and indirect influences. Effects may be considered as "nearly direct" if they have a fixed latency (of excitation or inhibition). Some of these effects are antidromic, others orthodromic. Effects may be considered indirect if there is instead a general excitation or suppression, without fixed latency.

Because of the diverse composition of a bundle it is clear that neither the direct nor the indirect effects can be taken *prima facie* as being related to the rewarding features of the stimulus. Ideally the search for the critical elements would be guided by the discovery of special neuronal activities correlated with peripheral rewards. The search for neuronal correlates of consummatory feeding behavior in an effort to discover these has not yet succeeded. The discovery of neuronal correlates of milk ejection could mark a positive case. However, it is not clear if stimulation of the paraventricular oxytocin cells is rewarding.

Several special methods have been tried to make direct identification of units correlated with brain reward. One method was to study the minimum interpulse (i.e., shock-shock) intervals for brain reward behavior and for units driven by the rewarding stimulus. In these experiments a train of shock pairs is applied (Deutsch, 1964). A set of parameters was chosen so that the second shock in each pair was required to maintain a suprathreshold stimulus train. Then the paired shocks were brought closer and closer together in time until the second shock became ineffective and the stimulus accordingly became subthreshold (ideally there was an abrupt drop in effectiveness at a fixed time interval). In this way, it was argued, the "refractory period" of the brain reward units could be discovered by behavioral tests. By this means it was determined that self-stimulation pedal behavior, in which the rewarding trains were rapidly repeated, did not stop until the intershock intervals were less than 0.6 msec; but runway behavior sequences, in which there was a longer time between rewarding trains, stopped when the intershock interval was less than 0.8 or 1.0 msec. Because stimulated feeding and drinking behaviors had the same 0.6-msec minimum interstimulus interval as the rapid pedal behavior (Rolls, 1973), it was likely that many different kinds of neurons had similar recovery times. In neurophysiological experiments, efforts were made to match these behaviorally determined minimum intershock times with the observed recovery times of units driven or accelerated by lateral hypothalamic stimulation (Rolls, 1971*a,* 1972, 1973). Some units recorded from the midbrain were observed to have recovery times of 0.8 or 1.0 msec; these were thought to be involved in an arousal mechanism but not in reward itself. The arousal mechanism was considered to be a prerequisite to brain reward behavior when longer intertrain intervals were involved. Neurons with 0.6 msec recovery times which were considered to be "reward" or "eating and drinking" neurons were recorded from the amygdala. All the reward neurons could not be in the amygdala as the behavior survived removal of the whole telencephalon (Huston and Borbely, 1974). However, this still might point to the olfactory forebrain as having some units that could be involved.

Another special method was to seek neurons that would be modified in opposite directions by rewarding and aversive brain stimulations on the view that such neurons might have a special relation to the underlying motive process (Keene, 1973). A family of neurons excited by aversive brain shocks and inhibited by rewarding ones was identified in the intralaminar system of the thalamus; and a second family accelerated by rewards and decelerated by punishments was observed with probes in the preoptic area.

A third method was to study the effects on local neurons of the medial forebrain bundle (Fig. 32) in the hope that these main target cells of the tracts in the bundle must be involved (Ito, 1972). Experiments showed that the nearest neurons to the brain reward were most often suppressed or inhibited, whereas more distant neurons (particularly those in the preoptic

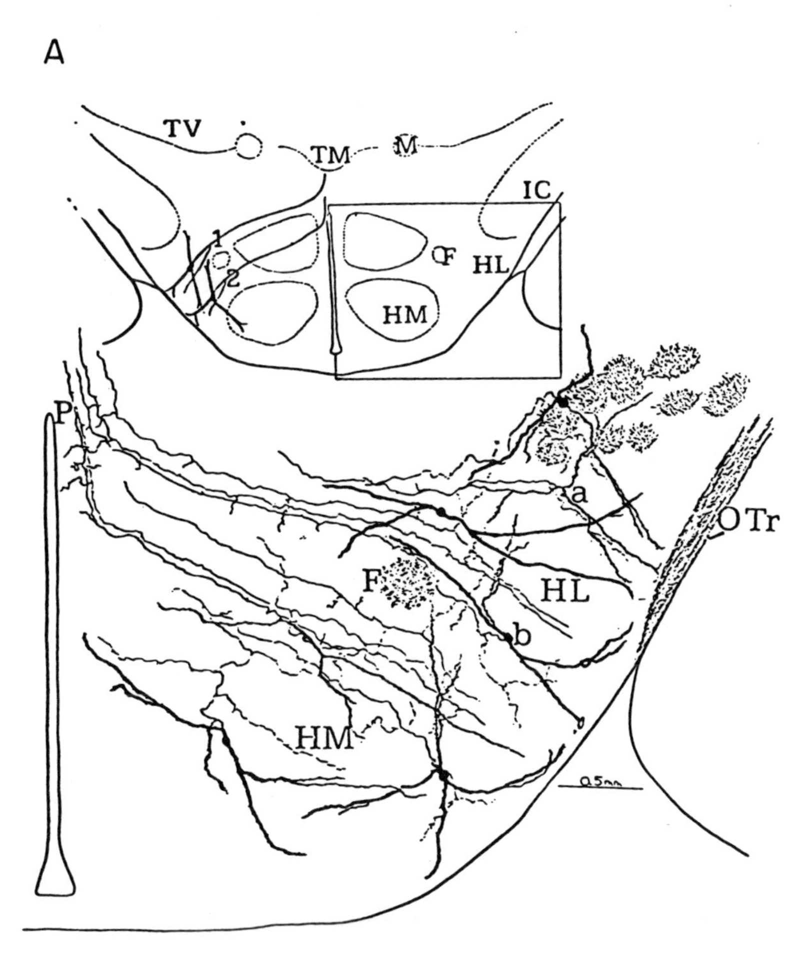

FIG. 32. A. Neurons of the medial forebrain bundle (Millhouse, 1969). 1 and 2, large neurons originating in medial forebrain bundle (MFB) path region and projecting into the periventricular system. TV, ventral thalamus. TM, medial thalamus. M, mammillothalamic tract. IC, internal capsule. F, fornix. HL, lateral hypothalamus. HM, medial hypothalamus. OTR, optic tract. a and b, path neurons showing the orientation of their dendrites in relation to descending fornix (F) and internal capsule (IC).

area) were more apt to be excited by the brain stimulation. Matching the rather surprising findings of Ito that lateral hypothalamic units were suppressed rather than excited by brain reward stimuli were data showing that these neurons were active during morphine withdrawal symptoms and were then suppressed by administration of morphine to addicted animals (Kerr et al., 1974).

Other studies of neurophysiological consequences of rewarding brain stimulation followed prior notions of where emotion mechanisms might lie (Ito and Olds, 1971). Neurons were driven in the cingulate cortex. Sec-

C

Experiment	*Hours of withdrawal*	*Site of recording*	*Morphine*			*Naloxone*		
			A	*B*	*C*	*A*	*B*	*C*
52	16	VMN	+	−	−	−	−	−
55	48	VMN	+	+	+	−	−	−
57	40	VMN	+	+	0	−	−	−
62	52	VMN	+	+	+	−	−	−
67	48	VMN	+	+	+	−	−	−
52	16	LHA	−	−	0	+	+	+
57	40	LHA	−	−	−	+	+	+
62	52	LHA	−	−	−	−	+	+
65	48	LHA	0	−	−	+	+	+

FIG. 32. B. Firing pattern of these units before and during self-stimulation (Ito, 1972). Full trace was 400 msec; large spikes (going off the figure) in the second half are artifacts of the self-administered brain shock. The other spikes are responses of medial forebrain bundle path neurons; these are greatly attenuated in their firing during the rewarding electrical shock train. C. Experimental results from Kerr et al. (1974) showing that the same neurons are activated during naloxone-induced "morphine drive" and quieted by "morphine reward." Interestingly, their medial neighbors are reciprocally affected. 0, unaffected. VMN, ventromedial nucleus of the hypothalamus; LHA, lateral hypothalamic area (region of the path neurons).

ondary effects were recorded in dorsal hippocampus where large neuronal spikes, presumably from pyramidal cells, were regularly suppressed and smaller ones (most likely from a different population) were sometimes excited. Neurons were driven in midbrain locations, mainly in those areas whose stimulation did not itself yield rewarding effects (Routtenberg and Huang, 1968). Electrophysiological slow waves were recorded from various parts of the olfactory forebrain system that gives rise to the descending medial forebrain bundle (Porter et al., 1959). Because of the absence of any special evidence for the involvement of the recorded responses in rewarding effects, the question of brain activity requisite or sufficient for reward is still open, and the facts unknown. It is interesting, in view of the theories about the monoamines, that activity of the monoamine neurons of the locus coeruleus was correlated to some degree with waking and paradoxical sleep (Chu and Bloom, 1973) and with the consumption of natural reinforcers (German and Fetz, 1974).

Some attention was given to the monoamine question in experiments on the lateral hypothalamic and preoptic area unit responses, but the results were ambiguous. Tetrabenazine, which releases and then quickly depletes amine stores, suppressed self-stimulation and caused the "inhibitory" responses of nearby lateral hypothalamic units to disappear. Because the same drug suppressed the brain responses and behavior, it appeared that the inhibitory brain responses might be a necessary part of the brain reward effect (Olds and Ito, 1973*a*). However, chlorpromazine, which is supposed to act by blocking adrenergic receptors, also halted brain reward behavior. This drug did not diminish the inhibitory brain responses, but it did curtail the more anterior excitatory responses (Olds and Ito, 1973*b*). Thus both sets of responses were in question as correlates of self-stimulation. With tetrabenazine the anterior excitatory responses survived while self-stimulation was suppressed; with chlorpromazine the more posterior inhibitory responses survived while self-stimulation was suppressed. It might be that both sets of responses were required in order to elicit the behavior. Still, if the lateral hypothalamic responses were mediated by norepinephrine as might be supposed, it was surprising that they survived the treatment with chlorpromazine.

Is there a pattern emerging from these data? If there is, it points to a family of units located in the path of the medial forebrain bundle having quite the opposite character from what would be expected on the basis of the rewarding effects of stimulating this bundle. Neurons in this area were active during instrumental behavior but suppressed during consummatory behavior—if instrumental behavior was not occurring simultaneously (Hamburg, 1971). They are active in hungry animals and further accelerated by Pavlovian signals that promise rewards (Linseman and Olds, 1973). They are also active during the aversive drug withdrawal condition (Kerr et al., 1974), and are decelerated or turned off by rewarding brain stimulation and by morphine administration (Ito, 1972; Kerr et al., 1974). Therefore they may well be involved in the mediation of strivings. Their firing rates do not go up and down with the physiological drive state. That is, they stop responding in the still-hungry animal when it is given a dish of food, and they can be aroused by "learned" signals. They may well go up and down with the behavioral drive state. On this basis they would appear to be correlated partly with something called drive and partly with something psychologists have long referred to as learned drive.

Summary and Conclusions

A. Stimulation Map

The reward map was made of locations where electrical stimulation caused mammals to come back for more. Rats, cats, and monkeys had much the same map. Humans pushed buttons to stimulate the same regions, although they often seemed confused as to why they were doing it. The map covered most of the hypothalamus and its satellites through the brain. In the hypothalamus it extended from far anterior to far posterior, from far lateral to midline. While probes placed in the hypothalamus often failed to cause reward behavior, there was no clear separation of anatomical locations. There were possibly individual differences between animals; at least there were some "uncooperative" rats that could be "cured" by a dose of amphetamine. A paradox was that the hypothalamus was also the home of aversive effects of electrical stimulation. If opposed aversive effects were not immediately obvious, they could usually be demonstrated by more careful analysis. Because the whole hypothalamus was covered by a reward map, and aversive countereffects were always in evidence, it might seem that the hypothalamus was homogeneous. It was not.

Rewarding effects of stimulation predominated in the far lateral parts and in some far medial ones. In these cases the animal was apparently at home with self-stimulation. No negative signs were seen during brain pedal behavior, and careful methods were required to reveal them. Aversive effects in these cases were evidenced only by the fact that continuously applied trains were interrupted periodically by the animal. This was possibly done only so that the stimulus might start again, the assumption being that onsets were more positive than the continuation of trains. An alternative was that these stimulations yielded unmixed rewards when applied in short doses, but had real aversive effects when the train endured too long. In any event there was a predominance of positive effects when stimulation was applied in far lateral and far medial areas.

In a large "in-between" area, there is an obvious mixture of positive and aversive effects. The animal pedal-pressed regularly and fast if closeted with an electrical stimulus; but if there was a way out, it was taken. There was no amount of stimulation in these areas that seemed just right. The animal behaved as if it could not stand it but could not resist it.

In this same middle area lay another paradox of the reward maps. Here the same electrical stimulus provoked both drives and rewards. The drives changed depending partly on the location of the stimulus. In anterior hypothalamus there were sex responses caused by stimulation and responses that adjusted the body temperature. In the anterior part of the middle hypothalamus there were both eating and drinking responses but the latter predominated. In the posterior part of the middle hypothalamus there were more eating and drinking responses, but here the eating responses predominated. In the posterior part of the hypothalamus sex responses were evoked again. Because there were many overlapping effects and sex responses were evoked in areas on both sides of the feeding and drinking areas, the idea of sharp localizations was rejected. However, because this in-between area could be mapped into four successive regions where stimulation caused temperature, drinking, eating, and sex responses, respectively, as the most likely responses, the idea of totally unlocalized drive systems was rejected. Obviously the truth lay somewhere in between.

One feature of the in-between answer was discovered; it was really quite surprising. The drive targets of these stimulations were found to be changeable by a simple training procedure. Animals were stimulated regularly in the presence of a drive object; after a while the stimulus began to evoke an appropriate drive state, i.e., one with the available drive object as its target. If probes were placed in a feeding point (where stimulation evoked feeding), and if 1 min trains of stimulation were applied every 5 min all night in the presence of water, the feeding point changed: In the morning it was a drinking point! This was called the Valenstein effect (Valenstein et al., 1968).

If drives were mapped into different areas of the brain to begin with, it seemed wrong that they could be modified by training. One possible answer to this puzzle is that a drive center might be predetermined by its sensitivity to visceral afferents or to particular hormones, but it still might need to be attached by learning to appropriate drive objects. The Valenstein effect might be evidence that electrical stimulation could pervert this normal learning mechanism. Assume that the stimulus was applied in a "hunger center" but that gradually the training artificially caused the animal to respond as if water were a hunger drive object. At present such a redirection of drives seem to me the most likely explanation of this surprising changeableness of the targets of the supposed drive centers.

To recapitulate the picture developed by the hypothalamic map of brain stimulation effects: there were far lateral and far medial areas where reward predominated, and in-between areas where aversive effects and drive effects were overlapped with reward.

This stimulation map matched the maps of several catecholamine neuronal systems. These are neurons containing the two specialized *slow* neurochemical transmitters: norepinephrine and dopamine. The far lateral and far medial areas contained *dopamine* neurons and the in-between areas contained *norepinephrine* neurons mixed with acetylcholine neurons. Acetylcholine is the more well-known *fast* chemical messenger. Thus all the reward

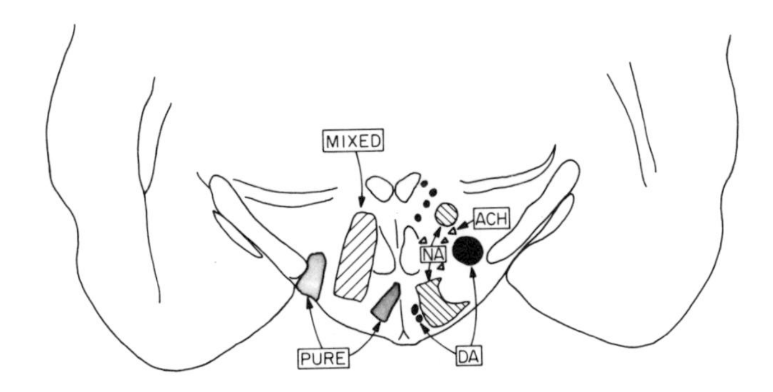

FIG. 33. Correlation of self-stimulation and neurotransmitter maps in the hypothalamus. Areas where stimulation effects were nearly "purely positive" (shaded), or mixed but predominantly positive (hatched). Chemical maps showing signs of the acetylcholine (ACH) transmitter system (triangles); norepinephrine (NA) axons or terminals (hatched); and dopamine (DA) neurons or pathways (black) (Jacobowitz and Palkovits, 1974).

areas were permeated by catecholamine slow-transmitter pathways. This led to a view that catecholamine neurons (or at least some of them) might be reward neurons (Stein, 1964*a;* Crow, 1972*b*). The intermixed aversive and drive effects might result from the intermixing of catecholamine and acetylcholine fibers in the in-between areas.

Thus the data suggested a dopamine system (or a pair of them) where reward predominated. Then another norepinephrine reward system mixed with an acetylcholine drive system (Fig. 33). This still left one question: What is the reason for the difference between dopamine neurons which characterized the more positive areas and the norepinephrine neurons which characterized the more mixed regions.

B. Lesion Map

Lesion studies divided the hypothalamus and its neighbors into a focus where lesions had one effect, and a set of three surrounding areas where different kinds of opposed effects were observed. The focus was the same far lateral hypothalamus region where stimulation had predominantly positive effects. It included the nearby substantia nigra where one dopamine bundle had its main origin. Lesions here caused a loss of positive drive-reward behaviors and other voluntary or instrumental performances (even ones aimed to avoid noxious stimulation). If the animal was kept alive for a few days there was a surprisingly good recovery. Animals died if not force-fed at first, but they recovered if kept alive by force-feeding (Teitelbaum and Epstein, 1962).

After recovery the animals were heavily dependent on the cortex for drive behavior (Teitelbaum and Cytawa, 1965). A damaging manipulation of cortex by application of potassium chloride in normals had a 4- to 8-hr effect (abolishing all instrumental behavior for that period). In recovered lateral hypothalamus animals it had a much more devastating effect, causing the full 3-week recovery to be needed once again. This dependence on the cortex showed that recovery was not really complete. There were other signs. After the lesions the animal never again responded to cellular water deficits by drinking. It drank to wet the mouth and for a number of reasons that would seem irrelevant (if they did not serve luckily for the animal to keep it alive). Similarly it did not respond to glucose deficits by eating, and it failed to respond appropriately to sodium deficits. However, with its repertoire of redundant hunger controllers or learned feeding behaviors, it got along; it ate well and looked robust. It was as if a learned cortex repertoire of drive behaviors recovered although a hypothalamic originator or starter of these was gone.

Fitting this view, a most important food learning mechanism was also gone. The animal did not learn well to exclude foods on the basis of poisoning or illness. Normal rats responded to foods that preceded illness as if they were aversive. This was called the Garcia effect (Garcia and Ervin, 1968). Similarly in normals there was a learning of special positive reactions of foods that were correlated with recovery from illness. These food-learning phenomena of Garcia matched the drive-target learning that occurred when Valenstein stimulated these areas. The Garcia effects were lost when these same areas were lesioned (Schwartz and Teitlebaum, 1974).

There were three areas surrounding the lateral hypothalamus substantia nigra region where lesions had opposed effects. (1) Medial or "between" hypothalamus lesions cause the opposite of starvation. The animals ate too often; i.e., meals began too early (as if no visceral or chemical trigger was needed). (2) Lesions in the caudate nucleus (i.e., the extrapyramidal area which is in a reciprocal inhibitory relation to substantia nigra) in cats caused nonsensical instrumental behavior directed at anything that moved (Villablanca, 1974). Instead of going toward nothing it went toward everything. (3) Lesions in amygdala caused consummatory behavior toward dangerous objects (or toward untested foods) or toward wrong objects, e.g., eating or mating with nonfood or nonsex objects (Klüver and Bucy, 1937; Rolls and Rolls, 1973*a,b*).

The fact that lesions in a central area stopped reward behaviors and lesions in three surrounding areas caused different kinds of excessive approach behaviors suggested a multiple opponent process system. A central positive region in the lateral hypothalamus and substantia nigra might inhibit and be inhibited by the three surrounding regions. In such a system a shifting balance of excitation and inhibition would determine acceleration or deceleration of approach behavior, and electrical stimulation along the communicating links might well have double effects.

Another kind of experiment connected the lesion studies to the catecholamine paths. A special method that caused poisoning of the dopamine pathway from the substantia nigra induced all or almost all of the loss of positive behavior that occurred with far lateral lesions (Ungerstedt, 1971*b*). The animal failed to eat and failed at other things. Similar poisoning applied to one of the norepinephrine pathways caused many of the effects of "in-between" or medial hypothalamic lesions; in this case the animals overate because they started meals too soon (Ahlskog and Hoebel, 1973). If both catecholamines were involved in reward, it was difficult to guess why lesions in the two would have such opposed effects.

One interesting supposition was offered by Crow (Crow, 1972*b*, 1973). The norepinephrine pathway might carry *drive-reducing satiety* messages, which would be rewarding. The dopamine pathway might carry *drive-inducing incentive* messages, which would also be rewarding. Rewards both start and stop things depending on whether they are incentive rewards or terminal consummatory rewards which bear the seeds of their own demise. Crow suggested that incentive rewards (e.g., the smell of food and maybe also learned rewards) used the dopamine pathways. Final rewards (e.g., the taste of food) would act through the norepinephrine pathways. Thus lesions in the two paths might block mechanisms to start and stop eating, respectively.

C. Catecholamine Maps

Catecholamine maps are neurochemical maps. They seemed to identify a set of brain reward neurons and the beginnings of an interpretation of the brain reward behavior and other reward processes. Small clumps of neurons from focal centers in the hindbrain, midbrain, and boundaries of the forebrain send axons broadcast through the brain. There are several clumps and several overlapping sets of broadcast fibers. The small origins and the widely diffusing fibers made these look like command centers that could send yes-no commands to the whole brain. All of them had amine-containing fibers; i.e., the transmitters they used were norepinephrine, dopamine, and serotonin.

The norepinephrine fibers started farthest back and went farthest forward. They ran from a crossroads of the brain in the medulla to all of its outposts, the cerebellum, thalamus, paleocortex, and neocortex. The serotonin fibers started in the middle of the midbrain and ran a less well-defined course to many parts of the forebrain. The dopamine fibers started in the front part of the midbrain and nearby parts of hypothalamus. They ran a shorter course, ending mainly in structures below the cortex, i.e., in the extrapyramidal motor systems (which may be the main control system for purposive instrumental behavior) and in some special but poorly understood lower centers of the olfactory brain. Most likely they did not all end here, for dopamine itself was found along with norepinephrine in many parts of the cortex.

For all amine fiber systems one property stood out; i.e., there was a very small source of origin and a very wide spread of influence. The norepinephrine, serotonin, and dopamine systems seemed almost like a small triumvirate: three little men deep in the brain making its command decisions.

Chemical and neurophysiological studies showed the amines to have special properties. First, two of them—dopamine and norepinephrine—have a common substrate, tyrosine. Moreover, one (dopamine) was the normal precursor of the other, norepinephrine. Second, these differed from other transmitters in the mode of inactivation. Other neurotransmitters were limited in time by degradation (destruction) of the transmitter. The catecholamines were originally thought to be inactivated in this way via oxidation. Excessive supplies were degraded by this process under the influence of the monoamine oxidase enzyme; but this was not the normal route of inactivation. When catecholamines were secreted by nerve terminals the messages were limited in time by reuptake of the amine via a pumping action back into the nerve terminals where the neurochemical was thought to be repackaged into vesicles for reuse (or oxidized if supplies were excessive). Reuptake apparently allowed these neurons to replenish their stores from "free" amines in the interstitial fluid, possibly permitting them to borrow or steal from their neighbors. Third, the amines conveyed their message by causing a second messenger to be produced inside the target cell (this second messenger was cyclic AMP). This same second messenger was used to carry out the commands of the peptide hormones. It was possible to imagine it, therefore, as a common path that would demand both a hormone message and a simultaneous amine message to become active. Fourth, the amines had a mysterious exciter-inhibitor role. Drugs which stimulated their central actions often had excitatory influence on the animal. Yet direct application of amines onto neurons usually caused suppression of the neuronal spikes and slowing of activity. The catecholamines therefore might be stopping the normal action potentials but causing some special kind of activation. Fifth, the onset and offset of action was slow when compared with that of other transmitters.

Thus a considerable list of properties fitted the catecholamines for special functions: (1) the common substrate (tyrosine) between dopamine and norepinephrine, and the precursor role of dopamine to norepinephrine; (2) the reuptake mechanism, which apparently permitted the monoamine terminals to compete for scarce supplies; (3) the "second messenger" cyclic AMP, which formed a common step in the action of catecholamine and peptide hormones; (4) the deceleratory or inhibitory modulation, which nevertheless seemed to have excitatory consequences; (5) the slow onset and long duration of action; (6) the monoamine oxidases, which provided a negative feedback on available supplies (a planned scarcity—like the Federal Reserve Board).

While it was by no means clear what special function they mediated, their properties fit them for controlling behavioral priorities. This is because the repeating theme was competition for a limited resource, and the time constants involved were in the order of magnitude of behavioral episodes rather than of neurophysiological events.

Because their properties seemed to suit them for controlling behavioral priorities, it was interesting that experiments linked them to drive and reward systems in strong and intricate ways. These fibers pervaded the drive-reward systems in such a way as to match the drive-reward maps (German and Bowden, 1974). New maps based on the theory that these were reward neurons showed new rewarding locations tracking the norepinephrine pathway toward the medulla and the dopamine pathway toward the substantia nigra (Crow, 1971; Ritter and Stein, 1973). Drug studies indicated that catecholamine deficits stopped brain reward behaviors, and their excesses caused these behaviors to be augmented and thresholds to fall.

The broadcast fibers of these neurons formed networks or meshworks of terminals sufficiently diffuse to explain the relative lack of localization of the sites effective for drive and reward experiments. Where these fibers were concentrated, the stimulation effects were strong and had low thresholds; where they were less concentrated, the stimulation effects were weak and thresholds were higher.

There was still an enigma. Drugs which discharged amines from their terminals often augmented brain reward behavior. At first it seemed that the excess of amines caused by discharging amines *should* promote reward behavior; but second thought shows a problem. What was being electrically stimulated if the amines were already outside the fibers? A similar problem arose in some experiments in which the catecholamine fibers were cut. In these cases behavior could often be restored by amphetamine. Here it was as if the amines were important but the fibers were not. What was being stimulated if the amine fibers were cut? Three answers were given. Although not entirely satisfactory, these emphasize other remarkable properties of the amine systems. The first answer is that the excessive amines were pumped back into fibers or into other fibers and were quickly ready to be reused. This by itself was not very good because it did not tell us any advantage to freeing the amines in the first place. The second answer was more interesting. Amines may be pumped into some cortical and hypothalamic neurons which do not themselves manufacture them (Hökfelt and Fuxe, 1972). Thus it might be that amines carried to the cortex by catecholamine neurons would affect reward behavior mainly when ejected from these and taken up by cortex storage elements. This would still leave a problem. If the amines were already free, why did the animal self-stimulate their fibers? Maybe it was the cortex storage elements that were stimulated by some other afferent path in the hypothalamus or by antidromic stimulation of their descending axons. This would be somewhat unsatisfactory because these other fibers might just as well have been responsible for reward in the first place; at least it would remove the amine fibers from their role as the only reward neurons if other fibers in the medial forebrain bundle could play that role too. A better answer was that the self-stimulation behavior went on by some automatic and almost superstitious repetition compulsion, even though the animal was already fully rewarded by the free amines. This is not a bad answer. Amphetamine, which is one of the drugs used to free amines, often caused (in animals and humans) repetition of behavior in extinction or at other times when it was actually useless. Thus if the free amines were pumped into cortex neurons, and these were the ones correlated with the repetitious behavior, the behavior might continue even though the electrical stimulation no longer had a directly rewarding effect.

Another interesting question remains. Why did amphetamine help restore the behavior which was suppressed after catecholamine fibers were cut? The answer often given is that there was a rapid regrowth of catecholamine fibers. This was a special property of catecholamine fibers which seemed to add greatly to the likelihood that they were tied to both the stimulation and lesion effects. Amine fibers regrew and proliferated after cutting. They were not just like other fibers in this respect but were quite remarkable. By cutting a bundle from locus coeruleus to cerebellum in half, it was possible to double the number of its endings in the cerebellum, and to cause a whopping six fold increase of endings in the other leg of the same bundle far away in the hippocampus (Pickel, Segal, and Bloom, 1974). The recovery from lateral hypothalamic lesions seemed to be possibly explained by this kind of mechanism. It took approximately 3 to 4 weeks for the regrowth and proliferation of these endings to be completed, and it took about this time for recovery from lateral lesions to be completed. Brain self-stimulation also improved after probe implantation in what was originally a surprising course. From the time of implantation of probes until 3 weeks later the behavior improved. This is the time it would take the catecholamine fibers to proliferate after the damage caused by probe implantation. Other examples of improvement after damage exist. Placing a probe in such a way as to do excessive damage or implanting several probes sometimes yielded better brain reward in the end; or placing lesions in the brain reward system sometimes caused a surprising increase in brain reward behavior. These examples of recovery and even improvement after lesions fit the surprising property of the catecholamine fibers to regrow and proliferate.

In any event, the catecholamine system was corroborated by a number of studies with the drive-reward systems. The paths were the paths of reward. Poisoning the paths caused the same effects as the lesions. Regrowth in these paths was correlated with recovery in the lateral hypothalamic syndrome and with recovery or improvement of self-stimulation. Drugs that modified catecholamines modified brain reward behavior (and normal reward behavior). Therefore catecholamine neurons could be reward neurons. If they were, how would a catecholamine reward system work?

D. Drive Connections

Because of the great convergence of catecholamine pathways on the hypothalamus before they diverge to the rest of the brain, an important clue to how they work might be found in the hypothalamus itself.

The most striking family of neurons in the catecholamine path through the hypothalamus was a family of large neurons with axons spread as if to monitor the ascending and descending messages in this path (Millhouse, 1969). The descending messages were from the paleocortex (the projection center for "rewards"?). The ascending messages were those from the locus coeruleus and substantia nigra (ascending messages about visceral and learned rewards?). To understand the large neurons better, we would like to have two questions answered. What do rewards do to them? What do drives do?

These questions were studied by recording neuron spikes during drive-reward behavior. The answer was surprising at first. These neurons were often turned off when animals ate (Hamburg, 1971). If they were rewarding neurons they should be turned on. It is not clear that they were turned off by the reward itself. Actually they were turned off when instrumental striving behavior stopped, as the animal started to eat. If the animal was both eating and struggling at the same time, these neurons were turned on again. It was as if they were either turned on by information that striving was required and turned off by other information that the necessity was past, or they were correlates caused by the striving behavior.

That it was not just feedback from the behavior was demonstrated by Ito (1972), who showed that the brain reward signals also turned these neurons off, directly before any behavior was caused. The stimulus stopped them for several milliseconds. Thus two kinds of rewards turned them off: food and brain rewards.

What turns them on? I guessed they might become more active as the animal became more hungry, but it was hard to check this and to distinguish it from the general activity that built up as the animal got hungrier.

Two things, however, seemed to fit the notion that these might be drive (or learned drive) neurons. One was that they were turned on by a Pavlovian stimulus associated with reward (Linseman and Olds, 1973; Olds, 1973). It is well known that signals correlated with goals often trigger the correlated drives. Signals close to the goal also activated these neurons. Another set of experiments connected these neurons to the special drives of drug addiction. These neurons were turned on in addicted rats during withdrawal periods, and they were further activated by antimorphine drugs. On the other hand, they were quite abruptly quieted by morphine itself (Kerr et al., 1974). Once again they were on during drive but quieted by a reward.

These could therefore be the drive neurons, the ones involved in the

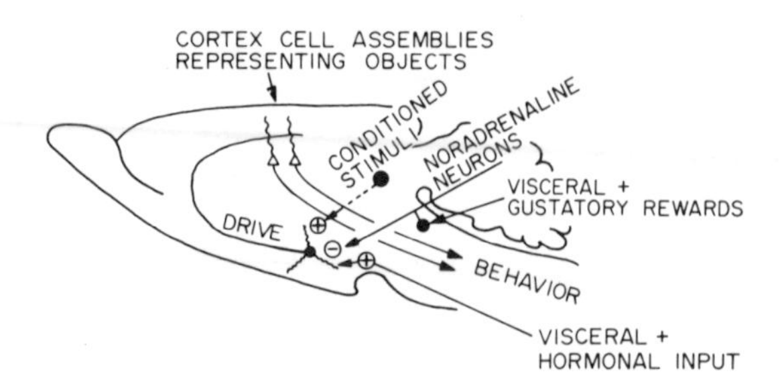

FIG. 34. "Drive reduction theory of reward." Norepinephrine (noradrenaline) neurons from the pons and medulla would be triggered by rewarding gustatory and visceral inputs. These would act to silence drive or learned drive neurons housed in or near the lateral hypothalamus (some of which might be dopamine neurons). Silencing drive neurons would cause them to become coupled to cortex cell assemblies active at the time. Excitatory inputs to drive neurons would come from visceral and hormonal factors and from conditioned stimuli.

Valenstein and Garcia effects. The catecholamine reward neurons might function to attenuate or silence them, thus causing a drive reduction kind of reward. By this action they might also attach or couple these neurons to correlated neuron firings in cortex (Fig. 34). Rearousal of the drive would then activate the attached set of cortex cell assemblies, causing the objects represented by them to become objects of pursuit. This might be a way for the Valenstein and Garcia effects to work.

Like any idea put together after the observations, this would need a good deal of testing. Still, it seemed a likely possibility that hypothalamic drive neurons were attenuated by catecholamine reward neurons.

E. The Hormones

A different idea about why the catecholamine neurons converged in the hypothalamus came from the brain hormone studies. These showed close interaction between the catecholamines and the hormones (Hökfelt and Fuxe, 1972).

Peptide hormones are generated by neurons in the brain, by other cells of the anterior pituitary, and similar cells in various organs. These peptide messengers are carried by the blood of the peripheral circulation and in special vascular systems such as the portal system. The portal system is a main window between the hormone systems of blood and the brain. Peptides are also carried by other fluids in the brain: in ventricles, specialized cells, and neurons. The effects of peptides are either directly on target glands or effectors, as in the milk ejection reflex, or on the pituitary where they trigger secondary control hormones; or their actions may be on the brain itself. It is the latter set of effects that needs to be further explored. Several findings pointed to direct brain actions.

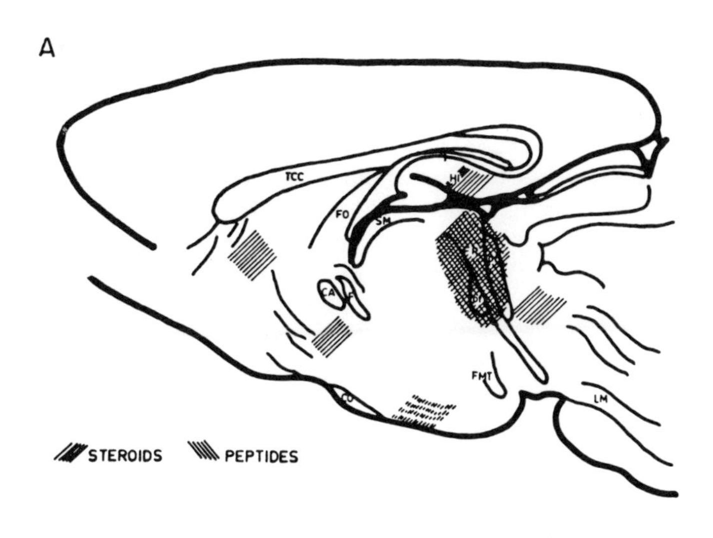

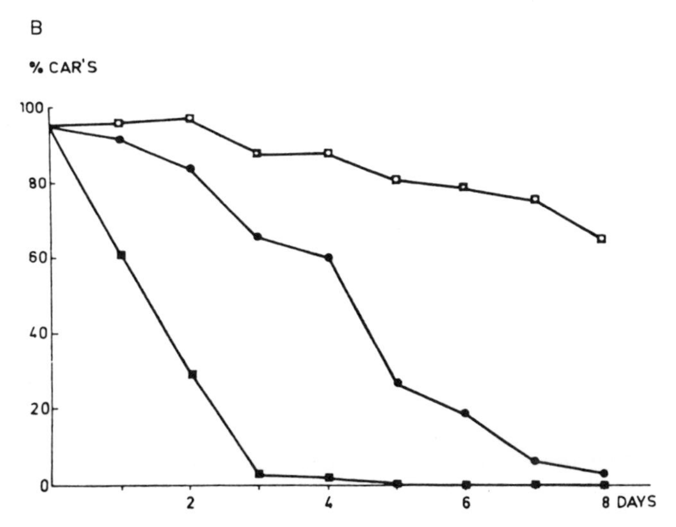

FIG. 35. Experiments of de Wied (1974). A. Regions of the brain where ACTH fractions caused "fear" reactions (cross-hatched) and where cortical steroids caused "bold" reactions (cross-hatched and single hatched). In much of the cross-hatch region electrical stimulation also caused negative reactions (Olds and Olds, 1963). TCC, truncus corporis callosum. HI, hippocampus. FO, fornix. SM, stria medullaris thalami. FR, fasciculus retroflexus. pf, nucleus parafascicularis. CA, commissura anterior. F, columna fornicis. FMT, fasciculus mamillothalamicus. CO, chiasma opticum. LM, lemniscus medialis. B. Persistence of conditioned avoidance reactions under the influence of an effective seven-peptide fragment of ACTH (*top trace*), and under control conditions (*middle trace*), and under the influence of a modified version of the seven-peptide fragment in which one of the peptides had been reversed from the L- to the D-stereoisomer (*bottom trace*). The effective fragment seemed to function as a "fear hormone" and the modified version had the opposite effect. (From de Wied, 1974.)

One interesting set of observations pointed to a hormone of the stress system (ACTH) as having specialized subparts that acted as "fear hormones" directly on brain centers. ACTH is a 39-member peptide. A six- or seven-member fragment of it acted from blood to cause fear. In much smaller quantities it had this action if applied in a brain center where electrical stimulation caused aversive effects (Fig. 35A) (de Wied, 1974).

A still more surprising aspect of these ACTH studies was that by a slight change in the spelling of the peptide word (inversion of one member of the peptide chain) the effect could be reversed; i.e., it could be changed from acting like a fear hormone to acting like a security hormone (Fig. 35B). These researches pointed to the possibility that the drive mechanisms of the brain might be mainly peptide events, i.e., changes in the chemical state of the brain, changes which would bias neuronal processes.

This made it interesting that catecholamines were involved in controlling hormonal states (Ganong, 1974). Catecholamines blocked the ACTH system and promoted three other systems—thyroid, growth hormone, and sex. More detailed pictures of catecholamine actions showed that they modulate the various steps in sequential procedures such as sex and reproduction. The catecholamines seemed to help trigger hormone events, and then the hormone process seemed to carry the momentum over longer periods.

If hormones were actually the determining factors in brain states they would need to have widespread influence, and the question arose whether they might be broadcast in brain like the catecholamine fibers. Would they have special fiber systems? Some peptides have been mapped in brain, and the results looked a little like the catecholamine maps—at least one peptide (thyroid-releasing hormone) appeared in the medial and lateral feeding centers in significant amounts (Fig. 36) (Brownstein, Palkovits, Saavedra, Bassiri, and Utiger, 1974; Winokur and Utiger, 1974). That they might be transported was one thing. How they would be transported was possibly best indicated by studies of oxytocin (Cross, 1973). This substance is released into the blood by neurons residing in the paraventricular nucleus of the hypothalamus. Its neurosecretory neurons have been studied carefully. The study of these cells was most important for showing that oxytocin cells had a type of activity during neurosecretion that was different from that observed normally. Between milk ejection episodes these neurons had fast and slow activity that looked normal. They appeared by accelerations and decelerations to be participating in normal neuronal processes. Approximately 15 sec prior to milk ejection, they raced at 50 spikes per second for approximately 2 sec and then became totally silent (Fig. 31) (Cross, 1973). The neurosecretion itself occurred approximately 7 sec after the burst. The burst of very fast activity and the period of silence might both have been involved. Why the rapid burst and the long silence appeared was not known. However, this picture suggested the possibility that the same cells might have two kinds of action, which would be represented by quite different

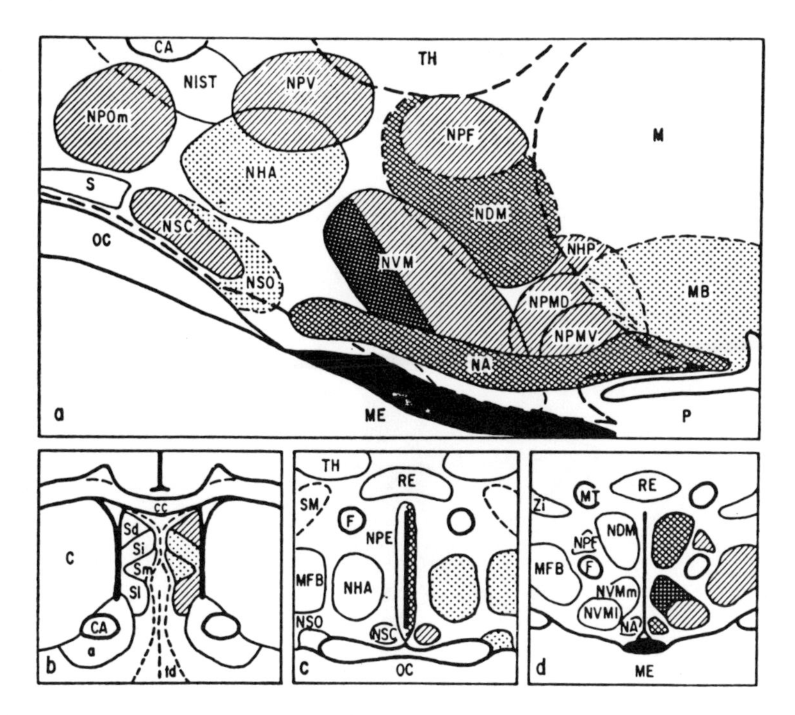

FIG. 36. Map of "thyroid-releasing hormone" (TRH), a three-member peptide chain in the hypothalamus and neighboring areas. Quantities of TRH range from 39 ng/mg protein (black) to less than 1 ng/mg (lightest stipple) with intermediate shades in between. The heaviest concentrations were in the median eminence (ME), medial part of the ventromedial nucleus (NVMm), the arcuate nucleus (NA), and the dorsomedial nucleus (NDM), respectively. Even the preoptic area (NPOm), medial forebrain bundle (MFB), and septal area (Sd, Si, Sm, Sl) had appreciable amounts. Other studies (Winokur and Utiger, 1974) mapped smaller concentrations even farther afield. a: Parasagittal section through the rat hypothalamus. b–d: Frontal sections. b: Septal region. c: Anterior hypothalamus. d: Tuberal region. C, nucleus caudatus. CA, commissura anterior. CC, corpus callosum. F, fornix. M, mesencephalon. MB, mammillary body. ME, median eminence. MFB, medial forebrain bundle. MT, tractus mammillothalamicus. NHA, anterior hypothalamic nucleus. NHP, posterior hypothalamic nucleus. NIST, nucleus interstitialis striae terminalis. NPE, periventricular nucleus (hypothalamus). NPF, parafascicular nucleus (thalamus). NPMD, medial premammillary nucleus (hypothalamus). NPMV, ventral premammillary nucleus (hypothalamus). NPV, paraventricular nucleus (hypothalamus). NSC, suprachiasmatic nucleus. NSO, supraoptic nucleus. NVMi, ventromedial nucleus (hypothalamus), inferior part. OC, chiasma opticum. P, pituitary. RE, nucleus reuniens thalami. S, nucleus preopticus suprachiasmaticus. SM, stria medullaris. TH, thalamus. ZI, zona incerta. a, nucleus accumbens. td, nucleus tractus diagonalis. (From Brownstein et al., 1974.)

recordings. The bursting and the silence might be involved in a peptide neurosecretory mechanism that would be quite independent from the more normal neuronal messages.

Two other observations related the catecholamines to peptide hormones. One was that some nerve endings in the hormone parts of the brain appeared to have two kinds of neurochemical vesicles carried in the same endings. One kind was typical for catecholamines, and the other for neuropeptides (Hökfelt and Fuxe, 1972). Thus catecholamines and peptides might

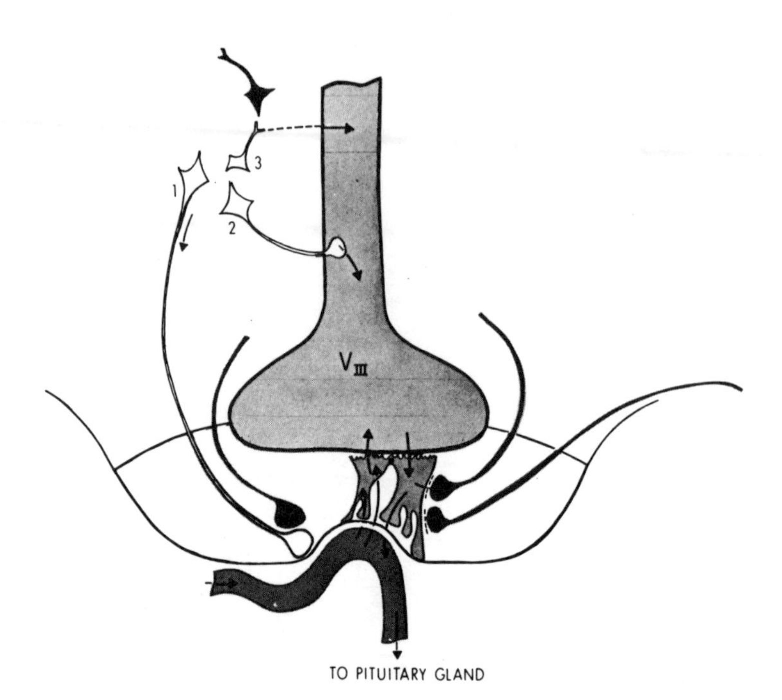

FIG. 37. Schematic portrayal of the evidence and theory of Knigge (Knigge et al., 1971). The elements are (1) the portal vessel (to the pituitary gland), (2) the median eminence (in lightest grey); (3) the tanycytes (in dark grey) connecting it to (4) the third ventricle (V iii). The neurons in white numbered 1, 2, and 3 are dopaminergic; those in black are noradrenergic. Knigge's view is that the third ventricle and the ventricular system in general is a chemical pool collecting from production points in the brain and from the blood and acting on (1) sensors along the walls, (2) through the blood on the adenohypophysis, and (3) possibly through transport mechanisms that act farther afield in the brain. The tanycytes and the portal vessel (and other similar arrangements at other "circumventricular organs") act as two-way windows between the blood and the ventricular pool and thus between the blood and the brain. Dopaminergic and noradrenergic innervation may function in regulating tanycyte function.

be co-occupants of the same fibers.

The other thing had to do with a set of tubules known as tanycytes, which linked the hormonal parts of the hypothalamus with the nearby blood supply (the portal system), and thence to the anterior pituitary. These were studied by Knigge et al. (1971). The system was thought to form a two-way window between hypothalamus (or the ventricle system) and the blood supply. Catecholamine neurons were observed ending on the tanycytes and Knigge says that "dopaminergic and noradrenergic innervation may function in regulating tanycyte function" (see Fig. 37).

All of these things suggested that peptides could be carried in catecholamine neurons or transport systems controlled by them. It is well known that amino acids become incorporated into small proteins, which are moved rather rapidly along neurons. This transport mechanism studied by Ochs (1974) could move peptide hormones from hypothalamus throughout the brain in catecholamine fibers, and these might be released by special messages in the amine fibers.

The study of peptide hormones therefore suggests a second scenario to show how a catecholamine reward system might work (Fig. 38). What if the catecholamine neurons were both drive and reward neurons? The catecholamine transmitters would then be set off by normal action patterns, and

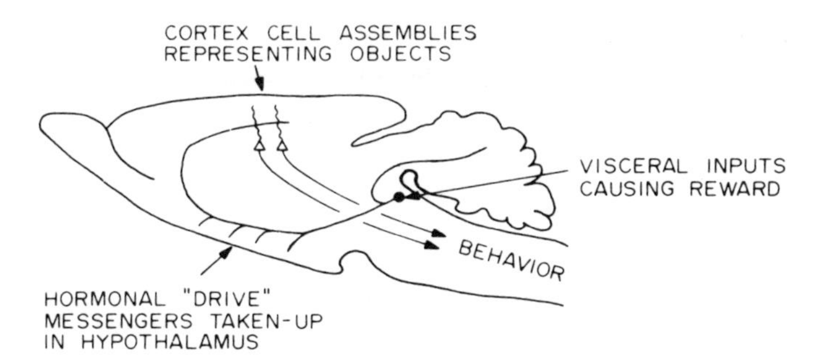

FIG. 38. Theory that catecholamine neurons might also be a peptide transport system. They would carry a reward message by one firing pattern that would release mainly catecholamines, and a drive message by a different firing pattern that would release mainly peptides. A rewarding input would couple these to active cell assemblies.

they could carry the reward message. In addition there would be a peptide hormone carried by active transport mechanisms in the same neuron; this could be the drive message, which would be released by a different pattern of activity in the same fibers. This would resolve in a new way one paradox of reward, i.e., the question of why a reward attaches a drive to a goal or to a special instrumental behavior. If a burst of catecholamine neuronal activity caused the neurons involved to become connected or coupled to coactive cortex cell assemblies, this coupling might serve later as a method whereby a drive could have a selective action on that cell assembly because drive and reward would "come down the same pipe."

This of course is not a likely possibility as things stand. If peptide messengers in the brain become better understood, however, they might well be found to carry drive messages, and their interactions with catecholamine neurons will require careful study.

F. Summary

First, stimulation and lesion studies possibly showed that a broadcast set of catecholamine fibers were reward neurons. It may be stimulation of these that caused reward behavior, and cutting them that at least temporarily suspended it. Because there were different effects of stimulation and lesions in the paths of the two catecholamines, it was suggested that one of them, norepinephrine, might be more involved in those rewards that come toward the end of a consummatory process and which carry the seeds of satiety and the demise of the drive system. The other catecholamine, dopamine, might be involved in those rewards that come at the beginning of the consummatory process (or in the promising phases of the instrumental process) which were involved, in a positive feedback way, with initiating events.

A possible mechanism for involvement of these catecholamine neurons in drive-reward interactions was considered: The catecholamine axons inhibited a set of drive neurons in the lateral hypothalamus. From the experiments of Valenstein and Garcia it was supposed that these neurons were prewired to basic drives on the input side but had variable drive-object-targets learned on the basis of good and bad aftereffects of consummatory behaviors. This learning was supposed to be mediated by changing the connection of the drive neurons in the cortex.

A different possible mechanism was also considered: Catecholamine fibers were also transport fibers for peptide hormones picked up in hypothalamic stations. These would be carried through the brain and their release would produce the drive states. In this case the same fibers might carry two messages. A drive message would be carried by one pattern of activity that would release peptides. A reward message would be carried by a different pattern of activity that would release amines. In this case the problem of how a reward connects a drive to a set of behaviors or objects would be resolved in an easily conceptualized way. Connecting a reward fiber would consist in connecting a drive fiber.

References

Adair, E. R., Casby, J. K., and Stolwijk, J. A. J. (1970): Behavioral temperature regulation in the squirrel monkey: Changes induced by shifts in hypothalamic temperature. *J. Comp. Physiol. Psychol.,* 72:17–27.

Ahlskog, J. E., and Hoebel, B. G. (1973): Overeating and obesity from damage to a noradrenergic system in the brain. *Science,* 182:166–169.

Albert, D. J., and Storlien, L. H. (1969): Hyperphagia in rats with cuts between the ventromedial and lateral hypothalamus. *Science,* 165:599–600.

Alcaraz, M., Guzman-Flores, C., Salas, M., and Beyer, C. (1969): Effect of estrogen on the responsivity of hypothalamic and mesencephalic neurons in the female cat. *Brain Res.,* 15:439–446.

Anand, B. K., and Brobeck, J. R. (1951): Hypothalamic control of food intake in rats and cats. *Yale J. Biol. Med.,* 24:123–140.

Anand, B. K., Chhina, G. S., Sharma, K. N., Dua, S., and Singh, B. (1964): Activity of single neurons in the hypothalamic feeding centers. *Am. J. Physiol.,* 207:1146–1154.

Andén, N.-E., Rubenson, A., Fuxe, K., and Hökfelt, T. (1967): Evidence for dopamine receptor stimulation by apomorphine. *J. Pharm. Pharmacol.,* 19:627–629.

Anderson, B., Gale, C. C., Hökfelt, B., and Larsson, B. (1965): Acute and chronic effects of preoptic lesions. *Acta Physiol. Scand.,* 65:45–60.

Anderson, B., Gale, C. C., and Sundsten, J. W. (1964): Preoptic influences on water intake. In: *Thirst in the Regulation of Body Water,* edited by M. J. Wayner, pp. 361–379. Macmillan (Pergamon), New York.

Anderson, B., and McCann, S. M. (1956): The effect of hypothalamic lesions on the water intake of the dog. *Acta Physiol. Scand.,* 35:312–320.

Angrist, B. M., Shopsin, B., and Gershon, S. (1971): The comparative psychotomimetic effects of stereoisomers of amphetamine. *Nature (Lond.),* 234:152–154.

Angyan, L. (1974): Sleep induced by hypothalamic self-stimulation in cat. *Physiol. Behav.,* 12:697–701.

Annau, Z., Heffner, R., and Koob, G. F. (1974): Electrical self-stimulation of single and multiple loci: Long term observations. *Physiol. Behav.,* 13:281–290.

Antelman, S. M., Lippa, A. S., and Fisher, A. E. (1972): 6-Hydroxydopamine, noradrenergic reward, and schizophrenia. *Science,* 175:919–923.

Appel, J. B., Sheard, M. H., and Freedman, D. X. (1968): Behavioral effects of amine-depleting lesions in the medial forebrain bundle. *Community Behav. Biol.* [*A*], 1:379–387.

Atrens, D. M., and von Vietinghoff-Riesch, F. (1972): The motivational properties of electrical self-stimulation of the medial and paraventricular hypothalamus. *Physiol. Behav.,* 9:229–235.

Balinska, H. (1968): The hypothalamic lesions: Effects on appetitive and aversive behaviors in rats. *Acta Biol. Exp.,* 28:47–56.

Balinska, H., Romaniuk, A., and Wyrwicka, W. (1964): Impairment of conditioned defensive reactions following lesions of the lateral hypothalamus in rabbits. *Acta Biol. Exp.,* 24:89–97.

Ball, G. G., and Adams, D. W. (1965): Intracranial stimulation as an avoidance or escape response. *Psychon. Sci.,* 39:39–40.

Bartholini, G., Pletscher, A., and Richards, J. (1970): 6-Hydroxydopamine-induced inhibition of brain catecholamine synthesis without ultrastructural damage. *Experientia,* 26:598–600.

Baumgarten, H. G., and Lachenmeyer, L. (1972): 5,7-Dihydroxytryptamine: Improvement in chemical lesioning of indoleamine neurons in the mammalian brain. *Z. Zellforsch. Mikrosk. Anat.,* 135:399–414.

Bernardis, L. L. (1970): Participation of the dorsomedial hypothalamic nucleus in the 'feeding center' and water intake circuitry of the weanling rat. *J. Neurovisc. Rel.,* 31:387–398.

Bernardis, L. L. (1972): Hypophagia, hypodipsia and hypoactivity following electrolytic lesions in the dorsomedial hypothalamic nuclei of mature rats of both sexes. *J. Neural Transm.,* 33:1–10.

Bernardis, L. L., Chlouverakis, C., Schnatz, J. D., and Frohman, L. A. (1974): Effect of dorsomedial hypothalamic lesions before and after placement of obesity-producing ventromedial hypothalamic lesions in the weanling male rat. *Brain Res.,* 69:67–75.

Bernardis, L. L., and Schnatz, J. D. (1971): Localization in the ventromedial hypothalamus of an area affecting plasma lipid levels. *J. Neurovisc. Rel.,* 23:90–99.

Bernardis, L. L., and Skelton, F. R. (1966): Growth and obesity following ventromedial hypothalamic lesions placed in female rats at four different ages. *Neuroendocrinology,* 1:265–275.

Bernardis, L. L., and Skelton, F. R. (1967): Growth and obesity in male rats after placement of ventromedial hypothalamic lesions at four different ages. *J. Endocrinol.,* 38:351–352.

Bishop, M. P., Elder, S. T., and Heath, R. G. (1963): Intracranial self-stimulation in man. *Science,* 140:394–396.

Bishop, M. P., Elder, T. S., and Heath, R. G. (1964): Attempted control of operant behavior in man with intracranial self-stimulation. In: *The Role of Pleasure in Behavior,* edited by R. G. Heath, pp. 55–81. Hoeber, New York.

Black, W. C., and Cooper, B. R. (1970): Reduction of electrically rewarded behavior by interference with monoamine synthesis. *Physiol. Behav.,* 5:1405–1409.

Bleier, R. (1972): Structural relationship of ependymal cells and their processes within the hypothalamus. In: *Brain-Endocrine Interaction, Median Eminance: Structure and Function. International Symposium on Brain-Endocrine Interaction Munich, 1971,* edited by K. M. Knigge, D. E. Scott, and A. Weindl, pp. 306–308. Karger, Basel.

Bloom, F. E. (1974): Dynamics of synaptic modulation: perspectives for the future. In: *The Neurosciences: Third Study Program,* edited by F. O. Schmitt and F. G. Worden, pp. 989–999. MIT Press, Cambridge, Massachusetts.

Bloom, F. E., Algeri, S., Groppetti, A., Revuelta, A., and Costa, E. (1969): Lesions of central norepinephrine terminals with 6-OH-dopamine: Biochemistry and fine structure. *Science,* 166:1284–1286.

Bogacz, J., St. Laurent, J., and Olds, J. (1965): Dissociation of self-stimulation and epileptiform activity. *Electroencephalogr. Clin. Neurophysiol.,* 19:75–87.

Booth, D. A. (1967): Localization of the adrenergic feeding system in the rat diencephalon. *Science,* 158:515–517.

Bose, S., Bailey, P. T., Thoa, N. B., and Pradhan, S. N. (1974): Effects of 5-hydroxytryptophane on self-stimulation in rats. *Psychopharmacologia,* 36:255–262.

Bower, G. H., and Miller, N. E. (1958): Rewarding and punishing effects from stimulating the same place in the rat's brain. *J. Comp. Physiol. Psychol.,* 51:669–674.

Bowman, W. C., Rand, M. J., and West, G. B. (1968): Sympathomimetics and drugs modifying their action. In: *Textbook of Pharmacology,* pp. 734–775. Blackwell Scientific Publications, Oxford.

Boyd, E. S., and Gardner, L. C. (1967): Effect of some brain lesions on intracranial self-stimulation in the rat. *Am. J. Physiol.,* 213:1044–1052.

Brady, J. V. (1960): Temporal and emotional effects related to intracranial electrical self-stimulation. In: *Electrical Studies on the Unanesthetized Brain,* edited by E. R. Ramey and D. S. O'Doherty. Hoeber, New York.

Brady, J. V., Boren, J. J., Conrad, D., and Sidman, M. (1957): The effect of food and water deprivation upon intracranial self-stimulation. *J. Comp. Physiol. Psychol.,* 50:134–137.

Breese, G. R., Howard, J. L., and Leahy, J. P. (1971): Effect of 6-hydroxydopamine on electrical self-stimulation of the brain. *Br. J. Pharmacol.,* 43:255–257.

Breese, G. R., and Traylor, T. D. (1971): Depletion of brain noradrenaline and dopamine by 6-hydroxydopamine. *Br. J. Pharmacol.,* 42:88–89.

Brobeck, J. R., Tepperman, J., and Long, C. N. H. (1943): Experimental hypothalamic hyperphagia in the albino rat. *Yale J. Biol. Med.,* 15:831–853.

Brodie, D. A., Moreno, O. M., Malis, J. L., and Boren, J. J. (1960): Rewarding properties of intracranial stimulation. *Science,* 131:929–930.

Broekkamp, C. L. E., and van Rossum, J. M. (1974): Effects of apomorphine on self-stimulation. *Psychopharmacologia,* 34:71–80.
Brown, S., and Trowill, J. A. (1970): Lever pressing performances for brain stimulation of FI and VI schedules in a single lever situation. *Psychol. Rep.,* 26:699–706.
Brown-Grant, K., Exley, D., and Naftolin, F. (1970): Peripheral plasma oestradiol and luteinizing hormone concentrations during the oestrus cycle of the rat. *J. Endocrinol.,* 48:295–296.
Brownstein, M. J., Palkovits, M., Saavedra, J. M., Bassiri, R. M., and Utiger, R. D. (1974): Thyrotropin-releasing hormone in specific nuclei of rat brain. *Science,* 185: 267–269.
Bruecke, F. T. V., Hornykiewicz, O., and Sigg, E. B. (1969): *The Pharmacology of Psychotherapeutic Drugs.* Springer-Verlag, New York.
Buchwald, N. A., Wyers, E. J., Lamprecht, C. W., and Heuser, G. (1961): The "caudate spindle." IV. A behavioral index of caudate-induced inhibition. *Electroencephalogr. Clin. Neurophysiol.,* 13:531–537.
Burkard, W. P., Jalfre, M., and Blum, J. (1969): Effects of 6-hydroxydopamine on behavior and cerebral amine content in rats. *Experientia,* 35:1295–1296.
Bursten, B., and Delgado, J. M. R. (1958): Positive reinforcement induced by intracranial stimulation in the monkey. *J. Comp. Physiol. Psychol.,* 51:6–10.
Cabanac, M., Stolwijk, J. A. J., and Hardy, J. D. (1968): Effect of temperature and pyrogens on single-unit activity in the rabbit's brain stem. *J. Appl. Physiol.,* 24:645–652.
Caggiula, A. R., and Hoebel, B. C. (1966): "Copulation-reward site" in the posterior hypothalamus. *Science,* 153:1284–1285.
Cantor, M. B. (1971): Signaled reinforcing brain stimulation establishes and maintains reliable schedule control. *Science,* 174:610–613.
Cantor, M. B., and LoLordo, V. M. (1970): Rats prefer signaled reinforcing brain stimulation to unsignaled ESB. *J. Comp. Physiol. Psychol.,* 71:183–191.
Cantor, M. B., and LoLordo, V. M. (1972): Reward value of brain stimulation is inversely related to uncertainty about its onset. *J. Comp. Physiol. Psychol.,* 79:259–270.
Chance, M. R. A., and Silverman, A. P. (1964): The structure of social behaviour and drug action. In: *Animal Behaviour and Drug Action,* edited by H. Steinberg, A. V. S. de Reuck, and J. Knight, pp. 65–79. Little Brown, Boston.
Chhina, G. S., and Anand, B. K. (1969): Responses of neurones in the hypothalamus and limbic system to genital stimulation in adult and immature monkeys. *Brain Res.,* 13:511–521.
Chhina, G. S., Anand, B. K., Singh, B., and Rao, P. S. (1971): Effect of glucose on hypothalamic feeding centers in deafferented animals. *Am. J. Physiol.,* 221:662–667.
Chu, N., and Bloom, F. E. (1973): Norepinephrine-containing neurons: Changes in spontaneous discharge patterns during sleeping and waking. *Science,* 179:908–910.
Cook, L. (1964): Effects of drugs on operant conditioning. In: *Animal Behaviour and Drug Action,* edited by H. Steinberg, A. V. S. de Reuck, and J. Knight, pp. 23–40. Little Brown, Boston.
Coons, E. E. (1964): Motivational correlates of eating elicited by electrical stimulation in the hypothalamic feeding area. Ph.D. thesis, Yale University.
Coons, E. E., and Cruce, J. A. F. (1968): Lateral hypothalamus: Food and current intensity in maintaining self-stimulation of hunger. *Science,* 159:1117–1119.
Coons, E. E., and Quartermain, D. (1970): Motivational depression associated with norepinephrine-induced eating from the hypothalamus: Resemblance to the ventromedial hyperphagic syndrome. *Physiol. Behav.,* 5:687–692.
Cooper, B. R., Black, W. C., and Paolino, R. M. (1971): Decreased forebrain and lateral hypothalamic reward after alpha-methyl-para-tyrosine. *Physiol. Behav.,* 6:425–429.
Cooper, B. R., Breese, G. R., Howard, J. L., and Grant, L. D. (1972*a*): Effect of central catecholamine alterations by 6-hydroxydopamine on shuttlebox avoidance acquisition. *Physiol. Behav.,* 9:727–731.
Cooper, J. R., Bloom, F. E., and Roth, R. H. (1974): *The Biochemical Basis of Neuropharmacology,* 2nd ed. Oxford University Press, New York.

Cooper, R. M., and Taylor, L. H. (1967): Thalamic reticular system and central grey: Self-stimulation. *Science,* 156:102–103.

Corbit, J. D. (1969): Behavioral regulation of hypothalamic temperature. *Science,* 166:256–258.

Corbit, J. D. (1970): Behavioral regulation of body temperature. In: *Physiological and Behavioral Temperature Regulation,* edited by J. D. Hardy, A. P. Gagge, and J. A. J. Stolwijk. Charles C Thomas, Springfield, Illinois.

Corbit, J. D. (1973): Voluntary control of hypothalamic temperature. *J. Comp. Physiol. Psychol.,* 83:394–411.

Coscina, D. V., and Balagura, S. (1970): Avoidance and escape behavior in rats with aphagia produced by basal diencephalic lesions. *Physiol. Behav.,* 5:651–657.

Coscina, D. V., Seggie, J., Godse, D. D., and Stancer, H. C. (1973): Induction of rage in rats by central injection of 6-hydroxydopamine. *Pharmacol. Biochem. Behav.,* 1:1–6.

Cox, V. C., Kakolewski, J. W., and Valenstein, E. S. (1969): Inhibition of eating and drinking following hypothalamic stimulation in the rat. *J. Comp. Physiol. Psychol.,* 68:530–535.

Cox, V. C., and Valenstein, E. S. (1965): Attenuation of aversive properties of peripheral shock by hypothalamic stimulation. *Science,* 149:323–325.

Crosby, E. C., Humphrey, T., and Lauer, E. W. (1962): *The Correlative Anatomy of the Nervous System.* Macmillan, New York.

Cross, B. A. (1966): The neural control of oxytocin secretion. In: *Neuroendocrinology, Vol. 1,* edited by L. Martini and W. F. Ganong, pp. 217–259. Academic Press, New York.

Cross, B. A. (1973): Unit responses in the hypothalamus. In: *Frontiers in Neuroendocrinology,* edited by W. F. Ganong and L. Martini, pp. 133–171. Oxford University Press, New York.

Cross, B. A., and Dyer, R. G. (1970*a*): Characterization of unit activity in hypothalamic islands with special reference to hormone effects. In: *The Hypothalamus,* edited by L. Martini, M. Motta, and F. Fraschini, pp. 115–122. Academic Press, New York.

Cross, B. A., and Dyer, R. G. (1970*b*): Effect of hypophysectomy on firing rates of hypothalamic neurons in diencephalic islands. *J. Endocrinol.,* 48:475–476.

Cross, B. A., and Dyer, R. G. (1971*a*): Unit activity in diencephalic islands: The effect of anesthetics. *J. Physiol.* (*Lond.*), 212:467–481.

Cross, B. A., and Dyer, R. G. (1971*b*): Cyclic changes in neurones of the anterior hypothalamus during the oestrus cycle, and the effects of anesthesia. In: *Steroid Hormones and Brain Function,* edited by R. Gorski and C. H. Sawyer, pp. 95–102. University of California Press, Los Angeles.

Cross, B. A., and Dyer, R. G. (1972): Ovarian modulation of unit activity in the anterior hypothalamus of the cyclic rat. *J. Physiol.* (*Lond.*), 222:25P.

Cross, B. A., Moss, R. L., and Urban, I. (1971): Effects of iontophoretic application of acetylcholine and noradrenaline to antidromically identified paraventricular neurones. *J. Physiol.* (*Lond.*), 214:30P (abstr.).

Crow, T. J. (1970): Enhancement by cocaine of intra-cranial self-stimulation in the rat. *Life Sci.,* 9:375–381.

Crow, T. J. (1971): The relation between electrical self-stimulation sites and catecholamine-containing neurones in the rat mesencephalon. *Experientia,* 27:662.

Crow, T. J. (1972*a*): A map of the rat mesencephalon for electrical self-stimulation. *Brain Res.,* 36:265–273.

Crow, T. J. (1972*b*): Catecholamine-containing neurones and electrical self-stimulation. 1. A review of some data. *Psychol. Med.,* 2:414–421.

Crow, T. J. (1973): Catecholamine-containing neurones and electrical self-stimulation. 2. A theoretical interpretation and some psychiatric implications. *Psychol. Med.,* 3:66–73.

Crow, T. J., and Arbuthnott, G. W. (1972): Function of catecholamine-containing neurons in mammalian central nervous system. *Nature* (*Lond.*), 238:245–246.

Crow, T. J., Spear, P. J., and Arbuthnott, G. W. (1972): Intracranial self-stimulation

with electrodes in the region of the locus coeruleus. *Brain Res.*, 36:275–287.
Cunningham, D. J., Stolwijk, J. A. J., Murakami, N., and Hardy, J. D. (1967): Responses of neurons in the preoptic area to temperature, serotonin and epinephrine. *Am. J. Physiol.*, 213:1570–1581.
Dafny, N., and Feldman, S. (1970): Single cell activity in the hypothalamus in intact and adrenalectomized rats. *Physiol. Behav.*, 5:873–878.
Dahlström, A., and Fuxe, K. (1964): Evidence for the existence of monoamine-containing neurons in the central nervous system. *Acta Scand.* [*Suppl.*], 62(232):1–55.
de la Torre, J. C. (1972): *Dynamics of Brain Monoamines.* Plenum, New York.
Delgado, J. M. R. (1969): *Physical Control of the Mind.* Harper & Row, New York.
Delgado, J. M. R., Roberts, W. W., and Miller, N. E. (1954): Learning motivated by electrical stimulation of the brain. *Am. J. Physiol.*, 179:587–593.
Deutsch, J. A. (1960): *The Structural Basis of Behavior.* Chicago University Press, Chicago.
Deutsch, J. A. (1964): Behavioral measurement of the neural refractory period and its application to intracranial self-stimulation. *J. Comp. Physiol. Psychol.*, 58:1–9.
Deutsch, J. A., and Albertson, T. E. (1974): Refractory period and adaptation in prolonged brain reward. *Behav. Biol.*, 11:275–279.
Deutsch, J. A., and Howarth, C. I. (1962): Evocation by fear of a habit learned for electrical stimulation of the brain. *Science*, 136:1057–1058.
Deutsch, J. A., and Howarth, C. I. (1963): Some tests of a theory of intracranial self-stimulation. *Psychol. Rev.*, 70:444–460.
de Wied, D. (1974): Pituitary-adrenal system hormones and behavior. In: *The Neurosciences, Third Study Program,* edited by F. O. Schmitt and F. G. Worden, pp. 653–666. MIT Press, Cambridge, Massachusetts.
Dews, P. B. (1958): Studies on behavior. IV. Stimulant actions of methamphetamine. *J. Pharmacol. Exp. Ther.*, 122:137–147.
Dresse, A. (1966): Importance du système mesencephalo-telencephalique noradrenergique comme substratum anatomique du comportement d'autostimulation. *Life Sci.*, 5:1003–1014.
Dyball, R. E. J. (1971): Oxytocin and ADH secretion in relation to electrical activity in antidromically identified supraoptic and paraventricular units. *J. Physiol.* (*Lond.*), 214:245–256.
Dyball, R. E. J., and Dyer, R. G. (1971): Plasma oxytocin concentrations and paraventricular neurone activity in rats with diencephalic islands and intact brains. *J. Physiol.* (*Lond.*), 216:227–235.
Dyer, R. G., and Cross, B. A. (1972): Antidromic identification of units in the preoptic and anterior hypothalamic areas projecting directly to the ventromedial and arcuate nuclei. *Brain Res.*, 43:254–258.
Dyer, R. G., Pritchett, C. J., and Cross, B. A. (1972): Unit activity in the diencephalon of female rats during the oestrus cycle. *J. Endocrinol.*, 53:151–160.
Ellinwood, E. H., Jr. (1971): "Accidental conditioning" with chronic methamphetamine intoxication: Implications for a theory of drug habituation. *Psychopharmacologia,* 21:131–138.
Ellison, G. D., and Bresler, D. E. (1974): Tests of emotional behavior in rats following depletion of norepinephrine, or serotonin, or of both. *Psychopharmacologia,* 34:275–288.
Ellison, G. D., Sorenson, C. A., and Jacobs, B. L. (1970): Two feeding syndromes following surgical isolation of the hypothalamus in rats. *J. Comp. Physiol. Psychol.*, 70:173–188.
Epstein, A. N. (1960): Reciprocal changes in feeding behavior produced by intrahypothalamic chemical injections. *Am. J. Physiol.*, 199:969–974.
Epstein, A. N. (1971): The lateral hypothalamic syndrome: Its implications for the physiological psychology of hunger and thirst. In: *Progress in Physiological Psychology, Vol. 4,* edited by E. Stellar and J. M. Sprague, pp. 263–317. Academic Press, New York.
Epstein, A. N., Fitzsimmons, J. T., and Rolls, B. J. (1970): Drinking induced by injection of angiotensin into the brain of the rat. *J. Physiol.* (*Lond.*), 210:454–474.

Ernst, A. M. (1967): Mode of action of apomorphine and dexamphetamine on gnawing compulsion in rats. *Psychopharmacologia,* 10:316–323.

Falck, B., Hillarp, N. A., Thieme, G., and Thorpe, H. (1962): Fluorescence of catecholamines and related compounds condensed with formaldehyde. *J. Histochem. Cytochem.,* 10:348–354.

Farber, J., Steiner, S., and Ellman, S. J. (1972): The pons as an electrical self-stimulation site. *Psychophysiology,* 9:105 (abstr.).

Feldman, S., and Sarne, Y. (1970): Effect of cortisol on single cell activity in hypothalamic islands. *Brain Res.,* 23:67–75.

Findlay, A. L. R. (1972): Hypothalamic inputs: methods, and five examples. *Prog. Brain Res.,* 38:163–190.

Fisher, A. E. (1969): The role of limbic structures in the central regulation of feeding and drinking behavior. *Ann. N.Y. Acad. Sci.,* 157:894–901.

Fisher, A., and Coury, J. N. (1962): Cholinergic tracing of a central neural circuit underlying the thirst drive. *Science,* 138:691–693.

Fog, R. (1969): Stereotyped and non-stereotyped behavior in rats induced by various stimulant drugs. *Psychopharmacologia,* 14:299–304.

Fog, R. (1970): Behavioral effects in rats of morphine and amphetamine and a combination of the two drugs. *Psychopharmacologia,* 16:305–312.

Fog, R. L., Randrup, A., and Pakkenberg, H. (1967): Aminergic mechanisms in corpus striatum and amphetamine-induced stereotyped behavior. *Psychopharmacologia,* 11:179–183.

Franklin, K. B. J., and Herberg, L. J. (1974): Ventromedial syndrome: The rat's "finickiness" results from the obesity, not from the lesions. *J. Comp. Physiol. Psychol.,* 87:410–414.

Frigyesi, T. L., Ige, A., Iulo, A., and Schwartz, R. (1971): Denigration and sensorimotor disability induced by ventral tegmental injection of 6-hydroxydopamine in the cat. *Exp. Neurol.,* 33:78–87.

Fuxe, K. (1965): Evidence for the existence of monoamine neurons in the central nervous system. IV. Distribution of monoamine nerve terminals in the central nervous system. *Acta Physiol. Scand.* [*Suppl.* 247], 64:37–85.

Gallistel, C. R. (1969*a*): The incentive of brain-stimulation reward. *J. Comp. Physiol. Psychol.,* 69:713–721.

Gallistel, C. R. (1969*b*): Failure of pretrial stimulation to affect reward electrode preference. *J. Comp. Physiol. Psychol.,* 69:722–729.

Gallistel, C. R. (1973): Self-stimulation: the neurophysiology of reward and motivation. In: *The Physiological Basis of Memory,* edited by J. A. Deutsch. Academic Press, New York.

Gallistel, C. R. and Beagley, G. (1971): Specificity of brain-stimulation reward in the rat. *J. Comp. Physiol. Psychol.,* 76:199–205.

Gallistel, C. R., Rolls, E. T., and Greene, D. (1969): Neuron function inferred from behavioral and electrophysiological estimates of refractory period. *Science,* 166:1028–1030.

Gallo, R. V., Johnson, J. H., Goldman, B. D., Whitmoyer, D. I., and Sawyer, C. H. (1971): Effects of electrochemical stimulation of the ventral hippocampus on hypothalamic electrical activity and pituitary gonadotropin secretion in female rats. *Endocrinology,* 89:704–713.

Ganong, W. F. (1974): Brain mechanisms regulating the secretion of the pituitary gland. In: *The Neurosciences, Third Study Program,* edited by F. O. Schmitt and F. G. Worden, pp. 549–563. MIT Press, Cambridge, Massachusetts.

Garcia, J., and Ervin, F. R. (1968): Gustatory-visceral and telereceptor-cutaneous conditioning—adaptation in internal and external milieus. *Community Behav. Biol.* [*A*], 1:389–415.

German, D. C., and Bowden, D. M. (1974): Catecholamine systems as the neural substrate for intracranial self-stimulation: A hypothesis. *Brain Res.,* 73:381–419.

German, D. C., and Fetz, E. E. (1974): Activity of locus ceruleus units responsive to stimulation at reinforcing sites in alert monkey. Fourth Annual Meeting of the

Society of Neurosciences, St. Louis, p. 225.
Gibson, S., McGeer, E. G., and McGeer, P. L. (1970): Effect of selective inhibitors of tyrosine and tryptophan hydroxylases on self-stimulation in rats. *Exp. Neurol.,* 27:283–290.
Gibson, W. E., Reid, L. D., Sakai, M., and Porter, P. B. (1965): Intracranial reinforcement compared with sugar water reinforcement. *Science,* 148:1357–1359.
Gold, R. M. (1970): Hypothalamic hyperphagia without ventromedial damage. *Physiol. Behav.,* 5:23–25.
Goodman, L. S., and Gilman, A. (1955): *The Pharmacological Basis of Therapeutics,* 2nd ed. Macmillan, New York.
Grossman, S. P. (1960): Eating and drinking elicited by direct adrenergic or cholinergic stimulation of hypothalamus. *Science,* 132:301–302.
Grossman, S. P. (1971): Changes in food and water intake associated with an interruption of anterior or posterior fiber connections of the hypothalamus. *J. Comp. Physiol. Psychol.,* 75:23–31.
Grossman, S. P., and Grossman, L. (1971): Food and water intake in rats with parasagittal knife cuts medial or lateral to the lateral hypothalamus. *J. Comp. Physiol. Psychol.,* 74:148–156.
Haller, E. W., and Barraclough, C. A. (1970): Alternations in unit activity of hypothalamic ventromedial nuclei by stimuli which affect gonadotropic hormone secretion. *Exp. Neurol.,* 29:111–120.
Hamburg, M. D. (1971): Hypothalamic unit activity and eating behavior. *Am. J. Physiol.,* 220:980–985.
Hamilton, C. L. (1963): Interactions of food intake and temperature regulation in the rat. *J. Comp. Physiol. Psychol.,* 56:476–488.
Hamilton, C. L., and Brobeck, J. R. (1964): Food intake and temperature regulation in rats with rostral hypothalamic lesions. *Am. J. Physiol.,* 207:291–297.
Hardy, J. D., Hellon, R. F., and Sutherland, K. (1964): Temperature sensitive neurones in the dog's hypothalamus. *J. Physiol. (Lond.),* 175:242–253.
Harvey, J. A., and Lints, C. E. (1971): Lesions in the medial forebrain bundle: Relationship between pain sensitivity and telencephalic content of serotonin. *J. Comp. Physiol. Psychol.,* 74:28–36.
Haymaker, W., Anderson, E., and Nauta, W. J. H. (1969): *The Hypothalamus.* Charles C Thomas, Springfield, Illinois.
Heath, R. G. (1954): *Studies in Schizophrenia.* Harvard University Press, Cambridge, Massachusetts.
Heath, R. G. (1964): Pleasure responses of human subjects to direct stimulation of the brain: physilogic and psychodynamic considerations. In: *The Role of Pleasure in Human Behavior,* edited by R. G. Heath, pp. 219–243. Hoeber, New York.
Hellon, R. F. (1967): Thermal stimulation of hypothalamic neurones in unanesthetized rabbits. *J. Physiol. (Lond.),* 193:381–395.
Hellon, R. F. (1970): The stimulation of hypothalamic neurones by changes in ambient temperature. *Pfluegers Arch.,* 321:56–66.
Herberg, L. J. (1963*a*): Seminal ejaculation following positively reinforcing electrical stimulation of the rat hypothalamus. *J. Comp. Physiol. Psychol.,* 56:679–685.
Herberg, L. J. (1963*b*): Determinants of extinction in electrical self-stimulation. *J. Comp. Physiol. Psychol.,* 56:686–690.
Hess, W. R. (1954): *Diencephalon: Autonomic and Extrapyramidal Functions.* Grune & Stratton, New York.
Hetherington, A. W. (1944): Non-production of hypothalamic obesity in the rat by lesions rostral or dorsal to the ventro-medial hypothalamic nuclei. *J. Comp. Neurol.,* 80:33–45.
Hetherington, A. W., and Ranson, S. W. (1942*a*): The relation of various hypothalamic lesions to adiposity in the rat. *J. Comp. Neurol.,* 76:475–499.
Hetherington, A. W., and Ranson, S. W. (1942*b*): Effect of early hypophysectomy on hypothalamic obesity. *Endocrinology,* 31:30–34.
Hitt, J. C., Bryon, D. M., and Modianos, D. T. (1973): Effects of rostral medial fore-

brain bundle and olfactory tubercle lesions upon sexual behavior of male rats. *J.*

Hitt, J. C., Hendricks, S. E., Ginsberg, S. I., and Lewis, J. H. (1970): Disruption of male, but not female, sexual behavior in rats by medial forebrain bundle lesions. *J. Comp. Physiol. Psychol.,* 73:377–384.

Hodos, W. H. (1965): Motivational properties of long durations of rewarding brain stimulation. *J. Comp. Physiol. Psychol.,* 59:219–224.

Hoebel, B. G. (1968): Inhibition and disinhibition of self-stimulation and feeding: Hypothalamic control and post-ingestional factors. *J. Comp. Physiol. Psychol.,* 66:89–100.

Hoebel, B. G., and Teitelbaum, P. (1962): Hypothalamic control of feeding and self-stimulation. *Science,* 135:357–377.

Hoebel, B. G., and Teitelbaum, P. (1966): Weight regulation in normal and hypothalamic hyperphagic rats. *J. Comp. Physiol. Psychol.,* 61:189–193.

Hökfelt, T., and Fuxe, K. (1972): On the morphology and the neuroendocrine role of the hypothalamic catecholamine neurons. In: *Brain-Endocrine Interaction, Median Eminance: Structure and Function. International Symposium. on Brain-Endocrine Interaction, Munich, 1971,* edited by K. M. Knigge, D. E. Scott, and A. Weindl, pp. 181–223. Karger, Basel.

Hull, C. L. (1943): *Principles of Behavior.* Appleton-Century-Crofts, New York.

Huston, J. P., and Borbely, A. A. (1974): The thalamic rat: General behavior, operant learning with rewarding hypothalamic stimulation, and effects of amphetamine. *Physiol. Behav.,* 12:433–448.

Ito, M. (1972): Excitability of medial forebrain bundle neurons during self-stimulating behavior. *J. Neurophysiol.,* 35:652–664.

Ito, M., and Olds, J. (1971): Unit activity during self-stimulation behavior. *J. Neurophysiol.,* 34:263–273.

Iversen, L. L. (1967): *The Uptake and Storage of Noradrenaline in Sympathetic Nerves,* University Press, Cambridge, England.

Iverson, S. D. (1974): 6-Hydroxydopamine: A chemical lesion technique for studying the role of amine neurotransmitters in behavior. In: *The Neurosciences: Third Study Program,* edited by F. O. Schmitt and F. G. Worden, pp. 705–711. MIT Press, Cambridge, Massachusetts.

Jacobowitz, D. M., and Palkovits, M. (1974): Topographic atlas of catecholamine and acetylcholinesterase-containing neurons in the rat brain. I. Forebrain (telencephalon, diencephalon). *J. Comp. Neurol.,* 157:13–28.

Jouvet, M. (1974): Monoaminergic regulation of the sleep-waking cycle in the cat. In: *The Neurosciences, Third Study Program,* edited by F. O. Schmitt and F. G. Worden, pp. 49–508. MIT Press, Cambridge, Massachusetts.

Kawakami, E., Terasawa, E., and Ibuki, T. (1970): Changes in multiple unit activity of the brain during the estrous cycle. *Neuroendocrinology,* 6:30–48.

Keene, J. J. (1973): Reward-associated inhibition and pain-associated excitation lasting seconds in single intralaminar thalamic units. *Brain Res.,* 64:211–224.

Keesey, R. (1962): The relation between pulse frequency, intensity, and duration and the rate of responding for intracranial stimulation. *J. Comp. Physiol. Psychol.,* 55: 671–678.

Keesey, R. E. (1964): Duration of stimulation and the reward properties of hypothalamic stimulation. *J. Comp. Physiol. Psychol.,* 58:201–207.

Keesey, R. E. (1966): Hypothalamic stimulation as a reinforcer of discrimination learning. *J. Comp. Physiol. Psychol.,* 62:231–236.

Keesey, R. E., and Goldstein, M. D. (1968): Use of progressive fixed-ratio procedures in the assessment of intracranial reinforcement. *J. Exp. Anal. Behav.,* 11:293–301.

Keesey, R. E., and Powley, T. L. (1968): Enhanced lateral hypothalamic reward sensitivity following septal lesions in the rat. *Physiol. Behav.,* 3:557–562.

Kent, E., and Grossman, S. P. (1969): Evidence for a conflict interpretation of anomalous effects of rewarding brain stimulation. *J. Comp. Physiol. Psychol.,* 69:381–390.

Kent, M. A., and Peters, R. H. (1973): Effects of ventromedial hypothalamic lesions on hunger-motivated behavior in rats. *J. Comp. Physiol. Psychol.,* 83:92–97.

Kerr, F. W., Triplett, J. N., and Beeler, G. W. (1974): Reciprocal (push-pull) effects of morphine on single units in the ventromedian and lateral hypothalamus and influences on other nuclei; with a comment on methadone effects during withdrawal from morphine. *Brain Res.,* 74:81–103.

Klüver, H., and Bucy, P. C. (1937): Psychic blindness and other symptoms following bilateral temporal lobectomy in rhesus monkey. *Am. J. Physiol.,* 119:352–353.

Knigge, K. M., Scott, D. E., and Weindl, A., editors. (1972): *Brain Endocrine Interactions.* Karger, Basel.

Knigge, K. M., Joseph, S. A., Scott, D. E., and Jacobs, J. J. (1971): Observations on the architecture of the arcuate-median eminence region after deafferentiation, with reference to the organization of hypothalamic RF-producing elements. In: *The Neuroendocrinology of Human Reproduction,* edited by H. C. Mack and A. I. Sherman, pp. 6–22. Charles C Thomas, Springfield, Ill.

Knott, P. D., and Clayton, K. N. (1966): Durable secondary reinforcement using brain stimulation as the primary reinforcer. *J. Comp. Physiol. Psychol.,* 61:151–153.

Koe, B. K., and Weissman, A. (1966): p-Chlorophenylalanine, a specific depletor or brain serotonin. *J. Pharmacol. Exp. Ther.,* 154:499–516.

Kornblith, C., and Olds, J. (1968): T-maze learning with one trial per day using brain stimulation reinforcement. *J. Comp. Physiol. Psychol.,* 66:488–491.

Krasne, F. B. (1962): General disruption resulting from electrical stimulation of the ventromedial hypothalamus. *Science,* 138:822–823.

Krenjevic, K. (1974): Chemical nature of synaptic transmission in vertebrates. *Physiol. Rev.,* 54:418–540.

Kuhar, M. J., Pert, C. B., and Snyder, S. H. (1973): Regional distribution of opiate receptor binding in monkey and human brain. *Nature (Lond.),* 245:447–450.

Leibowitz, S. F. (1974): Adrenergic receptor mechanisms in eating and drinking. In: *The Neurosciences, Third Study Program,* edited by F. O. Schmitt and F. G. Worden, pp. 713–720. MIT Press, Cambridge, Massachusetts.

Le Magnen, J., Devos, M., Gaudilliere, J-P., Louis-Sylvestre, J., and Tallon, S. (1973): Role of a lipostatic mechanism in regulation by feeding of energy balance in rats. *J. Comp. Physiol. Psychol.,* 84:1–23.

Lewis, J. J. (1964): *An Introduction to Pharmacology.* Williams & Wilkins, Baltimore.

Libet, B., and Owman, C. (1974): Concomitant changes in formaldehyde-induced fluorescence of dopamine interneurons and in slow inhibitory post-synaptic potentials of the rabbit superior cervical ganglion, induced by stimulation of the preganglionic nerve or by a muscarinic agent. *J. Physiol. (Lond.),* 237:635–662.

Lincoln, D. W. (1967): Unit activity in the hypothalamus, septum, and preoptic area of the rat: Characteristics of spontaneous activity and the effect of oestrogen. *J. Endocrinol.,* 37:127–189.

Lincoln, D. W., and Wakerley, J. B. (1972): Accelerated discharge of paraventricular neurosecretory cells correlated with reflex release of oxytocin during suckling. *J. Physiol. (Lond.),* 222:23–24 P.

Lindvall, O., and Björklund, A. (1974): The organization of the ascending catecholamine neuron systems in the rat brain as revealed by the glyoxylic acid fluorescence method. *Acta Physiol. Scand.* [*Suppl.* 412], 1974.

Linseman, M. A., and Olds, J. (1973): Activity changes in rat hypothalamus, preoptic area and striatum associated with Pavlovian conditioning. *J. Neurophysiol.,* 36: 1038–1050.

Lisk, R. D. (1968): Copulatory activity of the male rat following placement of preoptic-anterior hypothalamic lesions. *Exp. Brain Res.,* 5:306–313.

Loomer, H. P., Saunders, J. C., and Kline, N. S. (1957): A clinical and pharmacodynamic evaluation of iproniazid as a psychic energizer. *Psychiatr. Res. Rep. Am. Psychiatr. Assoc.,* 8:129–141.

Magour, S., Cooper, H., and Faehndrich, Ch. (1974): The effect of chronic treatment with d-amphetamine on food intake, body weight, locomotor activity and subcellular distribution of drug in rat brain. *Psychopharmacologia,* 34:45–54.

Malmo, R. B. (1961): Slowing of heart rate following septal self-stimulation in rats.

Science, 133:1128–1130.

Margules, D. L. (1969): Noradrenergic synapses for the suppression of feeding behavior. *Life Sci.,* 8:693–704.

Margules, D. L. (1970*a*): Alpha-adrenergic receptors in hypothalamus for the suppression of feeding behavior by satiety. *J. Comp. Physiol. Psychol.,* 73:1–12.

Margules, D. L. (1970*b*): Beta-adrenergic receptors in the hypothalamus for learned and unlearned taste aversions. *J. Comp. Physiol. Psychol.,* 73:13–21.

Margules, D. L., and Olds, J. (1962): Identical "feeding" and "rewarding" systems in the lateral hypothalamus of rats. *Science,* 135:374–375.

Mark, V. H., and Ervin, F. R. (1970): *Violence and the Brain.* Harper & Row, New York.

Marshall, J. F., and Teitelbaum, P. (1973): A comparison of the eating in response to hypothermic and glucoprivic challenges after nigral 6-hydroxydopamine and lateral hypothalamic electrolytic lesions in rats. *Brain Res.,* 55:229–233.

Marshall, J. F., and Teitelbaum, P. (1974): Further analysis of sensory inattention following lateral hypothalamic damage in rats. *J. Comp. Physiol. Psychol.,* 86:375–395.

McKenzie, G. M. (1972): Role of the tuberculum olfactorium in stereotyped behavior induced by apomorphine in the rat. *Psychopharmacologia,* 23:212–220.

Melzak, R., and Wall, P. D. (1965): Pain mechanisms: A new theory. *Science,* 150: 971–979.

Mendelson, J. (1966): Role of hunger in T-maze learning for food by rats. *J. Comp. Physiol. Psychol.,* 62:341–349.

Mendelson, J. (1967): Lateral hypothalamic stimulation in satiated rats: The rewarding effects of self-induced drinking. *Science,* 157:1077–1079.

Miliaressis, E., and Cardo, B. (1973): Self-stimulation versus food reinforcement: Comparative study of two different nervous structures, the lateral hypothalamus and the ventral tegmental area of the mesencephalon. *Brain Res.,* 57:75–83.

Miller, N. E. (1957): Experiments on motivation. *Science,* 126:1271–1278.

Miller, N. E. (1960): Motivational effects of brain stimulation and drugs. *Fed. Proc.,* 19:846–854.

Miller, N. E., Bailey, C. J., and Stevenson, J. A. F. (1950): Decreased "hunger" but increased food intake resulting from hypothalamic lesions. *Science,* 112:256–259.

Millhouse, O. E. (1969): A Golgi study of the descending medial forebrain bundle. *Brain Res.,* 15:341–363.

Modianos, D. T., Flexman, J. E. and Hitt, J. C. (1973): Rostral medial forebrain bundle lesions produce decrements in masculine, but not feminine sexual behavior in spayed female rats. *Behav. Biol.,* 8:629–636.

Mogenson, G. J. (1965): An attempt to establish secondary reinforcement with rewarding brain stimulation. *Psychol. Rep.,* 16:163–167.

Mogenson, G. J., and Morgan, C. W. (1967): Effects of induced drinking on self-stimulation of the lateral hypothalamus. *Exp. Brain Res.,* 3:111–116.

Mogenson, G. J., and Stevenson, J. A. F. (1966): Drinking and self-stimulation with electrical stimulation of the lateral hypothalamus. *Physiol. Behav.,* 1:251–254.

Morgane, P. J. (1961): Medial forebrain bundle and "feeding centers" of the hypothalamus. *J. Comp. Neurol.,* 117:1–26.

Morrison, C. F. (1967): Effects of nicotine on operant behavior of rats. *Int. J. Neuropharmacol.,* 6:229–240.

Morrison, S. D., and Mayer, J. (1957): Adipsia and aphagia in rats after lateral subthalamic lesions. *Am. J. Physiol.,* 191:248–254.

Moss, R. L., Dyball, R. E. J., and Cross, B. A. (1972*a*): Excitation of antidromically identified neurosecretory cells of the paraventricular nucleus by oxytocin applied iontophoretically, *Exp. Neurol.,* 34:95–102.

Moss, R. L., Urban, I., and Cross, B. A. (1972*b*): Microelectrophoresis of cholinergic and aminergic drugs on paraventricular neurons. *Am. J. Physiol.,* 223:310–318.

Motta, M., Fraschini, F., and Martini, L. (1969): "Short" feedback mechanisms in the control of anterior pituitary function. In: *Frontiers of Neuroendocrinology,* edited by W. F. Ganong and L. Martini, pp. 211–253. Oxford University Press, New York.

Murgatroyd, D., and Hardy, J. D. (1970): Central and peripheral temperatures in behavioral thermoregulation of the rat. In: *Physiological and Behavioral Temperature Regulation,* edited by J. D. Hardy, A. P. Gagge, and J. A. J. Stolwijk. Charles C Thomas, Springfield, Illinois.

Murphy, J. T., and Renaud, L. P. (1969): Mechanisms of inhibition in the ventromedial nucleus of the hypothalamus. *J. Neurophysiol.,* 32:85–102.

Nakajima, S., and Iwasaki, T. (1973): Dependence of the anterior olfactory area self-stimulation upon the lateral hypothalamic area. *Physiol. Behav.,* 11:827–831.

Nakamura, K., and Thoenen, H. (1972): Increased irritability: A permanent behavior change induced in the rat by intraventricular administration of 6-hydroxydopamine. *Psychopharmacologia,* 24:359–372.

Nakayama, T., Eisenman, J. S., and Hardy, J. D. (1961): Single unit activity of anterior hypothalamus during local heating. *Science,* 134:560–561.

Nakayama, T., Hammel, H. T., Hardy, J. D., and Eisenman, J. S. (1963): Thermal stimulation of electrical activity of single units of the preoptic region. *Am. J. Physiol.,* 204:1122–1126.

Neill, D. B., Boggan, W. O., and Grossman, S. P. (1974): Behavioral effects of amphetamine in rats with lesions in the corpus striatum. *J. Comp. Physiol. Psychol.,* 86:1019–1030.

Newman, B. L. (1961): Behavioral effects of electrical self-stimulation of the septal area and related structures in the rat. *J. Comp. Physiol. Psychol.,* 54:340–346.

Newman, L. M. (1972): Effects of cholinergic agonists and antagonists on self-stimulation behavior in the rat. *J. Comp. Physiol. Psychol.,* 79:394–413.

Nicoll, R. A., and Barker, J. L. (1971): Excitation of supraoptic neurosecretory cells by angiotensin II. *Nature* [*New Biol.*], 233:172–174,

Nobin, A., and Björklund, A. (1973): Topography of the monoamine neuron system in the human brain as revealed in fetuses. *Acta Physiol. Scand.* [*Suppl.*], 388:1–40.

Norgren, R., and Leonard, C. M. (1973): Ascending central gustatory pathways. *J. Comp. Neurol.,* 150:217–238.

Nymark, M. (1972): Apomorphine provoked stereotypy in the dog. *Psychopharmacologia,* 26:361–368.

Ochs, S. (1974): Systems of material transport in nerve fibers (axoplasmic transport) related to nerve function and trophic control. *Ann. N.Y. Acad. Sci.,* 228:202–223.

Olds, J. (1955): Physiological mechanisms of reward. In: *Nebraska Symposium on Motivation,* edited by M. R. Jones, pp. 73–138. University of Nebraska Press, Lincoln.

Olds, J. (1956*a*): A preliminary mapping of electrical reinforcing effects in the rat brain. *J. Comp. Physiol. Psychol.,* 49:281–285.

Olds, (1956*b*): Runway and maze behavior controlled by basomedial forebrain stimulation in the rat. *J. Comp. Physiol. Psychol.,* 49:507–512.

Olds, J. (1958*a*): Effects of hunger and male sex hormone on self-stimulation of the brain. *J. Comp. Physiol. Psychol.,* 51:320–324.

Olds, J. (1958*b*): Satiation effects in self-stimulation of the brain. *J. Comp. Physiol. Psychol.,* 51:675–678.

Olds, J. (1958*c*): Self-stimulation of the brain. *Science,* 127:315–324.

Olds, J. (1958*d*): Discussion. In: *CIBA Foundation Symposium on the Neurological Basis of Behavior,* edited by G. E. W. Wolstenholme and C. M. O'Connor, p. 89. Churchill, London.

Olds, J. (1962): Hypothalamic substrates of reward. *Physiol. Rev.,* 42:554–604.

Olds, J. (1964): The induction and suppression of hypothalamic self-stimulation behavior by mirco-injection of endogenous substances at the self-stimulation site. *Proceedings of the Second International Congress on Endocrinology, London, August 1964.* Excerpta Medica International Congress Series No. 83, pp. 597–605. Excerpta Medica, Amsterdam.

Olds, J., Allan, W. S., and Briese, E. (1971): Differentiation of hypothalamic drive and reward centers. *Am. J. Physiol.,* 221:368–375.

Olds, J., Killam, K. F., and Bach y Rita, P. (1956): Self-stimulation of the brain used as a screening method for tranquilizing drugs. *Science,* 124:265–266.

Olds, J., and Milner, P. (1954): Positive reinforcement produced by electrical stimulation of septal area and other regions of rat brain. *J. Comp. Physiol. Psychol.,* 47: 419–427.
Olds, J., and Olds, M. E. (1964): The mechanisms of voluntary behavior. In: *The Role of Pleasure in Behavior,* edited by R. G. Heath, pp. 23–53. Hoeber, New York.
Olds, J., and Peretz, B. (1960): A motivational analysis of the reticular activating system. *Electroencephalogr. Clin. Neurophysiol.,* 12:445–454.
Olds, J., and Sinclair, J. C. (1957): Self-stimulation in the obstruction box. *Am. Psychol.,* 12:464 (abstr.).
Olds, J., Travis, R. P., and Schwing, R. C. (1960): Topographic organization of hypothalamic self-stimulation functions. *J. Comp. Physiol. Psychol.,* 53:23–32.
Olds, J., Yuwiler, A., Olds, M. E., and Yun, C. (1964): Neurohumors in hypothalamic substrates of reward. *Am. J. Physiol.,* 207:242–254.
Olds, M. E. (1970): Comparative effects of amphetamine, scopolamine, chlordiazepoxide, and diphenylhydantoin on operant and extinction behavior with brain stimulation and food reward. *Neuropharmacology,* 9:519–532.
Olds, M. E. (1972): Comparative effects of amphetamine, scopolamine and chlordiazepoxide on self-stimulation behavior. *Rev. Can. Biol.,* 31:25–47.
Olds, M. E. (1973): Short-term changes in the firing pattern of hypothalamic neurons during Pavlovian conditioning. *Brain Res.,* 58:95–116.
Olds, M. E. (1974): Effect of intraventricular norepinephrine on neuron activity in the medial forebrain bundle during self-stimulation behavior. *Brain Res.,* 80:461–477.
Olds, M. E. (1975): Effects of intraventricular 6-hydroxydopamine and replacement therapy with norepinephrine, dopamine, and serotonin on self-stimulation in diencephalic and mesencephalic regions in the rat. *Brain Res.* (*in press*).
Olds, M. E., and Domino, E. F. (1969): Comparison of muscarinic and nicotinic cholinergic agonists on self-stimulation behavior. *J. Pharmacol. Exp. Ther.,* 166: 189–204a.
Olds, M. E., and Hogberg, D. (1964): Subcortical lesions and maze retention in the rat. *Exp. Neurol.,* 10:296–304.
Olds, M. E., Hogberg, D., and Olds, J. (1964): Tranquilizer action on thalamic and midbrain escape behavior. *Am. J. Physiol.,* 206:515–520.
Olds, M. E., and Ito, M. (1973*a*): Noradrenergic and cholinergic action on neuronal activity during self-stimulation behavior in the rat. *Neuropharmacology,* 12:525–539.
Olds, M. E., and Ito, M. (1973*b*): The effects of chlordiazepoxide, chlorpromazine and pentobarbital on neuronal excitability in the medial forebrain bundle during self-stimulation behavior. *Neuropharmacology,* 12:1117–1133.
Olds, M. E., and Olds, J. (1962): Approach-escape interactions in rat brain. *Am. J. Physiol,* 203:803–810.
Olds, M. E., and Olds, J. (1963): Approach-avoidance analysis of rat diencephalon. *J. Comp. Neurol.,* 120:259–295.
Olds, M. E., and Olds, J. (1969): Effects of lesions in medial forebrain bundle on self-stimulation behavior. *Am. J. Physiol.,* 217:1253–1254.
Oltmans, G. A., and Harvey, J. A. (1972): Lateral hypothalamic syndrome and brain catecholamine levels after lesions of the nigrostriatal bundle. *Physiol. Behav.,* 8:69–78.
Oomura, Y., Ono, T., Ooyama, H., and Wayner, M. J. (1969): Glucose and osmosensitive neurones of the rat hypothalamus. *Nature* (*Lond.*), 222:282–284.
Oomura, Y., Oomura, H., Yamamoto, T., and Naka, F. (1967): Reciprocal relationship of the lateral and ventromedial hypothalamus in the regulation of food intake. *Physiol. Behav.,* 2:97–115.
Palkovits, M., and Jacobowitz, D. M. (1974): Topographic atlas of catecholamine and acetylcholinesterase-containing neurons in the rat brain. II. Hindbrain (mesencephalon, rhombencephalon). *J. Comp. Neurol.,* 157:29–42.
Paxinos, G., and Bindra, D. (1972): Hypothalamic knife cuts: Effects on eating, drinking, irritability, aggression, copulation in male rat. *J. Comp. Physiol. Psychol.,* 79:219–229.
Paxinos, G., and Bindra, D. (1973): Hypothalamic and midbrain neural pathways involved in eating, drinking, irritability, aggression and copulation in rats. *J. Comp.*

Physiol. Psychol., 82:1–14.
Perez-Cruet, J., Black, W. C., and Brady, J. V. (1963): Heart rate: Differential effects of hypothalamic and septal self-stimulation. *Science,* 140:1235–1236.
Perez-Cruet, J., McIntire, R. W., and Pliskoff, S. S. (1965): Blood pressure and heart rate changes in dogs during hypothalamic self-stimulation. *J. Comp. Physiol. Psychol.,* 60:373–381.
Pfaff, D. W., and Gregory, E. (1971*a*): Correlation between pre-optic area unit activity and the cortical electroencephalogram: Difference between normal and castrated male rats. *Electroencephalogr. Clin. Neurophysiol.,* 31:223–230.
Pfaff, D. W., and Gregory, E. (1971*b*): Olfactory coding in olfactory bulb and medial forebrain bundle of normal and castrate male rats. *J. Neurophysiol.,* 34:208–216.
Phillips, A. G. (1970): Enhancement and inhibition of olfactory bulb self-stimulation by odours. *Physiol. Behav.,* 5:1127–1131.
Phillips, A. G., and Fibiger, H. C. (1973): Dopamine and noradrenergic substrates of positive reinforcement: Differential effects of *d*- and *l*-amphetamine. *Science,* 179: 575–577.
Phillips, A. G., and Mogenson, G. J. (1969): Self-stimulation of the olfactory bulb. *Physiol. Behav.,* 4:195–197.
Phillis, J. W. (1970): *The Pharmacology of Synapses.* Pergamon Press, New York.
Pickel, V. M., Segal, M., and Bloom, F. E. (1974): Axonal proliferation following lesions of cerebellar peduncles: A combined fluorescence microscopic and radioautographic study. *J. Comp. Neurol.,* 155:43–60.
Pliskoff, S. S., Wright, J. E., and Hawkins, T. D. (1965): Brain stimulation as a reinforcer: Intermittent schedules. *J. Exp. Anal. Behav.,* 8:75–88.
Porter, R. W., Conrad, D. G., and Brady, J. V. (1959): Some neural and behavioral correlates of electrical self-stimulation of the limbic system. *J. Exp. Anal. Behav.,* 2:43–55.
Poschel, B. P. H. (1963): Is centrally-elicited positive reinforcement associated with onset or termination of stimulation? *J. Comp. Physiol. Psychol.,* 56:604–607.
Poschel, B. P. H. (1968): Do biological reinforcers act via the self-stimulation areas of the brain? *Physiol. Behav.,* 3:53–60.
Poschel, B. P. H., and Ninteman, F. W. (1964): Excitatory (antidepressant) effects of monoamine oxidase inhibitors on the reward system of the brain. *Life Sci.,* 3:903–910.
Poschel, B. P. H., and Ninteman, F. W. (1966): Hypothalamic self-stimulation: Its suppression by blockade of norepinephrine biosynthesis and reinstatement by metaamphetamine. *Life Sci.,* 5:11–16.
Poschel, B. P. H., and Ninteman, F. W. (1968): Excitatory effects of 5-HTP on intracranial self-stimulation following MAO blockade. *Life Sci.,* 7:317–323.
Poschel, B. P. H., and Ninteman, F. W. (1971): Intracranial reward and the forebrain's serotonergic mechanism: Studies employing para-chlorophenylalanine and para-chloroamphetamine. *Physiol. Behav.,* 7:39–46.
Powley, T. L., and Keesey, R. E. (1970): Relationship of body weight to the lateral hypothalamic feeding syndrome. *J. Comp. Physiol. Psychol.,* 70:25–36.
Prescott, R. G. W. (1966): Estrous cycle in the rat: Effects on self-stimulation behavior. *Science,* 152:796–797.
Randrup, A., and Munkvad, I. (1970): Biochemical, anatomical and psychological investigations of stereotyped behavior induced by amphetamines. In: *Amphetamines and Related Compounds,* edited by E. Costa and S. Garattini, pp. 695–713. Raven Press, New York.
Reid, L. D., Hunsicker, J. P., Lindsay, J. L., Gallistel, C. L., and Kent, E. W. (1973): Incidence and magnitude of the "priming effect" in self-stimulating rats. *J. Comp. Physiol. Psychol.,* 82:286–293.
Reynolds, R. W. (1958): The relationship between stimulation voltage and hypothalamic self-stimulation in the rat. *J. Comp. Physiol. Psychol.,* 51:193–198.
Ritter, S., and Stein, L. (1973): Self-stimulation of noradrenergic cell group (A6) in locus coeruleus of rats. *J. Comp. Physiol. Psychol.,* 85:443–452.

Roberts, W. W. (1958): Rapid escape learning without avoidance learning motivated by hypothalamic stimulation in cats. *J. Comp. Physiol. Psychol.,* 51:391–399.

Roll, S. K. (1970): Intracranial self-stimulation and wakefulness: Effects of manipulating ambient brain catecholamines. *Science,* 168:1370–1372.

Rolls, B. J., and Rolls, E. T. (1973*a*): Effects of lesions in the basolateral amygdala on fluid intake in the rat. *J. Comp. Physiol. Psychol.,* 83:240–247.

Rolls, E. T. (1971*a*): Contrasting effects of hypothalamic and nucleus accumbens septi self-stimulation on brain stem single unit activity and cortical arousal. *Brain Res.,* 31:275–285.

Rolls, E. T. (1972): Activation of amygdaloid neurons in reward, eating and drinking elicited by electrical stimulation of the brain. *Brain Res.,* 82:15–22.

Rolls, E. T. (1973): Refractory periods of neurons directly excited in stimulus-bound eating and drinking in the rat. *J. Comp. Physiol. Psychol.,* 82:15–22.

Rolls, E. T., and Rolls, B. J. (1973*b*): Altered food preferences after lesions in the basolateral region of the amygdala in the rat. *J. Comp. Physiol. Psychol.,* 83:248–259.

Rose, M. D. (1974): Pain reducing properties of rewarding electrical brain stimulation in the rat. *J. Comp. Physiol. Psychol.,* 87:607–617.

Rostrosen, J., Wallach, M. B., Angrist, B., and Gershon, S. (1972): Antagonism of apomorphine-induced stereotypy and emesis in dogs by thioridazine, haloperidol and pimozide. *Psychopharmacologia,* 26:185–194.

Roth, S. R., Schwartz, M., and Teitelbaum, P. (1973): Failure of recovered lateral hypothalamic rats to learn specific food aversions. *J. Comp. Physiol. Psychol.,* 83:184–197.

Routtenberg, A. (1971): Forebrain pathways of reward in Rattus norvegicus. *J. Comp. Physiol. Psychol.,* 75:200–276.

Routtenberg, A., and Huang, Y. H. (1968): Reticular formation and brainstem unitary activity: Effects of posterior hypothalamic and septal-limbic stimulation at reward loci. *Physiol. Behav.,* 3:611–617.

Routtenberg, A., and Lindy, J. (1965): Effects of the availability of rewarding septal and hypothalamic stimulation on bar pressing for food under conditions of deprivation. *J. Comp. Physiol. Psychol.,* 60:158–161.

Routtenberg, A., and Malsbury, C. (1969): Brainstem pathways of reward. *J. Comp. Physiol. Psychol.,* 68:22–30.

Routtenberg, A., and Olds, J. (1963): Attenuation of response to an aversive brain stimulus by concurrent rewarding septal stimulation. *Fed. Proc.,* 22:515 (abstr.).

Routtenberg, A., and Sloan, M. (1974): Self-stimulation in the frontal cortex of Rattus norvegicus. *Behav. Biol.,* 7:564–572.

Ruf, K., and Steiner, F. A. (1967): Steroid-sensitive single neurons in rat hypothalamus and midbrain: Identification by microelectrophoresis. *Science,* 156:667–669.

Satinoff, E., and Rutstein, J. (1970): Behavioral thermoregulation in rats with anterior hypothalamic lesions. *J. Comp. Physiol. Psychol.,* 71:77–82.

Satinoff, E., and Shan, S. Y. Y. (1971): Loss of behavioral thermoregulation after lateral hypothalamic lesions in rats. *J. Comp. Physiol. Psychol.,* 77:302–312.

Sawyer, C. H., Kawakami, M., Meyerson, B., Whitmoyer, D. I., and Lilley, J. J. (1968): ACTH, dexmethasone and asphyxia on electrical activity of the rat hypothalamus. *Brain Res.,* 10:213–226.

Scheel-Kruger, J. (1972): Behavioural and biochemical comparison of amphetamine derivatives, cocaine, benztropine and tricyclic anti-depressant drugs. *Eur. J. Pharmacol.,* 18:63–73.

Schwartz, M., and Teitelbaum, P. (1974): Dissociation between learning and remembering in rats with lesions in the lateral hypothalamus. *J. Comp. Physiol. Psychol.,* 87:384–398.

Schwartzbaum, J. S. (1965): Discrimination behavior after amygdalectomy in monkeys: Visual and somesthetic learning and perceptual capacity. *J. Comp. Physiol. Psychol.,* 60:314–319.

Sclafani, A., Berner, C. N., and Maul, G. (1973): Feeding and drinking pathways between medial and lateral hypothalamus in the rat. *J. Comp. Physiol. Psychol.,*

85:29–51.

Scott, J. W. (1967): Brain stimulation reinforcement with distributed practice: Effects of electrode locus, previous experience, and stimulus intensity. *J. Comp. Physiol. Psychol.,* 63:175–183.

Scott, J. W., and Pfaffman, C. (1967): Olfactory input to the hypothalamus: Electrophysiological evidence. *Science,* 158:1592–1594.

Segal, M., and Bloom, F. (1974): The action of norepinephrine in the rat hippocampus. I. Iontophoretic studies. *Brain Res.,* 72:79–97.

Sem-Jacobsen, C. W. (1968): *Depth-Electrographic Stimulation of the Human Brain and Behavior.* Charles C Thomas, Springfield, Illinois.

Shepherd, M., Lader, M., and Rodknight, R. (1968): *Clinical Psychopharmacology.* Lea & Febiger, Philadelphia.

Sidman, M., Brady, J. V., Boren, J. J., Conrad, D., and Schulman, A. (1955): Reward schedules and behavior maintained by intracranial self-stimulation. *Science,* 122:830–831.

Siggins, G. R., Hoffer, B. J., and Bloom, F. E. (1969): Cyclic adenosine monophosphate: Possible mediator for norepinephrine effects on cerebellar Purkinje cells. *Science,* 165:1018–1020.

Simpson, B. A., and Iverson, S. D. (1971): Effects of substantia nigra lesions on the locomotor and stereotyped responses to amphetamine. *Nature (Lond.),* 230:30–32.

Simpson, J. B., and Routtenberg, A. (1973): Subfornical organ: Site of drinking elicitation by angiotenson II. *Science,* 181:1172–1175.

Singer, J. J. (1968): Hypothalamic control of male and female sexual behavior in female rats. *J. Comp. Physiol. Psychol.,* 66:738–742.

Singh, D. (1973): Effects of preoperative training on food-motivated behavior of hypothalamic hyperphagic rats. *J. Comp. Physiol. Psychol.,* 84:38–46.

Skinner, B. F. (1938): *The Behavior of Organisms.* Appleton-Century-Crofts, New York.

Skinner, B. F. (1948): "Superstition" in the pigeon. *J. Exp. Psychol.,* 38:168–172.

Snyder, S. H. (1972): Catecholamines in the brain as mediators of amphetamine psychosis. *Arch. Gen. Psychiatry,* 27:169–179.

Snyder, S. H. (1974): Catecholamines as mediators of drug effects in schizophrenia. In: *The Neurosciences, Third Study Program,* edited by F. O. Schmitt and F. G. Worden, pp. 721–732. MIT Press, Cambridge, Massachusetts.

Spear, N. E. (1962): Comparison of the reinforcing effect of brain stimulation on Skinner box, runway, and maze performance. *J. Comp. Physiol. Psychol.,* 55:679–684.

Spies, G. (1965): Food versus intracranial self-stimulation reinforcement in food deprived rats. *J. Comp. Physiol. Psychol.,* 60:153–157.

Stark, P., and Boyd, E. S. (1963). Effects of cholinergic drugs on hypothalamic self-stimulation response rates of dogs. *Am. J. Physiol.,* 205:745–784.

Stark, P., Boyd, E. S., and Fuller, W. R. (1964): A possible role of serotonin in hypothalamic self-stimulation in dogs. *J. Pharmacol. Exp. Ther.,* 146:147–153.

Stark, P., Fuller, R. W., Hartley, L. W., Schaffer, R. J., and Turk, J. A. (1970): Dissociation of the effects of p-chlorophenylalanine on self-stimulation and on brain serotonin. *Life Sci.,* 9:41–48.

Stein, L. (1958): Secondary reinforcement established with subcortical stimulation. *Science,* 127:466–467

Stein, L. (1964*a*): Amphetamine and neural reward mechanisms. In: *Ciba Foundation Symposium on Animal Behavior and Drug Action,* edited by H. Steinberg, A. V. S. de Reuck, and J. Knight, pp. 91–113. Churchill, London.

Stein, L. (1964*b*): Self-stimulation of the brain and the central stimulant action of amphetamine. *Fed. Proc.,* 23:836–850.

Stein, L. (1964*c*): Reciprocal action of reward and punishment mechanisms. In: *The Role of Pleasure in Behavior,* edited by R. G. Heath, pp. 113–119. Hoeber, New York.

Stein, L. (1965): Facilitation of avoidance behavior by positive brain stimulation. *J. Comp. Physiol. Psychol.,* 60:9–19.

Stein, L. (1966): Psychopharmacological aspects of mental depression. *Can. Psychiatr. Assoc. J.,* 11:34–49.

Stein, L. (1968): Chemistry of reward and punishment. In: *Psychopharmacology: A Review of Progress 1957–1967,* Public Health Service Publication No. 1836, edited by D. H. Efron, pp. 105–123. U.S. Government Printing Office, Washington, D.C.

Steiner, S. S., Beer, B., and Shaffer, M. M. (1969): Escape from self-produced rates of brain stimulation. *Science,* 163:90–91.

Steiner, S. S., Bodnar, R. J., Ackerman, R. F., and Ellman, S. J. (1973): Escape from rewarding brain stimulation of dorsal brainstem and hypothalamus. *Physiol. Behav.,* 11:589–591.

Steiner, S. S., and Ellman, S. J. (1972): Relation between REM sleep and intracranial self-stimulation. *Science,* 177:1122–1124.

Stinus, L., and Thierry, A.-M. (1973): Self-stimulation and catecholamines. II. Blockade of self-stimulation by treatment with alpha-methylparatyrosine and the reinstatement by catecholamine precursor administration. *Brain Res.,* 64:189–198.

Stricker, E. M., and Zigmond, M. J. (1974): Effects on homeostasis of intraventricular injections of 6-hydroxydopamine in rats. *J. Comp. Physiol. Psychol.,* 86:973–994.

Svensson, T. H. (1971): Functional and biochemical effects of a d- and l-amphetamine on central catecholamine neurons. *Naunyn Schmiedebergs Arch. Pharmalcol.,* 271:170–180.

Taylor, K. M., and Snyder, S. H. (1970): Amphetamine: Differentiation by d- and l-isomers of animal behavior involving central norepinephrine or dopamine. *Science,* 168:1487–1489.

Taylor, K. M., and Snyder, S. H. (1971): Differential effects of *d*- and *l*-amphetamine on behavior and on catecholamine disposition in dopamine and norepinephrine containing neurons of rat brain. *Brain Res.,* 28:295–309.

Teitelbaum, P. (1955): Sensory control of hypothalamic hyperphagia. *J. Comp. Physiol. Psychol.,* 48:156–166.

Teitelbaum, P. (1971): The encephalization of hunger. In: *Progress in Physiological Psychology, Vol. 4,* edited by E. Stellar and J. H. Sprague, pp. 319–350. Academic Press, New York.

Teitelbaum, P., and Cytawa, J. (1965): Spreading depression and recovery from lateral hypothalamic damage. *Science,* 147:61–63.

Teitelbaum, P., and Epstein, A. N. (1962): The lateral hypothalamic syndrome: Recovery of feeding and drinking after lateral hypothalamic lesions. *Psychol. Rev.,* 69:74–90.

Tenen, S. S. (1967): The effects of p-chlorophenylalanine, a serotonin depletor on avoidance acquisition, pain sensitivity, and related behavior in the rat. *Psychopharmacologia,* 10:204–219.

Terman, M., and Terman, J. S. (1970): Circadian rhythm of brain self-stimulation behavior. *Science,* 168:1242–1244.

Trendelenburg, U. (1959): The supersensivitity caused by cocaine. *J. Pharmacol. Exp. Ther.,* 125:55–65.

Trowill, J. A., and Hynek, K. (1970): Secondary reinforcement based on primary brain stimulation reward. *Psychol. Rep.,* 27:715–718.

Ungerstedt, U. (1970): Is interruption of the nigro-striatal system producing the "lateral hypothalamus syndrome?" *Acta Physiol. Scand.,* 80:35A–36A.

Ungerstedt, U. (1971*a*): Aphagia and adipsia after 6-hydroxydopamine induced degeneration of the nigro-striatal dopamine system. *Acta Physiol. Scand.* [*Suppl.* 367], 95–122.

Ungerstedt, U. (1971*b*): Postsynaptic supersensivity after 6-hydroxydopamine induced degeneration of the nigro-striatal dopamine system. *Acta Physiol. Scand.,* [*Suppl.* 367], 69–93.

Ungerstedt, U. (1971*c*): Stereotaxic mapping of the monoamine pathways in the rat brain. *Acta Physiol. Scand.* [*Suppl.* 367], 1–48.

Ungerstedt, U. (1974*a*): Brain dopamine neurons and behavior. In: *The Neurosciences, Third Study Program,* edited by F. O. Schmitt and F. G. Worden, pp. 695–704. MIT

Press, Cambridge, Massachusetts.
Ungerstedt, U. (1974*b*): Functional dynamics of central monoamine pathways. In: *The Neurosciences, Third Study Program,* edited by F. O. Schmitt and F. G. Worden, pp. 979–988. MIT Press, Cambridge, Massachusetts.
Uretsky, N. J., and Iverson, L. L. (1970): Effects of 6-hydroxydopamine on catecholamine containing neurones in the rat brain. *J. Neurochem.,* 17:269–278.
Ursin, R., Ursin, H., and Olds, J. (1966): Self-stimulation of hippocampus in rats. *J. Comp. Physiol. Psychol.,* 61:353–359.
Valenstein, E. S. (1965): Independence of approach and escape reactions to electrical stimulation of the brain. *J. Comp. Physiol. Psychol.,* 60:20–30.
Valenstein, E. S. (1973*b*): Commentary. In: *Brain Stimulation and Motivation,* edited by E. S. Valenstein, pp. 162–172. Scott, Foresman, Glenview, Illinois.
Valenstein, E. S., and Beer, B. (1964): Continuous opportunity for reinforcing brain stimulation. *J. Exp. Anal. Behav.,* 7:183–184.
Valenstein, E. S., and Campbell, J. F. (1966): Medial forebrain bundle lateral hypothalamic area and reinforcing brain stimulation. *Am. J. Physiol.,* 210:270–274.
Valenstein, E. S., Cox, V. C., and Kakolewski, J. W. (1968): Modification of motivated behavior elicited by electrical stimulation of the hypothalamus. *Science,* 157:552–554.
Valenstein, E. S., Cox, V. C., and Kakolewski, J. W. (1970): Reexamination of the role of the hypothalamus in motivation. *Psychol. Rev.,* 77:16–31.
Van Atta, L., and Sutin, J. (1971): The response of single lateral hypothalamic neurons to ventromedial nucleus and limbic stimulation. *Physiol. Behav.,* 6:523–536.
Van Delft, A. M. L., and Kitay, J. I. (1972): Effect of ACTH on single unit activity in the diencephalon of intact and hypophysectomized rats. *Neuroendocrinology,* 9:188–196.
Villablanca, J. (1974): Presentation of films of kittens and cats with bilateral ablations of the caudate nuclei. Conference on Brain Mechanisms in Mental Retardation, Oxnard, California, January 1974. Jointly sponsored by NICHHD, NIH, and Mental Retardation Research Center, University of California, Los Angeles.
Vincent, J. D., Arnauld, E., and Bioulac, B. (1972): Activity of osmosensitive single cells in the hypothalamus of behaving monkey during drinking. *Brain Res.,* 44:371–384.
Vincent, J. D., and Hayward, J. N. (1970): Activity of single cells in osmoreceptor-supraoptic nuclear complex in the hypothalamus of the waking rhesus monkey. *Brain Res.,* 23:105–108.
Wampler, R. S. (1973): Increased motivation in rats with ventromedial hypothalamic lesions. *J. Comp. Physiol. Psychol.,* 84:268–274.
Ward, H. P. (1959): Stimulus factors in septal self-stimulation. *Am. J. Physiol.,* 196:779–782.
Ward, H. P. (1960): Basal tegmental self-stimulation after septal ablation in rats. *Arch. Neurol.,* 3:158–162.
Ward, H. P. (1961): Tegmental self-stimulation after amygdaloid ablation. *Arch. Neurol.,* 4:657–659.
Weiskrantz, L. (1956): Behavioral changes associated with ablation of the amygdaloid complex in monkeys. *J. Comp. Physiol. Psychol.,* 49:381–391.
Wetzel, M. C. (1963): Self-stimulation aftereffects and runway performance in the rat. *J. Comp. Physiol. Psychol.,* 56:673–678.
Wetzel, M. C. (1968): Self-stimulation anatomy: Data needs. *Brain Res.,* 10:287–296.
Wetzel, M. C., Howell, L. G., and Bearie, K. J. (1969): Experimental performance of steel and platinum electrodes with chronic monophasic stimulation of the brain. *J. Neurosurg.,* 31:658–669.
Wheatley, M. D. (1944): The hypothalamus and affective behavior in cats: A study of the effects of experimental lesions with anatomical correlations. *Arch. Neurol. Psychiatry,* 52:296–316.
Wilkinson, H. A., and Peele, T. L. (1962): Modification of intracranial self-stimulation by hunger satiety. *Am. J. Physiol.,* 203:537–540.
Winokur, A., and Utiger, R. D. (1974): Thyrotropin-releasing hormone: Regional dis-

tribution in rat brain. *Science,* 185:265–267.

Wise, C. D., Berger, B. D., and Stein, L. (1973): Evidence of alpha-noradrenergic reward receptors and serotonergic punishment receptors in the rat brain. *Biol. Psychiatry,* 6:3–21.

Wise, C. D., and Stein, L. (1969): Facilitation of brain self-stimulation by central administration of norepinephrine. *Science,* 163:299–301.

Wit, A., and Wang, S. C. (1968): Temperature-sensitive neurons in preoptic/anterior hypothalamic region: Effects of increasing ambient temperature. *Am. J. Physiol.,* 215:1151–1159.

Wolf, G. (1964): Effect of dorsolateral hypothalamic lesions on sodium appetite elicited by deoxycorticosterone and by acute hyponatremia. *J. Comp. Physiol Psychol.,* 58:396–402.

Wurtz, R. H., and Olds, J. (1963): Amygdaloid stimulation and operant reinforcement in the rat. *J. Comp. Physiol. Psychol.,* 56:941–949.

Wyrwicka, W., and Dobrzecka, C. (1960): Relationship between feeding and satiation centers of the hypothalamus. *Science,* 132:805–806.

Yunger, L. M., and Harvey, J. A. (1973): Effect of lesions in the medial forebrain bundle on three measures of pain sensitivity and noise-elicited startle. *J. Comp. Physiol. Psychol.,* 83:173–183.

Subject Index